AF781828

THE LEGAL ESSAYS OF MICHAEL BAYLES

Law and Philosophy Library

VOLUME 57

Managing Editors

FRANCISCO J. LAPORTA, *Department of Law, Autonomous University of Madrid, Spain*

ALEKSANDER PECZENIK, *Department of Law, University of Lund, Sweden*

FREDERICK SCHAUER, *John F. Kennedy School of Government, Harvard University, Cambridge, Mass., U.S.A.*

Former Managing Editors
AULIS AARNIO, MICHAEL D. BAYLES†, CONRAD D. JOHNSON†, ALAN MABE

Editorial Advisory Board

AULIS AARNIO, *Research Institute for Social Sciences, University of Tampere, Finland*
ZENON BAŃKOWSKI, *Centre for Law and Society, University of Edinburgh*
PAOLO COMANDUCCI, *University of Genua, Italy*
ERNESTO GARZÓN VALDÉS, *Institut für Politikwissenschaft, Johannes Gutenberg Universität Mainz*
JOHN KLEINIG, *Department of Law, Police Science and Criminal Justice Administration, John Jay College of Criminal Justice, City University of New York*
NEIL MacCORMICK, *European Parliament, Brussels, Belgium*
WOJCIECH SADURSKI, *European University Institute, Department of Law, Florence, Italy*
ROBERT S. SUMMERS, *School of Law, Cornell University*
CARL WELLMAN, *Department of Philosophy, Washington University*

The titles published in this series are listed at the end of this volume.

THE LEGAL ESSAYS OF MICHAEL BAYLES

Edited by

WADE L. ROBISON

Ezra A. Hale Professor in Applied Ethics, Rochester Institute of Technology

KLUWER LAW INTERNATIONAL

THE HAGUE / LONDON / NEW YORK

A C.I.P. Catalogue record for this book is available from the Library of Congress.

ISBN 90-411-1835-7

Published by Kluwer Law International,
P.O. Box 85889, 2508 CN The Hague, The Netherlands.

Sold and distributed in North, Central and South America
by Kluwer Law International,
101 Philip Drive, Norwell, MA 02061, U.S.A.
kluwerlaw@wkap.com

In all other countries, sold and distributed
by Kluwer Law International, Distribution Centre,
P.O. Box 322, 3300 AH Dordrecht, The Netherlands.

Printed on acid-free paper

All Rights Reserved
© 2002 Kluwer Law International
Kluwer Law International incorporates
the imprint of Martinus Nijhoff Publishers.

No part of this work may be reproduced, stored in a retrieval system, or transmitted
in any form or by any means, electronic, mechanical, photocopying, microfilming, recording
or otherwise, without written permission from the Publisher, with the exception
of any material supplied specifically for the purpose of being entered
and executed on a computer system, for exclusive use by the purchaser of the work.

Printed in the Netherlands.

CONTENTS

INTRODUCTION

WADE L. ROBISON

Michael Bayles had an uncanny ability to lay out a problem with clarity and power so that one felt, at the end, that one had a full conceptual grasp of the issues involved and of the points of entry for understanding and criticism. His analysis of the criminal law system in the first essay, 'Dismantling the Criminal Law System,' is a paradigmatic example of this ability.

He discusses there 'four different models for undesirable behavior,' the traditional system which relies on punishment, a treatment system, a social reform system, and a social defense system (18). In the process of laying out these four systems, he delineates the nature of punishment, the nature of criminal responsibility and the role that excuses and ignorance, mistake and accident, and duress play in the conceptual framework of criminal responsibility. He pinpoints the three ways in which we may try to 'dismantle' the criminal law system by noting that the process requires three steps--that conduct be made criminal, that it be applicable to groups of individuals, and that it involve punishment. We may thus decriminalize conduct, immunize some from being criminalized, e.g. mental defectives, and remove punishment from the system (by e.g. substituting treatment).

In discussing the social reform model, he lays out the main features of determinism since that model presupposes that it is the environment that is primarily responsible for undesirable behavior. Change the environment, and we will change the behavior. In laying out the social defense model, he examines preventive detention in its various forms, from bail to third offense rules, since preventive detention is the most obvious way in which to defend the social system from undesirable behavior. He is able, without an extended analysis, to question whether the requirement for bail is fair since it depends upon income and social status, neither of which are necessarily connected to criminal conduct. Some are thus detained unfairly.

The end result of this analysis is that we have a thorough and tidy conceptualization of the main elements of the criminal law system with, along the way, thorough and tidy conceptualizations of punishment, responsibility, and determinism, to name just three. The essay makes a wonderful introduction to the criminal justice system and a quick way to see how moral questions may be raised about the system and how change could be effected in the system. Who could ask for anything more?

But Bayles gives us more. In discussing the issue of whether Bentham assumed that 'people make rational choices when engaging in crime' (18), Bayles distinguishes, in his response, the question whether that assumption is an empirical proposition and the question whether, whatever its empirical status, it lays down a condition for the operation of the criminal justice system.

These are distinct questions, easily and often confused, and separating them is crucial to understanding debates about the criminal justice system. Since most murders are crimes of passion between people who know each other, it is at least questionable whether those murders, or at least some of those murders, are the result of rational calculations. Similarly, in the United States only about a fifth of the states now preclude those with mental retardation, that is, IQ's below 70, from being executed,[1] but if one feature of mental retardation is an inability to calculate means to ends, to think rationally, that is, about what one is doing and the consequences of one's actions, then it is conceptually confused to subject such individuals to the criminal justice system. They fail to fulfil one of the necessary conditions for the application of the system, namely, that they are rational calculators. And, of course, that conceptual mistake is paired with the moral wrong that results. Similarly, drug laws may be attacked for assuming that those who take drugs are as rational in their choices as alcoholics were assumed to be when alcoholism was treated as a crime.

In other words, the practical import of the conceptual distinction between treating a proposition as an empirical claim and treating it as a condition for the application of a model for controlling undesirable behavior is enormous. So Bayles has not only given us a conceptual framework for understanding the various models for controlling such behavior, but also a tool for critiquing the application of the most prevalent of those models.

It is difficult to write clearly in any discipline, and philosophy seems to present to its practitioners more problems than any other discipline. On the one hand, the drive for truth and its conditional nature in our world mean that few propositions, if any, can be maintained without an inordinate supply of conditionals. It takes good judgment to come to know which conditionals need expression and which can be ignored. On the other hand, the abstract character of philosophy's concepts and the

[1]Raymond Bonner and Sara Rimer, 'Executing the Mentally Retarded Even as Laws Begin to Shift,' *New York Times* (August 7, 2000), A1 & A14.

inherent complexities of explaining what is complex in a way that is understandable to both practitioners and 'the vulgar,' as the Empiricists would have it, mean that only a few gifted philosophers will succeed in stating clearly its abstract but generally contingent truths. We need only to peruse any collection of philosophical writings to come to see how very difficult it is to achieve clarity. So when I praise Michael Bayles for being clear and, more important, for being so clear as to open up for view and for criticism complex subjects, that is no small praise. Such an ability ought to be the envy of philosophers, and the writings a model of philosophical writing.

The best evidence for the clarity of the following essays is found in reading them, and it heartens a commentator to know that he or she can do no better summarizing such essays than the author did in writing. Such knowledge lightens a commentator's burdens. 'Read the essays yourself! And learn.'

Bayles was a utilitarian, and as one reads through these essays, one is witness to the advantages of being a utilitarian. Taking a utilitarian stance towards problems means determining what courses of action are possible and then laying out the consequences of these possible alternative courses of action. Bayles does such a clear job of laying out and opening up complex subjects for view because, I suspect, he brings to them his utilitarian commitments.

Asking, for instance, what we have contracts and what sustains contract law is to ask, for a utilitarian, how contracts serve us in the long term to produce a greater good, and asking what changes could be made in contract law to make it better makes us look at the ends we currently have, compare them to ends we ought to achieve, and then see what changes ought to be made in what we now do that would allow us to achieve those new ends or achieve better the ends we already have.

Being a utilitarian forces us, that is, into a causal frame of mind. 'Change a cause, and you change the effect' is a principle for understanding, and when applied to such practical issues as our criminal justice system and contract law, it means that we are that much closer to understanding what effects particular causal factors have in what we get and so much closer to being able to regulate those effects so as better to achieve better ends than we currently get.

The reader will find no sustained attempt to justify utilitarianism or any other general feature of Bayles's thought in these essays. They were not designed to probe such matters. They rather illustrate as well as any essays could how very effective a public voice a philosopher can have who is knowledgeable and clear and concerned, as Bayles was, with making things clear so that those who want to change them would know where to begin and how best to proceed.

All this praise is not to suggest that Bayles's essays are without difficulties. I once introduced Michael for a talk by pointing out that there are four possible kinds of essays and talks -- those that are true and look true, those that are false and look false, those that are false and look true, and those that are true and look false. Obviously, I noted, the essays strived for would seem to be those that are true and look true, and I then said, by way of introduction, and as a joke, 'Professor Bayles is at least halfway there!'

But the best essays, the ones, that is, that make it into the canon and are read and reread, are those that are true but look false. These pique a reader's curiosity and call for refutation, but, being true, resist it. So other practitioners of the craft work on the topic, trying to figure out what it is about the subject chosen that has led to an essay that looks false and, not succeeding in finding anything that is false which could lead to such an appearance, give the essay stature.

Many of Bayles's essays are problematic in just this way: they appear false, at least in regard to some of their claims, but resist refutation. The last in this anthology, on marriage being a bad business deal, has that look about it. 'Why,' one wants to ask, 'if it is such a bad business deal, do so many get married?'

Perhaps we are not such rational self-interested calculators as economists would have us think? Perhaps it is completely misplaced to think of marriage as a deal at all, let alone a business deal? Perhaps some variable that would make a difference to its being a business deal has been left out? Perhaps the criteria being used to determine that it is a bad business deal are mistaken?

These and other questions instantly begin to pile up in one's mind, tumbling over each other as the essay's thesis generates more and more. *Something* seems wrong about it, and so it behooves us to try to find out what it is that is causing the appearance of falsity. Yet when one looks at it in detail and examines the care with which Bayles has constructed his arguments, noting, for instance, that the situation varies in different states because different states handle marriage law and particularly marital property in very different ways, one finds it hard to figure out what exactly has gone wrong, if anything. So perhaps he is right? So perhaps those who are thinking about getting married for reasons other than children ought to think twice about the economics of it all?

The essay illustrates well Bayles's ability to marshall plausible arguments for an implausible thesis. The very best essays in philosophy generate questions. They do not settle matters, but unsettle our understandings by forcing us to confront propositions which strike us as off-the-mark or odd or 'not quite right' while giving us good reasons for thinking that, nonetheless, they are true. The best of Michael Bayles's essays achieve this goal. We are forced to question ourselves and our understandings, and one could ask for no more from a philosopher.

I have made some minor changes in the text of some of these articles such as, for instance, adding italics where a book is named and is italicized elsewhere in the article. Otherwise the articles are as they were printed except for what errors I have myself introduced and failed to discover. In particular, I have not made all the texts consistent with one another. The various journals in which these articles appear have different formats for their articles, and I was concerned that any attempt to standardize the articles would introduce more errors and, perhaps more important, frustrate those who wanted to quote the articles and those who wanted to double check the quotations with the originals. I judged it better that the articles be consistent with their originals than with each other.

The bibliography is as complete and accurate as I can make it, but I cannot guarantee its completeness and accuracy any more than I can guarantee the thoroughness and accuracy of the index. Mistakes seem to creep in. Besides, Bayles published a great deal, and some of what he refers to as his minor pieces occur in very out-of-the way publications that would make them difficult to track down if one did not already know of their existence. It is possible some such piece has escaped my notice, and if so, the fault is as much mine as any other errors in the anthology.

I cannot end without a note of regret that Myke Bayles is not with us these days. He would have relished the legal and moral intricacies of the Clinton impeachment, and the legal and moral delights of the Supreme Court decision in *Bush v. Gore* would have kept him, and so us, occupied for a long time to come. He brought a wealth of knowledge to whatever he touched, and we readers were blessed by that knowledge combined with a moral indignation tempered by a playful cynicism and by a sense that this sort of thing is part and parcel of the human condition, to be repeated time and again whenever human beings congregate and try to regulate their behavior through the rule of law. I learned much from him when he and I were friends, and I have learned much from his writings as I have chosen those to be reprinted and worked through them for this volume. He is missed.

DISMANTLING THE CRIMINAL LAW SYSTEM

The criminal law systems in the United States as well as those of most Western countries have been subject to much recent criticism. Crime rates have been increasing much faster than population size in almost every Western country. In the United States one group of critics has blamed the courts, especially the Supreme Court, for the rise in crime, claiming they have "handcuffed the police" by restrictions on police procedure. Another group of critics blames the prison system and society at large, contending prisons encourage rather than discourage criminal conduct. Further, they say, people trapped by racism and poverty have few alternatives to crime. But all the critics agree that the criminal law system is not working as intended.

The term "dismantle" originally meant to uncloak, to take off a mantel or cloak. It has also come to mean to strip of apparatus, take apart, or pull down. The Articles in this special issue are concerned with dismantling the criminal law system in both of these senses. First, they are concerned with uncovering the underlying principles and assumptions of the criminal law system. Second, many of them also suggest ways to strip the criminal law system of some of its elements or modify it in significant ways.

The purpose of this introduction is to provide an overall framework for considering the more detailed Articles which follow. Thus, it first distinguishes models of various types of systems for controlling undesirable behavior. The models are ideal types to which actual systems conform in varying degrees. Emphasis is placed upon the underlying philosophical principles and conceptions which distinguish the traditional criminal law system from those stressing treatment and preventive social reform. Second, it shows how various attacks on the criminal law system pertain to different elements of it. Finally, it indicates how the conceptions of criminal, treatment, and preventive social reform systems are involved in the specific problems of insanity, drug addition, and preventive detention.

I. THE CRIMINAL LAW SYSTEM

The criminal law system consists of all the various elements involved in the process which results in punishment of some persons. So conceived, the criminal law system includes at least the following elements: substantive and procedural rules, principles, policies, decisions, judges,

W. L. Robison (ed.), The Legal Essays of Michael Bayles, 1–20.
© 2002 *Kluwer Law International. Printed in the Netherlands.*

lawyers, courtrooms, police, penitentiaries, and probation agencies. But if one thus defines the criminal law system by its result--punishment for some people--one must be able to distinguish punishment from similar results of other systems. The process-product distinction is somewhat artificial as applied to a criminal law system, but it is a useful pedagogic device for clarifying the conceptual differences between criminal, treatment, and preventive social reform systems.

There are five basic elements in a widely accepted philosophical definition of punishment.[1] First, it involves an evil or deprivation; second, it is for an offense against the rules; third, it is (or is supposed to be) of an offender for his offense; fourth, it is imposed by human beings; and fifth, those persons administering it have authority to do so by the system of rules against which the offense was committed. However, this definition of punishment does not immediately distinguish it from compulsory treatment. Both involve an evil, deprivation of liberty, and both are imposed by human beings granted authority to do so by the system of rules. To distinguish punishment and treatment requires an elucidation of the first three elements in the definition.

The first difference concerns the nature of the offense in the second element. Punishment is for, and most criminal offenses require, a discrete item of behavior (an act); however, not all of them do, *e.g.*, vagrancy. Treatment, on the other hand, is not for a discrete item of behavior but a condition or status,[2] *e.g.*, being mentally ill. Frequently, of course, behavior is used as evidence of a status, but the behavior is merely a symptom of the underlying status to be treated. Thus, discrete items of behavior are not logically or conceptually required for treatment. Indeed, it is quite compatible with the concept of treatment to seek to change a status before it results in undesirable behavior.

The difference between punishment for a discrete item of behavior and treatment for a status leads to a second difference between them. The immediate aim of punishment is to prevent the occurrence of specified sorts of behavior, while the immediate aim of treatment is to alter or change a status.[3] This difference in aim is very important to the first

---

[1]*See* H.L.A. HART, PUNISHMENT AND RESPONSIBILITY 4-6 (1968); Flew, *The Justification of Punishment*, in THE PHILOSOPHY OF PUNISHMENT 85-87 (H. Acton ed. 1969).

[2]"Status" is used throughout to mean being in a certain state or condition.

[3]This discussion of the distinction between punishment and treatment generally follows H. PACKER, THE LIMITS OF THE CRIMINAL SANCTION 17-34 (1968). However, where Packer speaks of the "justifying aims" of punishment and treatment, I follow Hart and

element in the definition, namely, punishment involves an evil. In punishment, the intention is to inflict an evil upon an offender. One may attempt to avoid certain types of evil, *e.g.*, physical pain; still some evil is imposed. If one's intention were to provide an overall benefit, then it would not be punishment but reward. In treatment, while evil may be inflicted, it is not part of the intention or purpose, since the overall purpose is to benefit the person treated. It is perfectly possible to seek to remove all evil; whatever evil is involved is considered unavoidable. The deprivation of liberty involved in compulsory commitment is viewed as analogous to the unavoidable pain in having a decayed tooth filled.

The third element of the definition of punishment, that it be of an offender for his offense, is also important in distinguishing it from treatment. For a person to be an offender, this element requires he must be somehow responsible for his offense. In treatment, it is irrelevant whether or not a person is responsible for his status. People are treated for illness, and usually they are not responsible for being ill. Of course, a person may be responsible for his illness by having neglected to take proper care of himself, but it is in any event irrelevant since the immediate aim is simply to change his status.

The requirement of criminal responsibility is central to the traditional criminal law system. There are three basic conditions for criminal responsibility. First, a person must engage in voluntary behavior (perform an act). A person is not responsible for involuntary, *e.g.*, purely reflexive, behavior.[4] Second, the act must cause or pose a risk of causing a result (harm, *actus reus*) which the law seeks to prevent. This causal condition for responsibility serves to eliminate vicarious and collective responsibility from the model of the criminal law system. Third, the person must have the appropriate mental conditions or mens rea.

The doctrine of mens rea has been at the center of many attacks upon the criminal law. Indeed; one proposal for dismantling the criminal law system is simply to abolish the requirement of mens rea.[5] There has also been much philosophical controversy concerning what the mens rea requirement involves.[6] A traditional view considers it to require some positive mental state of the actor which is usually evidenced by acting

speak of their "immediate aims." This leaves open the question of what reasons, if any, justify them. *See* HART, *supra* note 1, at 6-8.

[4]For a discussion of the importance of the behavior being voluntary, *see* HART, *supra* note 1, at 90-112; Thalberg, *Hart on Strict Liability and Excusing Conditions,* 81 ETHICS 150 (1971).

[5]*See* K. MENNINGER, THE CRIME OF PUNISHMENT (1968); B. WOOTTON, CRIME AND THE CRIMINAL LAW (1963).

[6]*See, e.g.*, PACKER, *supra* note 3, at 103-8.

purposely, knowingly, recklessly, or negligently. On a view of this sort, excuses such as accident, mistake, and duress indicate the absence of required mental state. On the other hand, some recent writers have defined men rea simply in terms of the absence of a valid excuse.[7] On this view, mens rea simply operates to exclude responsibility for some actions.

Legal excuses indicate that a person was not responsible, while justifications indicate that the person did not perform a prohibited act. Thus, justifications do not involve a denial of responsibility. The underlying philosophical principle of excuses is that a person is not responsible for an action if he could not have avoided it, could not have done otherwise. Two types of excuses have traditionally been recognized. One type rests upon ignorance, *i.e.*, a person can not reasonably be expected to avoid performing an action if he cannot foresee that harm might result from it. Mistake and accident are the main excuses of this sort. The other type of excuses rests upon an actor's lack of control of his behavior. Duress is a legal excuse of this type.

Thus, the criminal law system is a complex process resulting in punishment of some people. It defines prohibited acts and determines who has and has not performed them. Of those who have, it attempts to distinguish between those who were responsible and those who were not. Finally, punishment is imposed on those who were responsible for performing prohibited actions. A treatment system, on the other hand, logically need not require the performance of discrete behavior or that a person be responsible. Nor does it purposely impose an evil; any evil involved is incidental to changing a person's status.

II. ATTACKS ON THE CRIMINAL LAW SYSTEM

There are three main ways of dismantling, in the sense of tearing down, the criminal law system. First, offenses can be eliminated by repealing substantive laws, *i.e., by decriminalization of conduct*. Second, the responsibility requirement may be attacked in either of two ways. The criminal law may be declared inapplicable to groups of people (juveniles, for example) on the ground that they cannot be responsible, i.*e*., *divestment of people*,[8] or the responsibility condition may be eliminated as a requirement of conviction. The latter approach may involve eliminating

---

[7] *See, e.g.,* HART, *The Ascription of Responsibility and Rights*, in ESSAYS ON LOGIC AND LANGUAGE 145 (A. Flew ed. 1951).

[8] Kittrie includes both decriminalization and divestment under the latter term. But these are distinct methods of dismantling the criminal law system and should have separate names. *See* N. KITTRIE, THE RIGHT TO BE DIFFERENT 4 (1971).

any of the three elements required for responsibility, but most attention has focused on the act and mens rea requirements. Third, one can seek to eliminate punishment. More specifically, most attacks of this type have been aimed at eliminating the prison system at least as it has traditionally operated.

These three methods of dismantling the criminal law system roughly correspond to different stages of the criminal law process. The first method eliminates grounds for arrest or detainment. The second method affects the conviction process. People are either removed from the process or the requirements for conviction are modified by eliminating one or more of the conditions for responsibility. The latter makes conviction easier, but the criminal law system is being changed toward another type of system. The third method is concerned with sentencing. A general outline of the attempts and success to date of each of these lines of attack may be useful.

Many theoretical arguments have been advanced in recent years for decriminalization of much conduct. Perhaps the best known discussion of decriminalization is the so-called Hart-Devlin debate.[9] The arguments concern what types of conduct should be criminal. Essentially four types of reasons for making conduct criminal have been discussed: to prevent harm to others, to prevent people from harming themselves, to prevent offense to others, and to enforce the popular morality. Hart has criticized the last reason. Elimination of laws to enforce popular morality would decriminalize fornications, homosexual conduct between consenting adults, etc. But laws based upon the second and third reasons have also come under attack.[10]

Many of the arguments for decriminalization are moralistic ones, that is, they argue there is no justifiable reason for making some conduct criminal. Practical lines of reasoning may be more effective in producing change. One argument simply declares it is not possible to effectively enforce all the laws now on the books.[11] Since they cannot all be

---

[9]*See* P. DEVLIN, THE ENFORCEMENT OF MORALS (1965); H.L.A. HART, LAW, LIBERTY, AND MORALITY (1963). *See also* B. MITCHELL, LAW, MORALITY, AND RELIGION IN A SECULAR SOCIETY (1967).

[10]For discussions of the third reason, see Feinberg, *"Harmless Immoralities" and Offensive Nuisances*, in ISSUES IN LAW AND MORALITY (N. Care & T. Trelogan eds.) (forthcoming); Bayles, *Offensive Conduct and the Law*, in *id.*; Feinberg, *Rejoinder*, in *id.* For discussions of laws to prevent people from harming themselves, see Bayles, *Criminal Paternalism*, in LIMITS OF LAW: NOMOS XV (J. Pennock & J. Chapman eds.) (Forthcoming); Dworkin, *Paternalism*, in MORALITY AND THE LAW 107 (R. Wasserstrom ed. 1971); Feinberg, *Legal Paternalism*, 1 CAN J. OF PHIL. 105 (1971).

[11]*See* PACKER, *supra* note 3, at 270-95.

enforced, one might as well legalize the less harmful conduct (marijuana, gambling) and devote scarce enforcement resources to more serious crimes. Another argument contends that many laws result in more, rather than fewer, crimes. For example, laws against gambling, drugs, and alcohol pave the way for large scale organized crime.[12] The repeal of the prohibition amendment probably represents the most significant application of these arguments. Indeed, the problems of prohibition are frequently pointed to by those who wish to decriminalize marijuana use.

In practice the effort to decriminalize conduct has not been effective. While some success has been achieved with respect to consensual sex offenses, the number of offenses which are *mala prohibita* has increased rapidly. The federal government is now pushing for laws making it illegal not to buckle auto seat-belts, and the criminal law has also reached long tentacles into the business world. Many new economic offenses have been created. Interestingly, however, there has been a strong tendency to eliminate the requirement of responsibility by use of strict liability.

The method of dismantling the criminal law by divestment has been the most successful to date. The focus of this attack is upon using the mental conditions for responsibility to eliminate large groups of people from the criminal law system. Certain groups of people, it is contended, do not have the requisite mental conditions. In this century two large classes of people have been removed from the reaches of the criminal law system, namely juveniles and the mentally abnormal. Juveniles, however, have been placed in a system which is halfway between a punishment and a treatment system, although it was intended to be the latter. Pressure has also been increasing to divest the criminal law of drug addicts. Much of the focus of the attempt to dismantle the criminal law system by divestment has been centered on broadening the *M'Naghten*[13] test of insanity, *e.g.*, irresistible impulse,[14] the *Durham* rule [15] and diminished responsibility.[16]

At the same time, other attempts to dismantle the criminal law system have taken the opposite approach. Instead of broadening the excuses, the

[12]*See* Smith & Pollack, *Crimes Without Victims*, 77 CASE & COM. 9 (No. 4, 1972).
[13]M'Naghten's Case, 8 Eng. Rep. 718 (H.L. 1843).
[14]*See* Davis v. United States, 165 U.S. 373, 378 (1897); Parsons v. State, 81 Ala. 577, 596-97, 2 So. 854, 866-67 (1887).
[15]Durham v. United States, 214 F.2d 862, 874-75 (D.C. Cir. 1954), *overruled*, United States v. Brawner, Crim. No. 22,714 (D.C. Cir., Jun. 23, 1972) (en banc) (*Durham* rule replaced by MODEL PENAL CODE §4.01 (1) (Proposed Official Draft 1962)).
[16]*See* People v. Bassett, 69 Cal. 2d 122, 443 P.2d 777, 70 Cal. Rptr. 193 (1968): People v. Wolff, 61 Cal. 2d 795, 394 P.2d 959, 40 Cal. Rptr. 271 (1964).

mens rea requirement and excuses have been eliminated. As noted above, a large number of strict liability offenses have been added to most criminal law system. Strict liability essentially eliminates the mens rea requirements. Thus, attempts to dismantle the criminal law system have been working in two opposite directions with respect to the mental conditions for responsibility.

Finally, attempts have been made to alter or abolish the prison system. Incarceration is not, of course, the only method of punishment. But since corporal and capital punishment[17] have virtually disappeared, the two main methods of punishment now in use are deprivation of liberty and of wealth. Some European systems rely much more on fines than is customary in the United States. In view of the high rate of recidivism and overcrowding or prisons, attempts are being made to make less use of incarceration. Various techniques are involved, the most obvious being suspended sentences and probation for first offenders. Other techniques change the nature of prisons by instituting temporary release as in work release programs. These practices do not necessarily eliminate punishment, but they do change considerably its traditional form. The overall trend is towards treatment or rehabilitation instead of punishment per se. But so long as incarceration is involved and the other parts of the criminal law system such as responsibility remain intact, punishment remains.

III. Responsibility or Treatability

Much of the criticism and dismantling of the criminal law system have centered on the requirement of responsibility, especially the mental conditions for responsibility. The general features of criminal responsibility have already been outlined. A contrasting notion is that of treatability. As responsibility is a requirement for the imposition of punishment, so treatability is a requirement for the imposition of treatment. But treatability is a simpler concept. The conditions for treatability are that a person have an undesirable condition or status and that there be a method for changing his condition or status to a more desirable one. Many proposals for dismantling the criminal law system seek to substitute treatability for responsibility.[18] The full substitution of treatability for

[17]*See* Furman v. Georgia, 408 U.S. 238 (1972).

[18]Some people may fall outside of both punishment and treat-systems, being neither responsible nor treatable. There may not be a known method for changing their status. In practice, treatment systems have tended to ignore the requirement that a status be correctable. But logically a third system--social defense--is involved. A social defense system takes whatever steps necessary to prevent dangerous persons from engaging in

responsibility would eliminate both the act and men rea requirements. Of course, mixed systems are possible in which the act requirement is retained, but the requirement of an act is not logically involved in the concept of a treatment system.

Two general lines of attack--one practical and scientific, the other philosophical--have been made upon criminal responsibility by those favoring a treatment system. The practical attack centers on the difficulty courts have in determining whether a person could avoid doing what he did. Because of this difficulty, the law has always relied upon objective tests: could or would a reasonable man have known or done such and such. Use of objective tests, of course, means that some people who do not have normal abilities will be convicted when they in fact could not have avoided doing what they did. Moreover, this determination has been vastly complicated by the rise of psychology. Psychologists and psychoanalysts have shown that much less behavior is within a person's conscious control than was previously though. Can most blacks raised in ghettos keep from becoming drug addicts or turning to crime? Could a white collar embezzler have actually resisted the temptation, given that society has taught him to seek consumer goods and a higher standard of living? When all the root causes of a crime are brought to light by a sympathetic psychiatrist and defense lawyer, one may not be sure the defendant could have avoided doing what he did.

A variation of this argument claims that there is no sharp distinction between being able and not being able to control one's conduct. People have varying degrees of control over different actions. Consider whether or not the following people can refuse the offer: a man who has just eaten a steak dinner offered a piece of blubber to chew; an obese person offered a piece of his favorite candy after dinner; a marijuana user offered a joint; a smoker offered a cigarette; an alcoholic offered a drink; and, a heroin addict beginning withdrawal offered a fix. One may claim each of these people can refuse the offer, but it will obviously be much easier for some than others. Further, the defense of diminished responsibility seems to recognize that mental disability may result in degrees of ability to avoid actions. So the argument is that courts cannot accurately determine a person's ability to avoid a specific action. Instead of pursuing the question of whether or not a person could control his conduct, one suggestion is that the only question should be whether or not he is treatable. If he has an undesirable but correctable status, he should be treated.

A philosophical attack on criminal responsibility seeks to show that ultimately it rests upon a status and that the most reasonable policy is to treat this status. A recent philosophical theory is that a person is

---

undesirable behavior.

blameworthy for an action only if it manifests a defect of character.[19] A defect of character is a bad or undesirable character trait. The concept of a character trait is difficult to explain, but R. B. Brandt suggests it must be either a social asset or liability and behavior manifesting it much be within a person's voluntary control. On this account the excuses fall into place as indicating actions which do not manifest a defect of character. Since a man who acts as a result of ignorance or duress does not manifest any evil intention or reprehensibility, this account of blame worthiness appears quite plausible. Further, it can easily be modified to the criminal law by substituting criminal responsibility for blameworthiness and restricting the acts to criminal offenses. A person is thus responsible for an offense if his act manifests a defect of character.

Upon this account, then, responsibility involves both act and character. There is not responsibility for an act unless character is involved. Some people are tempted to turn this theory against that requirement of responsibility. It is not clear, they argue, that actions manifesting character traits are voluntary as Brandt suggests. A character trait is a disposition to act in certain ways, and dispositions result in conduct in the appropriate circumstances. If a person is hungry and food is presented to him, he will eat it. If he does not, then he did not in fact have the disposition to eat, *i.e.*, he was not hungry. Further, people's characters are much less under their control than their actions--a man cannot avoid being greedy. Hence, if responsibility requires that people be able to avoid what they are responsible for, then since part of what they are held responsible for are character traits and these are usually not under their control, people probably are not responsible for most actions.

Proponents of this argument may then expand it to eliminate the requirement of an act and drop all discussion of responsibility. If acts are significant only as manifestations of defects of character, then, they contend, there is no reason to require an act of liability. Acts are not the only indicators of character. Psychological tests and other evidence may provide a good basis for determining that a person is greedy or violent. To wait until people commit crimes to take action is simply shutting the barn door after the horses have gone. The only reasonable approach is to enquire whether a person has a character trait apt to result in undesirable conduct, and if he does and it is correctable, to change it.

To summarize this argument: (1) People are only responsible for acts if they manifest a defect of character. (2) Undesirable character traits are

---

[19]*See, e.g.*, R. BRANDT, ETHICAL THEORY 461-71 (1959); Brandt, *Blameworthiness and Obligation*, in ESSAYS IN MORAL PHILOSOPHY 3 (A. Melden ed. 1958); Brandt, *A Utilitarian Theory of Excuses*, 78 PHIL. REV. 337 (1969).

almost certain to result in undesirable conduct. (3) People cannot usually avoid having the character traits they have. (4) People are frequently treatable, but never responsible, for that which they cannot avoid or control. (5) Therefore, people are frequently treatable but not usually responsible for their character traits. (6) Thus, treatment, not punishment, is generally appropriate. (7) Since people are to be treated to prevent undesirable conduct, there is no reason to require that they perform prohibited acts before being treated.

However, this line of reasoning is open to strong criticism. It may be said to rest upon confusing what one is responsible for and the conditions under which one is responsible. Specifically, one is responsible for prohibited actions. A defect of character is a necessary condition for one being responsible, but not what one is responsible for. Thus, the crucial question is not whether a person could avoid acting from them. A person may not be able to help being irascible, but he can refrain from punching others in the mouth. Not all behavior indicating irascibility is prohibited, and a person can control which types of irascible conduct he performs. Once this distinction is made, there is no reason to ask whether or not a person's character trait is within his control. Further, since a person is being punished for his act, not his character, there can be no justification for eliminating the requirement of an act.

IV. Determinism and Preventive Social Reform

Both punishment and treatment systems are oriented towards individuals; that is, they are both directed at specific persons for their actions or statuses. An alternative to both of them is socially directed. Instead of focusing on individuals, it focuses on the social conditions on which, it is held, the actions and statuses or individuals ultimately depend. As B. F. Skinner puts the point, "It is the environment which is 'responsible' for the objectionable behavior, and it is the environment, not some attribute of the individual, which must be changed."[20] Those who have argued for freedom, dignity, and punishment, Skinner contends, "cannot now accept the fact that all control is exerted by the environment and proceed to the design of better environments rather than of better men."[21]

There are many sources for such a view. One source is the traditional concern to prevent crime. The aim of penal laws is to ensure that fewer actions or certain types are performed. Punishment and treatment operate after the fact, after a crime has been committed or an undesirable status has

---

[20] B. Skinner, Beyond Freedom and Dignity 70 (Bantam/Vintage ed. 1971).
[21] *Id.* 77.

developed. But if the aim is to prevent undesirable conditions, then efforts should be directed at preventing their first appearance. The way to eliminate their appearance is preventive social reform.

The main attack on the criminal law system by advocates of a system of preventive social reform stems from the belief of some of them that determinism is incompatible with responsibility.[22] Determinism, they contend, is the scientific view, whereas responsibility rests upon a mystical, religious belief in uncaused actions. In the modern world, they say, it is unacceptable to continue to punish people on the basis of the outmoded, unscientific concept of responsibility. A crucial issue, then, is whether determinism is incompatible with responsibility. This is not a scientific but a philosophical issue.

For present purposes, determinism may perhaps best be defined as the claim that every event has a cause.[23] However, there are various definitions of "cause," and the meaning of determinism will necessarily vary with the definition used. Legally, a cause is frequently defined as a necessary condition of an event, *sine qua non*. But that definition is not widely used in science. Another definition more closely approximating scientific usage defines a cause as a set of sufficient conditions for an event. Thus, a cause is a set of conditions such that whenever conditions of this sort exist, an event of a specified type will occur.[24]

This central issue of the compatibility of determinism which responsibility may be developed from the following argument: For a person to be responsible for an action, it must be the case that he could have avoided the action and done otherwise. But if determinism is true, there is a set of sufficient conditions for every event. Thus, there are sufficient conditions for every action every person performs. Given these conditions, the action follows. Thus, given the conditions, a person could not have avoided an action or done otherwise. Hence, determinism is incompatible with responsibility.

Two general types of view--mechanistic or hard determinism and libertarianism or indeterminism--accept the foregoing argument. The hard

---

[22]Skinner asserts that "[t]he mistake...is to put the responsibility [for objectionable behavior] anywhere, to suppose that somewhere a causal sequence is initiated." *Id.* 72.

[23]For an introductory discussion of the principle of determinism, see J. HOSPERS, AN INTRODUCTION TO PHILOSOPHICAL ANALYSIS 308-320 (2d ed. 1971).

[24]This definition is probably not acceptable for the cause of an event. For example, if a man falls from a 10 story building, sufficient conditions exist for his death. However, if a marksman shoots and kills him before he lands, the marksman causes his death and not the fall even though the fall, etc., constitutes a set of conditions sufficient for his death. However, the analysis of causation is to complex to be pursued here.

determinists conclude that responsibility is illusory. No one is responsible for his actions.[25] The indeterminists, on the other hand, argue that responsibility exists and that determinism is false.[26]

The third general view--nonmechanistic or soft determinism--rejects the foregoing argument for the incompatibility of responsibility and determinism. First, the soft determinist points out that to say a person's actions are caused is not the same as to say they are compelled. Psychiatrists generally hold that all of a person's actions are caused, but they do not believe that all of them are compulsive. Circumstances, other people, or inner compulsions may compel actions. But if a normal person is trying to decide whether to have a hamburger or hot dog and finally chooses the latter, he was not compelled to choose it. Yet, there were causes for his choice, e.g., he likes hot dogs better. Compulsion, at best, refers to certain types of causes.

Second, the soft determinist argues that an action's being caused is compatible with the claim that the actor could have avoided it. To say "a person could have done otherwise" is equivalent to saying """he would have done otherwise if...". Precisely what should be filled in after the "if" depends upon the situation.[27] The main requirements for doing otherwise are that a person have the capacity, opportunity, and desire to do otherwise. For example, last night Harry Reader read *The Winds of War*. But he could have read *Babbitt.* He had the capacity to read *Babbitt* for he reads English. Further, he had the opportunity for it was there beside him on the bookshelf. But he did not want to read it as much as he wanted to read *The Winds of War.*

But, the hard determinist will object, the central point is that what a person wants to do is also caused. So there is a set of sufficient conditions for a person wanting to do one thing more than another. And so long as this is the case, the person could not have done otherwise. The soft determinist, however, admits there are causes for people wanting to do one thing rather than another. But among these causes are a person's character traits, which differ from other traits people have. Consider two boys who

---

[25]*See e.g.*, Edwards, *Hard and Soft Determinism*, in DETERMINISM AND FREEDOM IN THE AGE OF MODERN SCIENCE 104 (S. Hook ed. 1958); Hospers, *What Means This Freedom*, in *id.* 13.

[26]*See, e.g.*, Broad, *Determinism, Indeterminism, and Libertarianism,* in ETHICS AND THE HISTORY OF PHILOSOPHY: SELECTED ESSAYS 195 (1952); Campbell, *Is "Freewill" a Pseudo-Problem?*, 60 MIND 441 (1951).

[27]*See* P. NOWELL-SMITH, ETHICS 273-78 (1954); Nowell-Smith, *Ifs and Cans,* in FREE WILL AND DETERMINISM 322 (B. Berofsky ed. 1966).

both fail an exam, one because his is stupid, and the other because he is lazy.[28] The stupid boy is not thought responsible for his failing, but the lazy one is. The lazy one could have done otherwise, but not the stupid one.

The reason only the lazy boy is responsible is that only his trait is amenable to change by praise and blame, reward and punishment. Thus, a person is responsible for actions manifesting certain character traits simply because the traits in question are amenable to control. In particular cases punishment or reward may not be effective, but generally such traits and actions can be controlled by these devices. And this view is not incompatible with there being causes of actions. In fact, it requires actions to be caused. As David Hume long ago asserted, "'Tis indeed certain, that as all human laws are founded on rewards and punishments, 'tis suppos'd as a fundamental principle, that these motives have an influence on the mind, and both produce the good and prevent the evil actions."[29]

While the soft determinist does not believe that determinism is incompatible with responsibility, he may still advocate social reforms. There are many conditions which influence actions. The question for crime prevention may then become a practical issue--which techniques will best prevent crime. But the soft determinist, unlike the hard determinist, may be quite willing to continue the criminal law system and pursue social reform simultaneously, for he finds both procedures acceptable methods of controlling undesirable behavior.

V. Insanity, Addiction, and Preventive Detention

The general issues relating to punishment, treatment, and social reform systems are involved in each of the specific areas of insanity, addiction, and preventive detention. In each area there are questions of responsibility and the appropriate method of preventing undesirable behavior. The issue of legal insanity concerns a defendant's responsibility. Thus, each of the three main tests of legal insanity are to be viewed as indicating conditions in which a mentally abnormal person could not have avoided doing what he did.[30] The *M'Naghten* test emphasizes cognitive aspects of responsibility--a person's knowledge of the wrongness or nature and

---

[28]*See* ETHICS, *supra* note 27, at 300-06

[29]D. HUME, A TREATISE OF HUMAN NATURE 410 (L. Selby-Bigge ed. 1888).

[30]The Model Penal Code tests are here treated as a combination and rewording of the *M'Naghten* and irresistible impulse tests.

quality of his art.[31] It excuses from responsibility on the grounds of ignorance. The irresistible impulse test emphasizes a person's incapacity to control his behavior.[32] Finally, the *Durham* test excuses a person if his conduct was the product of mental disease or defect.[33] Since the issue is whether a person could have avoided doing what he did, if he could have, his illness will not be classified as a mental disease or defect.

All the tests deny responsibility due to the status of the defendant--his having a mental disease or defect. In effect, the mental state of the defendant makes him an inappropriate subject for responsibility and punishment. At the same time, each of the tests guides the defendant into a treatment process because in each case he obviously has acted in a way harmful to the community. Also, he is judged to have had (and likely still to have) a disease or defect. If the defendant's disease or defect is correctable, then the meets the criteria of treatability. Since there has been a tendency to assume all diseases and most defects are correctable, incarceration is a treatment program seems almost inevitable. And, in fact, persons who successfully plead insanity are usually confined in mental institutions.

This dismantling of the criminal law system at this point involves divesting it of the mentally abnormal defendants and substituting mass civil commitment programs. Since theoretically any evils inflicted on persons during treatment are only unavoidable aspects of a program designed to benefit them, they may be confined until cured so long as the benefit of the cure is thought to outweigh the evils of treatment. Persons being treated for physical diseases may decide to discontinue treatment if they do not think the benefit is worth the evils. But the mentally ill are not deemed competent to make such judgments. Thus, they are confined until others decide they are well or it is not worth trying to cure them (or the number of committed persons is so great there is no room to continue to hold them).

The social reform approach to insanity claims that social conditions cause people to become mentally ill. Thus, the first task of social reform is to identify those social conditions which "drive people crazy." Racism, poverty, unhappy marriages, and bad working conditions are some of the alleged causes of mental illness. So the chief task in preventing insanity is to build a sane society, *i.e.*, one which does not cause people to become mentally ill.

---

[31]M'Naghten's Case, 8 Eng. Rep. 718 (H.L. 1843).

[32]*See* Davis v. United States, 165 U.S. 373, 378 (1897); Parsons v. State, 81 Ala. 577, 596-97, 2 So. 854, 866-67 (1887).

[33]Durham v. United States, 214 F.2d 862, 874-75 (D.C. Cir. 1954). See note 15 *supra*.

Similar issues arise with addiction. There has not yet been complete divestment of addicts from the criminal law system. Further, many scholars advocate decriminalization rather than divestment. Addiction itself, not being an act but an illness, is not criminal in the United States,[34] but the acts engaged in by addicts--possession and use of drugs--are criminal. The situation is somewhat analogous to maintaining that people are not responsible for whooping cough, but are for coughing or possessing cough medicine. The tensions between responsibility for acts, treatability for status, and social reform are probably greatest with respect to drug addiction.

The main theoretical attempt to dismantle the criminal law system with respect to drug use has focused on decriminalizing it. Advocates of social reform contend that question of responsibility is not important, the point being that the criminalization of drugs causes more harm than good. Addicts are not deterred from drug use, and they turn to other types of crime to support their habits. Moreover, the distribution of illegal drugs provides organized crime with a lucrative activity. Thus, the way to solve the drug problem is to decriminalize drug related actions. The drug problem, it is frequently contended, is a clear example of social conditions creating a problem and then authorities trying to solve it by punishing those deemed responsible.

A major step toward decriminalization of drug use was the recent report of the National Commission on Marijuana and Drug Abuse.[35] After its investigation, the Commission recommended repealing laws making private possession and use of marijuana a crime.[36] Interestingly, the Commission recommended that a plea of marijuana intoxication not be a defense to any criminal charge under any circumstances. This recommendation treats marijuana intoxication differently from alcoholic intoxication despite their clinical similarities. The Commission justifies barring marijuana intoxication as a defense, even if it negates an element of an offense or is involuntarily induced, on the ground that marijuana does not involve physical dependence.[37] But, of course, a social drinker does not have a physical dependence on alcohol, yet he can claim intoxication as a defense.

The approach to dismantling the criminal law system by divestment

---

[34]*See* Robinson v. California, 370 U.S. 660 (1962).

[35]THE NAT'L COMM'N ON MARIHUANA AND DRUG ABUSE, MARIHUANA, A SIGNAL OF MISUNDERSTANDING (1972).

[36]*Id.* 190-95.

[37]*Id.* 201-02.

and treatment has also been advanced for addiction, especially addiction to the opiates. The use of opiates establishes a physical dependence with a need for increasingly larger doses. The result of unchecked usage is apt to be death. Thus, there is considerable ground for the claim that the opiate user harms himself. Since addiction of this sort has a physical basis and involves a lack of control over drug-related behavior, a sort of irresistible impulse, it is contended that addicts are not responsible for acts manifesting their condition, *i.e.*, for drug use.

One method of divestment of addicts is straightforward civil commitment for treatment. Given an addict's physical dependence and lack of control, he can be classified as ill or as having an undesirable status. Indeed, the authority of the Supreme Court stands behind such a classification.[38] Thus, civil commitment for treatment based solely on the status of being an addict is appropriate if one assumes that addiction is correctable.

Another and more common method of divestment occurs within the criminal process. This divestment occurs at the sentencing stage and substitutes treatment for punishment. Thus, it still requires an act and responsibility; a person much be convicted of committing a crime. Since addicts have an uncontrollable craving for drugs which are only available at high prices, they turn to other crimes to support their habits. Since stealing is not a direct manifestation of addiction, the addict is responsible for his crime. But then treatment is substituted for punishment. The treatment is neither for the criminal act nor the culpable mental state from which it originates, but for the nonculpable mental state of addiction. So this process of divestment is halfway between a punishment and a treatment system.

Finally, preventive detention also involves dismantling part of the criminal law system.[39] Preventive detention may occur either within or outside the criminal law system. Within the system, preventive detention may be either pretrial or posttrial detainment. However, both forms involve a modification of the criminal law system. While both of these forms of preventive detention require that a person be responsible for committing a prohibited act, he is not detained for that act. Instead, he is detained for a status, usually dangerousness.[40]

---

[38]*See* Robinson v. California, 370 U.S. 660 (1962).

[39]Preventive detention is detainment of persons to avoid undesirable effects upon them or the community.

[40]Most generally "dangerousness" means a disposition to commit additional criminal acts.

Posttrial preventive detention has existed in most countries for a long time and is widely accepted. It is found in persistent or habitual offender statutes. The defendant must usually have been convicted of two or more previous felonies. When convicted of another, his sentence is increased above the normal for first or second offenders. Thus, he must be responsible for committing a prohibited act, but the increased sentence cannot, by definition, be for that act since the crime of which he is convicted carries a lesser penalty. Neither is he punished for the previous crimes, since he has already been punished for them and further punishment would be a denial of due process. Thus, the person is being confined for the status of being a persistent offender. While detainment of persistent offenders rests upon status and might be thought to be an instance of a treatment system, no treatment other than detainment is forthcoming. Perhaps the reason for the lack of treatment is that absence of any known cure for being a persistent offender. In any event, in the absence of treatment, this form of detainment actually follows the model of a social defense system.[41]

A major dispute in the United States in recent years has centered on pretrial preventive detention. This form of detention also requires an act, but it need not be proven that the person is responsible for it. It is enough if he was arrested for a crime and sufficient evidence exists to bind him for trial. However, the person is neither detained for that alleged crime nor to assure his presence at trial. The District of Columbia preventive detention statute makes clear that the person is held to "assure the safety of the community" or to prevent obstruction of justice.[42] Again, the primary reason for keeping the person in custody is his status as dangerous. It is another instance of social defense.

In the absence of any known treatment, disputes over preventive detention are primarily between defenders of the traditional criminal law system and advocates of social defense. Defenders of the traditional system contend that pretrial preventive detention infringes the right to bail and the presumption of innocence. Beyond these issues, and of more interest of advocates of social defense, is the question of the effectiveness of pretrial detention and bail systems. For pretrial detention to greatly reduce crimes, one must either be able to accurately predict those who will commit crimes while awaiting trial or detain a large number of persons who are not dangerous. But it may be said, it is not possible to accurately predict who is apt to commit further crimes, and it would be obviously unjust to use a system in which many nondangerous persons would be

---

[41]For a definition of social defense systems, see note 18 *supra*.

[42]D.C. CODE §23-1322 (a) (1)-(3) (Supp. V. 1972).

detained. Further, if the period of time from arrest to trial were reduced from the 2 years frequently required to 2 months of less, defendants would not commit so many crimes while on pretrial release simply because they would have less time to do so.

On the other side, it can be argued that the bail system results in many indigent persons being detained prior to trial. Surely it would be more fair and rational to detain people because there is reason to believe they threaten the safety of the community than because they are poor. Since the latter status is not a disposition to act, there is no justification whatsoever to use it as a basis for detaining persons.

VI. Conclusion

Four different models for controlling undesirable behavior have been discussed: First, the traditional criminal law system which relies on punishment of person responsible for prohibited actions; second, the treatment system which relies upon correcting undesirable statuses; third, the social reform system which relies upon designing social institutions so that undesirable behavior and statuses do not arise; and fourth, the social defense system which is unconcerned with responsibility, treatment, or reform and relies upon doing whatever is necessary to prevent undesirable behavior, usually simply removing people from society.

No actual system exactly conforms to any of the models, although many legal scholars have sought to purify existing criminal law systems to make them more closely conform to the traditional model. But recently the ideal of the traditional system has increasingly come under attack by proponents of the other types of system. The future seems to portend further attempts and successes by those seeking to dismantle much of the criminal law system. Jeremy Bentham, perhaps the greatest criminal law theorist of all time, is usually criticized for assuming that people make rational choices when engaging in crime. But Bentham may have accurately stated the necessary conditions for a criminal law system to operate effectively. Its effectiveness appears to be restricted to highly rational behavior. And if the soft determinist is correct about responsibility, people are not responsible for behavior unless the threat or imposition of punishment can generally affect the character traits causing behavior of that sort. Thus, by it very conceptions the criminal law system is restricted to that behavior for which the threat and imposition of punishment can generally be effective.

Perhaps, then, those parts of existing criminal law systems not concerned with rational behavior should be dismantled. The criminal law is not the only legal technique for controlling behavior.[43] Other legal and nonlegal techniques may be more effective for controlling some of the behavior and persons currently within the province of criminal law systems.

---

[43]For an account of various legal techniques, see Summers, *The Technique Element in Law*, 59 CALIF. L. REV. 733 (1971). Joseph L. Sax has persuasively argued that the criminal law system is not the most effective legal technique for environmental protection. J. SAX, DEFENDING THE ENVIRONMENT (1971).

LEGISLATING MORALITY

John Stuart Mill's *On Liberty* initiated a controversy concerning the legislation of morality which has raged ever since. One would expect that by now at least the issues would be clear. However, several recent discussions indicate a difference of opinion even about what the issues are. The first three sections of this paper primarily aim to clarify the issues and the last three sections show that, properly understood, Mill is correct in maintaining that the state ought not legislate morality. In particular, three main arguments for legislating morality will be shown to be inadequate.

THE GENERAL ISSUE

Mill wrote that "the only purpose for which power can be rightfully exercised over any member of a civilized community, against his will, is to prevent harm to others."[1] This assertion involves two distinct claims: (1) preventing harm to others is a purpose for which a person's liberty may be limited, and (2) there is no other purpose for which a person's liberty may be limited. The concern herein is with the second claim, in particular, its denial that preventing immorality is a proper purpose for limiting liberty. While Mill did not restrict himself to legal limits on liberty, the issue is so restricted in this paper.

Some writers, especially those who disagree with Mill, take the second claim as asserting that there is some conduct which is not the law's business. For example, Martin P. Golding has recently written that Mill's statement is "the *locus classicus* of the position that there are spheres of conduct which are 'not the law's business'...."[2] There are two possible interpretations of the second claim as thus stated. First, one may interpret it as meaning that there is conduct which does not fall within the purposes for limiting liberty. This interpretation has given rise to the criticism of Mill that there is no self-regarding conduct, conduct which does not affect others.[3] But, it is clear that there is such conduct. For example, when I put

[1]J.S. MILL, ON LIBERTY 13 (C. Shields ed. 1956).

[2]M. GOLDING, PHILOSOPHY OF LAW 55-56 (1974).

[3]Mill does not deny that self-regarding conduct frequently affects others in some manner or other, only that it affects them in any manner which gives them a legitimate basis for possibly interfering with the liberty to engage in it. J.S. MILL, *supra* note 1, at 98-99. *See also* J. FEINBERG, SOCIAL PHILOSOPHY 31-32 (1973).

W. L. Robison (ed.), The Legal Essays of Michael Bayles, 21–40.
© 2002 *Kluwer Law International. Printed in the Netherlands.*

on my socks this morning, I did not affect others. However, so interpreted, the claim is trivial. For no matter what purposes one takes to be acceptable for limiting people's liberty, there will be conduct which is not the law's business, namely, that which does not fall within any of those purposes. Thus, even if one believes that one purpose for legally limiting liberty is to prevent immorality, there is conduct which is not the law's business, namely, that which is neither immoral nor harmful to others. Surely this trivial claim cannot be what Mill meant to assert and his critics to deny.

The second interpretation of the claim that there is conduct which is not the law's business requires description of the conduct in a way which is neutral with respect to the purposes for limiting liberty. For example, the conduct might be described as that which occurs in private rather than public. Indeed, critics of the Millian position frequently interpret its defenders as making just this distinction. Lord Devlin interprets the *Wolfenden Report*[4] in this manner[5] and Golding believes this is a basic criterion of H.L.A. Hart.[6] Of course, the critics have little difficulty showing that some neutrally described conduct is the law's business. Furthermore, the critics would not be satisfied with a showing that as a matter of fact conduct described in a certain manner was never the law's business; they insist that there must be no conceivable circumstances in which such conduct would be the law's business. As Devlin puts it, "You have to show that the vice is not of its nature one that is capable of injuring society. Only then can society safely sign away its power of control."[7] Since he does not think this showing can be made, Devlin concludes that there are "no theoretical limits to legislation against immorality."[8]

However, this interpretation makes an impossible demand of Mill and his defenders, one which Mill never attempted to meet. The demand is that one describe conduct without reference to its producing harm (or falling within any other purpose for limiting liberty) and show that it is logically impossible for such conduct to cause harm because there are no conceivable circumstances in which the conduct would cause harm. This requirement cannot be met, because it is always logically possible for two logically independent conditions to be causally related. Moreover, Mill did

---

[4]REPORT ON THE COMMITTEE ON HOMOSEXUAL OFFENCES AND PROSTITUTION (1957).

[5]P. DEVLIN, THE ENFORCEMENT OF MORALS 9 (1965).

[6]M. GOLDING, *supra* note 2, at 61.

[7]P. DEVLIN, *supra* note 5, at 110.

[8]*Id.* 14.

not claim that neutrally described conduct could never cause harm. He allowed that even speech, which he thought was entitled to the widest liberty, could be limited in some circumstances. That is, he admitted that even speech could cause harm.[9] Thus, one does not disagree with Mill if one asserts, as Golding does, that the limits of permissible legal interference with conduct have to be settled on a case by case basis.[10] That does not deny theoretical limits on legislation in any sense which Mill asserted. Thus, Golding must put forth some other argument in order to establish Devlin's claim, with which he agrees, that there are no theoretical limits on legislation.[11]

Mill was concerned with the ends or purposes which would warrant legal interference with liberty. Preventing harm to others, he claimed, is the "sole end" or "purpose" for which society is "warranted" in limiting liberty.[12] A person's own good or the opinion of others that it would be right for him to do or forbear are "good reasons" for trying to persuade a person to do or forbear, but not for legally limiting his liberty to act.[13] In short, Mill was concerned with reasons for limiting liberty or conduct. He denied that reasons other than harm to others are good ones for limiting conduct; he did not claim that there is a neutrally describable type of conduct which could never be limited. A reason for or against legislation which limits liberty is neither necessary nor sufficient. It is not sufficient, because even the prevention of harm to others is not a sufficient reason for legislation if it will cause more harm than it will prevent. It is not necessary, because there might be another reason which would be sufficient to justify legislation.

What Mill and other opponents of the legislation of morality deny is the legal moralist principle. Roughly, the legal moralist principle states that a good reason for legislation is that it will prevent immoral conduct. Mill and his defenders deny that the immorality of conduct, in and of itself, is ever a good reason for legislation limiting liberty. Supporters of the legal moralist principle claim the opposite. But, of course, since the reason is not sufficient, they do not claim that any conduct which is immoral should be legally limited. There may be reasons against legislating morality, *e.g.*, that it would involve invasion of privacy.

---

[9]J.S. MILL, *supra* note 1, at 67-68. *See also* Feinberg, *Limits to the Free Expression of Opinion*, in PHILOSOPHY OF LAW 135 (J. Feinberg & Gross eds. 1975).

[10]M. GOLDING, *supra* note 2, at 67.

[11]*Id.*; P. DEVLIN, *supra* note 5, at 14.

[12]J.S. MILL, *supra* note 1, at 13.

[13]*Id.*

A crucial problem which cannot be discussed herein is the proper method for establishing that a reason for limiting liberty is a good one. The method which will be followed here is to ask whether the legal moralist principle would be acceptable to a reasonable person[14] contemplating its use by others in enacting legislation to which he would be subject.

THE MORALITY TO BE LEGISLATED

The chief question concerning the meaning of legal moralism is which standard of morality is to be used. The first distinction to be made is between the use of popular and critical morality as the standard. Popular morality, sometimes called positive morality by writers on jurisprudence, is the generally accepted morality of a society. Critical morality is what one believes to be the correct morality.

It is sometimes claimed that the entire dispute between Mill and his defenders on the one side, and their critics on the other, is simply which critical morality is to be legislated. For example, Rolf E. Sartorius contends that both sides agree that other things being equal, wrong ought to be prevented.[15] H.L.A. Hart, Sartorius claims, must allow society to limit liberty to engage in conduct which morally harms an actor, since Hart allows society to do so if the conduct physically harms the actor. Thus, Sartorius believes there is no principled basis for distinguishing between wrongful conduct which can and cannot be legally limited. Sartorius consequently claims the issue may only be resolved by taking a stand on the morality of conduct.[16]

This interpretation of the issue, however, is incorrect. First, Sartorius is wrong in thinking that if one allows some paternalism (limiting liberty to prevent an actor harming himself), one must adopt legal

---

[14]A reasonable person is one who is open to evidence and persuasion by argument, and not mentally ill or unintelligent. A reasonable person makes decisions on the basis of all relevant readily obtainable information. Moreover, he can be persuaded by arguments pro and con. While not every psychological abnormality, *e.g.*, a mild neurosis, prevents a person from being reasonable, severe abnormalities involving reality distortion do. Finally, a reasonable person is intelligent in the sense of being able to understand principles and the types of legislation for which they provide reasons in various circumstances. Of course, it is assumed that the reader is a reasonable person. Bayles, *Comments: Offensive Conduct and the Law*, in ISSUES IN LAW AND MORALITY 120 (N. Care & T. Trelogan eds. 1973).

[15]Sartorius, *The Enforcement of Morality*, 81 YALE L.J. 891, 908 (1972).

[16]*Id.* 899-900.

moralism. Legal moralism does not require that conduct cause even moral harm to the actor, while paternalism does.[17] Second, morality and law differ with respect to the "sanction" normally used to secure compliance. Morality is normally "sanctioned" by appeals to respect for the rules, admonitions, etc. The law normally uses punishment and other coercive measures as sanctions.[18] Even if one must believe the immorality of conduct is a good reason for the imposition of moral "sanctions," one need not think it is a good reason for the imposition of legal sanctions. Thus, thinking conduct is immoral does not entail thinking there is a good reason for legally prohibiting it. Third, these reasons are used by others to justify legislation. The question is not whether one's belief that conduct is immoral is a good reason for limiting liberty, but whether one can assent to *others* legally limiting liberty to engage in conduct which *they* believe to be immoral. Thus, the issue is not which critical morality to legislate, but whether anyone's critical morality ought to be legislated.

Few contemporary writers defend the legislation of critical morality. An exception is H.J. McCloskey,[19] who contends that a stable society requires a shared morality. Moreover, McCloskey contends, if one is to legislate moral beliefs, then surely one must legislate those which one believes to be correct.

McCloskey fails to see the tension in his argument. If a shared morality is needed for stability, then the morality to be legislated will have to be generally accepted or its enforcement will lead to instability. Yet the point of legislating one's own critical rather than the popular one is to avoid having a morality with which one disagrees enforced. Moreover, the critical morality to be legislated is not one's own but that of the political authorities. On McCloskey's own grounds, he could not expect authorities to legislate a morality they did not believe to be correct, yet the political authorities may be elected representatives, corrupt tyrants, or Plato's philosopher kings.

A reasonable person would not accept the legal moralist principle based upon critical morality. If the critical morality adopted by the political authorities differs greatly from that generally accepted in society, then the legal moralist principle would support much legislation preventing citizens from acting in ways they think morally permissible or even obligatory or requiring them to act in ways they think morally wrong. Given the variations in people's views as to the correct morality, a reasonable person

---

[17]Bayles, *Criminal Paternalism*, in THE LIMITS OF LAW: NOMOS XV 178-79 (J. Pennock & J. Chapman eds. 1974).

[18]H.L.A. HART, THE CONCEPT OF LAW 175-76 (1961).

[19]McCloskey, *Liberalism*, 49 PHILOSOPHY 13, 18-21 (1974).

would not find the risk of loss of liberty worth the potential benefits, for it is quite likely he would not hold the same critical morality as the political authorities on some major issues or at least disagree about its application to specific issues. In short, legal moralism based upon critical morality is apt to lead to a dictatorship in the name of morality.

If popular morality is the standard used for legal moralism, it is much more likely a reasonable person will agree with the moral principles and rules used by the political authorities. He is less likely to be prevented from doing what he thinks is morally permissible or obligatory. Thus, most recent defenders of legal moralism believe that legal moralism based upon popular morality is more likely to be acceptable than legal moralism based upon critical morality.

Even if legal moralism uses popular morality as its standard, there is still a problem of defining the popular morality precisely. The most famous account is that presented by Lord Devlin. In determining the popular morality, Devlin believes legislators should use the views of what he variously calls "the man in the street," "the man in the Clapham omnibus," "the right-minded man," "the reasonable man," or "the man in the jury box." Such descriptions involve a number of requirements upon the judgments of people. As in jury decisions, judgments should be such that any twelve persons could unanimously agree upon them. The judgments are made only after all facts and arguments have been presented and considered calmly and dispassionately. The people are not to judge on the basis of reason, but on their feelings of "intolerance, indignation and disgust."[20]

Devlin's account of the popular morality has been severely criticized as removing the use of reason from determining what morality should be legally enforced. Some criticisms have overlooked the restrictions which Devlin thinks are implied by his conception, *e.g.*, hearing the facts and arguments. Perhaps the best criticism of Devlin on this point has been by Ronald Dworkin. Dworkin writes, "[W]hat is shocking and wrong is not his [Devlin's] idea that the community's morality counts, but his idea of what counts as the community's morality."[21]

Dworkin presents an alternative account of popular morality based upon a distinction between what he calls the anthropological and discriminatory senses of "moral position." The anthropological sense of moral position refers to any attitudes and views of a group about proper conduct.

---

[20]P. DEVLIN, *supra* note 5, at 14-16, 17, 90-91.

[21]Dworkin, *Lord Devlin and the Enforcement of Morals*, in MORALITY AND THE LAW 69 (R. Wasserstrom ed. 1971).

It is what an anthropologist would describe as the morality (and, perhaps, customs) of a society. The discriminatory sense of moral position denotes a subclass of anthropological morality by contrasting a sincere moral conviction about proper conduct with prejudices, rationalizations, parrotings of others, etc. According to Dworkin, Devlin's mistake is to use popular morality in the anthropological sense and thus ignore whether the moral beliefs are reasonable ones, *i.e.*, held in the discriminatory sense.[22]

Dworkin requires two main features for one's judgment to be the result of a moral position in the discriminatory sense. One must be prepared to give reasons for it, and these reasons must be consistent with one's other convictions and beliefs expressed both verbally and in conduct.[23] The reasons which may be presented cannot be arbitrary or mere prejudices based upon considerations generally deemed irrelevant, *e.g.*, the color of a person's eyes. Nor can they be based upon personal emotional reactions, *e.g.*, aversion to homosexuals, since one's emotional reactions are supposed to be based upon the morality of persons' conduct, not *vice versa*. If facts are cited as reasons, they must at least be plausible, not, for example, the belief that homosexual conduct causes brain damage. The reasons cannot be a mere recital of the views of others, although this restriction is not meant to exclude appeal to expert opinion about facts. A discriminatory moral position excludes claiming homosexual actions are wrong because, for example, most people in one's community think they are. Further, the requirement of consistency does not exclude qualifications, exceptions, and occasional backsliding from one's convictions, only reasons which one does not sincerely hold but merely proffers to win an argument or those inconsistent with other sincere beliefs.

Dworkin contends that these general restrictions as to what is a moral position are part of the concept of moral position used in ordinary discussion and argument, part of popular morality, not simply standards of a critical morality imposed upon society. Although one may wish to

---

[22]*Id.* 67. There are thus four possible moralities on which the legal moralist principle might be based. There are two versions based on critical morality, what an individual considers to be morally correct. McCloskey's version (1a) uses the moral judgments of an individual citizen, one's own. The other version (1b), which Plato held in THE REPUBLIC, uses the moral judgments of the individual political authority. There are also two versions based on popular morality, what the general public believes. Devlin's version (2a) uses popular morality in the anthropological sense ignoring whether there is a reasonable basis for the popular morality. Dworkin's version (2b) uses popular morality in the discriminatory sense; that is, it selects those generally held moral beliefs which have a reasonable basis.

[23]*Id.* 62-65.

provide a different set of requirements for a moral position in the discriminatory sense or describe the same ones differently, Dworkin is basically correct. His account brings an element of reasonableness into the conception of popular morality. Generally, Dworkin's conditions for what counts as a moral position in the discriminatory sense resemble conditions for the views being those of a reasonable person.

Viewing himself as subject to legislation based upon the legal moralist principle, a reasonable person would prefer to have it based upon Dworkin's discriminatory rather than Devlin's anthropological account of popular morality. Since unreasonable moral beliefs would not be legislated, he would not usually be prevented from performing an action which he reasonably judged to be moral. Even if he were prevented from doing something he thought was morally permissible or obligatory, at least he would know that most reasonable people in society deemed the actions morally wrong; he might then be less certain of his own conviction about it. Consequently, legal moralism using the standard of critical morality in the discriminatory sense appears to be the most plausible version. Critical morality, what legislators happen to believe to be morally correct, was shown above to be unacceptable.[24] Here, popular morality in the discriminatory sense has been shown to be more plausible as a basis for legislation than popular morality in the anthropological sense.

Can Morality Be Legislated?

There is an initial objection to legal moralism, prevalent in the United States, that one cannot legislate morality; adoption of the legal moralist principle would be pointless since such legislation could never be effective. The contention that one cannot legislate morality might mean a number of things. (1) It could mean that making a rule a legal one does not make it morally correct. If morality could be so legislated, then conduct might be perfectly moral one day and immoral the next, but the morality of conduct does not change in this way.[25]

An objection might be that since one has a moral duty to obey the law, a law making conduct illegal also makes it immoral. This objection is subtle; it depends upon the assumption that one has a moral duty or obligation to obey the law. Few scholars hold that this obligation is

---

[24]See text at note 19 *supra*.

[25]It might be objected that some people believe the Pope can legislate morality. The official view, however, is not that the Pope legislates morality but that his declarations make clear that conduct is immoral. The conduct was always immoral; the Pope merely promulgates that fact.

absolute, making it always immoral to disobey the law. Nonetheless, with a few qualifications or exceptions, many scholars and others would accept a prima facie obligation to obey the law. One must distinguish, however, between conduct wrong in itself and conduct wrong for some other reason. There is an old legal distinction between *mala in se* and *mala prohibita*. *Mala in se* are acts which are wrong in themselves, while *mala prohibita* are acts which are wrong only because they have been prohibited. For example, there is nothing inherently wrong with stating the weight of packages in terms of pounds and ounces, but if kilograms and grams are required as the units of measurement, then it is wrong. The contention that legislation cannot make conduct morally right or wrong pertains to the conduct in itself, not as prohibited. Thus, morality cannot be legislated in the sense that legislation cannot make conduct right or wrong in itself. But this point is irrelevant, because the conduct to be limited is already deemed immoral in itself.

(2) A second meaning of the claim that one cannot legislate morality is that legislation cannot get people to act in morally acceptable ways, *i.e.*, prevent immoral actions and obtain moral ones. The United States' failure in prohibiting the consumption of alcoholic beverages is cited as evidence of this claim since, during Prohibition, many people continued to drink alcohol. In fact, it is said the wife of Chief Justice Hughes of the Supreme Court used to embarrass him by serving alcoholic drinks at their parties. But one failure does not demonstrate that legislation cannot obtain conformity to moral standards of conduct.

Some types of immoral conduct have been made illegal. Laws against prostitution and gambling are usually considered legislation of popular morality and such laws frequently do prevent immoral conduct. The amount of gambling which occurs in Nevada where it is legal is much greater than that which occurs in Utah and other states where it is illegal.[26] Those who claim one cannot legislate morality frequently reply that gambling still occurs in Utah and other places where it is illegal, but the fact that such activities still occur is irrelevant. The question is whether less immoral conduct occurs than would occur were it legal. No one claims that one cannot legislate against harm to others merely because murders still occur even though they are illegal. Success in legislation against forms of conduct does not depend upon their complete elimination.

Hence, one can, at least sometimes, legislate morality in the sense of securing conduct in conformity with it. Sometimes, however, those who contend that one cannot legislate morality have something else in

---

[26]For a similar claim with respect to prohibition of homosexuality, see B. LEISER, LIBERTY, JUSTICE AND MORALS 61 (1973).

mind. (3) They may mean that legislation cannot get people to believe or accept the moral norm, *i.e.*, change their attitudes and beliefs about the morality of the conduct. H.L.A. Hart argues that one cannot legislate morality in this sense. No moral value, he claims, resides in mere conformity to standards of popular morality.[27] Instead, value resides in voluntary restraint, refraining from immoral actions due to respect for moral norms.[28] If it is suggested that threats help teach moral norms, then Hart would require empirical evidence to show that threats of legal sanctions are an effective way of teaching morality. Hart suggests it is implausible that they are, for most morality is taught in other ways. Further, the use of threats creates the dangers that the sole motive for conformity is fear of punishment and that without such fear people would not refrain from immoral conduct.[29]

Nonetheless, it is not clear that legal enforcement of morality cannot produce conformity to moral norms from morally good motives.[30] Aristotle defines moral virtues as habits of right action which are developed by acting rightly.[31] Many philosophers would give a similar account of moral virtues. Such developed habits or dispositions frequently create a desire to act in the appropriate ways. If moral conduct can be produced by legislation, it may lead to the development of the proper motives and dispositions. Children are frequently taught moral norms by being required to conform to them and punished when they do not. However, adults may be less receptive to this learning process, especially with respect to morals,[32] because many persons' moral beliefs are settled by the time they are in their middle teens and change only as a result of dramatic personal experiences.

Even if the legislation of morality does not provide moral motives, it may strengthen them. Basil Mitchell suggests that legal enforcement may strengthen motives such as self-interest and habit.[33] While these motives

---

[27]H.L.A. HART, LAW, LIBERTY AND MORALITY 57-58 (1963).

[28]*Id.*

[29]*Id.*

[30]See McCloskey, *supra* note 19, at 19. T. DUSTER, THE LEGISLATION OF MORALITY ch. 1 (1970), presents a detailed account of how the legal proscription of heroin in the United States led to a general moral disapproval of its use.

[31]ARISTOTLE, NICOMACHEAN ETHICS, bk. 2, ch. 1.

[32]Plamenatz, *Responsibility, Blame and Punishment* in PHILOSOPHY, POLITICS AND SOCIETY ser. 3, at 176 (P. Laslett & W.G. Runciman eds. 1967).

[33]B. MITCHELL, LAW, MORALITY AND RELIGION IN A SECULAR SOCIETY 76-79 (1967).

are not strictly moral ones, they can support moral motives to action and make it easier for one to do the morally correct thing. Hart argues as if one conforms to rules either because one thinks they are morally correct or because one fears punishment, but there are various motives for action besides a sense of duty and fear.

Legislation of morality may also indirectly provide a moral motive for conduct. If people believe that it is morally wrong to break the law, then they may conform from a moral motive because the conduct is illegal. The motive will not be that the conduct is wrong in itself, *malum in se*. Rather, it will be that the conduct is wrong because prohibited, *malum prohibitum*. Nonetheless, the motive is a distinctively moral one. The objection that one cannot legislate morality thus does not seem sufficiently strong to bar the possibility of adopting the legal moralist principle.

THE DEMOCRATIC ARGUMENT

Various arguments have been proposed to show that the legal moralist principle is acceptable. Some of these arguments support versions of legal moralism which have already been rejected[34] as less plausible than that based on the discriminatory popular morality explicated above. While authors such as Devlin,[35] Golding,[36] and Rostow[37] have not explicitly directed their arguments to support legal moralism based on discriminatory popular morality, most of their arguments also apply to it. Essentially, three different arguments for legal moralism have been developed.

The first argument may be called the democratic argument. It rests upon the principle that governmental policies should reflect the will of the people and that the people who live in a country have a right to the kind of society they want. The legal moralist principle based on the discriminatory popular morality does not support the legislation of morality unless almost everyone judges in the discriminatory sense that the conduct in question is morally wrong. There must be more than a mere majority who think so; there must be a strong consensus among the subjects that the conduct is immoral.[38] If most of the people believe conduct is immoral, then the failure to consider that fact in legislating implies that the political authorities are not responsive to the will of the people. A reasonable person would not wish to have the will of the people ignored, for he, as a probable member

---

[34]See text at notes 19 and 24 *supra*.

[35]P. DEVLIN, *supra* note 5.

[36]M. Golding, *supra* note 2, at 58-61.

[37]E.V. ROSTOW, THE SOVEREIGN PREROGATIVE 45-80 (1962).

[38]Dworkin, *supra* note 21, at 69.

of a qualified majority, would not want his opinion ignored.

This argument has been criticized by Hart. He claims a confusion is involved in the claim that commitment to democratic principles requires granting that the majority, even a qualified majority, has the right to legislate morality.[39] The confusion is between the principle that political power should be entrusted to the majority and the claim that the majority cannot be criticized. From the fact that a majority is more apt to rule wisely than a minority it does not follow that a majority may not be mistaken or that there are not some matters about which even a majority should not be permitted to legislate. That most people believe a type of conduct to be immoral does not imply that it is permissible for them to enforce it upon the rest, Hart argues

Hart's criticism does not quite hit the mark. A defender of the democratic argument does not claim the moral beliefs of the majority are correct ones. Indeed, he could not do so without making the relativist claim that the moral beliefs of each society are the correct ones for it. Instead, he argues that there is no conclusive way of deciding which views are correct and that democracies are founded on the belief that in morals each person is as rational as the next or at least has equal capacity to distinguish right from the next or at least has equal capacity to distinguish right from wrong. Hence, the only acceptable procedure is to let the majority enact moral beliefs if they see fit.

Two different questions seem to be confused at this point: whether a majority has a political or constitutional right to legislate against what it deems immoral and whether it is an acceptable principle of legislation to make laws against conduct merely because a majority of citizens deem it immoral. Not even Mill denied a majority the political or constitutional right to legislate its morals, but he did deny that it should do so.[40] The democratic argument seems to illegitimately shift from the undoubted political or constitutional right to pass legislation to its acceptability. A majority must think it is correct about matters of morals, and there may even be reasons for supporting it more likely to be so than a minority. It is another question whether that morality should be legally enforced. A majority might recognize a legislative principle not to enforce its moral views just because they are moral views. Even if the majority does not recognize that point, it may still be correct.

There are other strong criticisms of the democratic argument. The argument is restricted in scope because it applies only to countries which

---

[39]H.L.A. HART, *supra* note 27, at 79-80.

[40]J.S. MILL, CONSIDERATIONS ON REPRESENTATIVE GOVERNMENT 103 (C. Shields ed. 1958).

acceptable principles. Thus, the method of decision-making cannot without circularity be used to justify accepting certain principles. And the contention that a reasonable person could not accept a political system denying the will of the people is too general. In choosing acceptable principles of legislation, one is deciding what one's will is with respect to the kinds of legislation which should be passed.

The Conformity Argument

The second argument for the legal moralist principle may be called the conformity argument, the central contention of which is that the value of enforcing conformity to popular morality is sufficient to justify adopting the legal moralist principle. There are two elements of this argument. The first element is the value of conformity; the second that the punishment or loss of liberty involved is not in fact a sufficient reason against legislating conformity. The legislation of morality may produce conformity to moral rules. Further, it may even provide moral motives or at least motives supporting moral ones.[41] The legal moralist principle does not support legislation unless most of the people in a country believe the conduct to be prevented is immoral. Hence, there is a high probability that a subject of the political authority will think the conduct immoral. It is part of the very idea of thinking conduct to be immoral, as opposed to an individual ideal, to demand that others comply with a rule proscribing it.[42] That is, to believe that conduct is immoral is to believe that others ought not engage in it and to desire that they not do so. Thus, one will probably believe conformity to the morality to be desirable.

Second, the most extreme loss of liberty which might be involved in legislating morality is punishment. But punishment to prevent immoral conduct may not be an overall evil. Under a retributive view of punishment, reward and punishment should be allocated according to desert. To obtain a just distribution of reward and punishment, those who act wrongly should be punished. Under a reformative view of punishment, the wrongdoer may be made morally better by the punishment. Even under a deterrent view, at least other persons may be deterred from immoral conduct. Hence, on any prevalent view, punishment may constitute less of an evil when imposed for immoral conduct than when imposed for conduct which is morally permissible.

There are various criticisms of this conformity argument. First, if

---

41 See text at note 28 *supra*.

42 Strawson, *Social Morality and Individual Ideal*, in READINGS IN CONTEMPORARY ETHICAL THEORY 334 (K. Pahel & M. Schiller eds. 1970).

a deterrent view, at least other persons may be deterred from immoral conduct. Hence, on any prevalent view, punishment may constitute less of an evil when imposed for immoral conduct than when imposed for conduct which is morally permissible.

There are various criticisms of this conformity argument. First, if one believes a form of conduct to be immoral, then one not only desires that others not engage in it but is willing to make an effort to obtain conformity. But as noted above, the measures one is willing to use to obtain conformity need not include legislation.[43] One may believe that admonitions, praise or blame are the only proper measures to produce conformity to moral rules. Thus, one may not believe that legislation is a justifiable measure for producing conformity.

Second, the central claim of the conformity argument is that conformity to the popular morality of a society, no matter what it may be, is intrinsically valuable. Such a principle is surely false. The popular morality of a society consists of a set of beliefs, feelings, and attitudes about proper conduct which, to some extent at least, influence conduct. Suppose a society has a strongly anti-Semitic or anti-black morality. One cannot reasonably claim that conformity to the morality is desirable. Whether or not conformity to a morality is desirable depends upon what the morality is. Hence, a reasonable person cannot commit himself to the claim that conformity to any and every popular morality is intrinsically valuable. His judgment of its value will have to depend upon his assessment of the correctness of particular moralities.

If conformity to moral beliefs is not in itself valuable, it follows that the fact that conduct is contrary to those beliefs is not a reason for preventing it. Conduct contrary to popular morality would merely be conduct contrary to what persons other than the actor think should be done, resulting only in others being annoyed and perhaps feeling aversion. These feelings on the part of others, regardless of their basis, are not necessarily evils to be avoided or to be prevented by law. So, unless one believes that people's moral beliefs, whatever they may be, and their feelings of aversion or revulsion to conduct contrary to those beliefs are to be protected and avoided, the mere fact that conduct is contrary to popular morality is not an acceptable reason for legislating against it.

It may be claimed that these criticisms of the conformity argument assume that a reasonable person does not share the popular morality, while the chances are very great that he will share it.To the contrary, while it is true that for any specific moral rule the chances are that he will not disagree with popular morality, the chances are also very high that he will disagree

---

[43]See text at note 18 *supra*.

with at least some rules of popular morality. Hence, there is a strong likelihood that acceptance of legal moralism will involve his being prevented from performing some type of action which he thinks is morally permissible or obligatory or being required to perform an action he thinks is immoral. He will likely give up the legislation of his moral beliefs when he agrees with the popular morality to avoid having the popular morality legislated when he disagrees, because he thereby gains moral autonomy albeit at the expense of annoyance and aversion to some conduct of others.

THE DISINTEGRATION ARGUMENT

The disintegration argument has been vigorously advanced by Devlin.[44] His account of it will be presented although his view of what is popular morality has already been rejected.[45] Devlin argues that morality is essential to the existence of society and, by analogy with treason, that society has a right to preserve whatever is essential to its existence.

A society, Devlin contends, is not merely a group of people living together, but a group of people sharing certain ideas concerning a way of life as well as political matters. Part of this way of life involves the morality of the group. Hence, a public or popular morality is part of the very idea of a society. For example, in most Western countries, monogamous marriage is a central social structure. The ideal of a monogamous marriage grounds most of sexual morality, and were the society not monogamous, one should probably say it was a different society. Actions contrary to those elements of morality forming the basis of the social structure affect society.

If there is a shared popular morality, then, Devlin claims, society has a right to enforce that morality by the use of law. "[I]f society has the right to make a judgment and has it on the basis that a recognized morality is as necessary to society as, say, a recognized government," Devlin argues, "then society may use the law to preserve morality in the same way it uses it to safeguard anything else that is essential to its existence."[46] He draws an analogy with treason.[47] Treason can be made illegal because it is directed towards the destruction of government and a government is essential for the existence of a society. Societies also often collapse from internal pressures, and frequently the first step in such pressures is the

---

[44]P. DEVLIN, *supra* note 5.

[45]See text at notes 21-24 *supra*.

[46]P. DEVLIN, *supra* note 5, at 11.

[47]*Id.* 13.

breakdown of a common morality. This fact indicates that immorality may threaten society as much as treason. "There are no theoretical limits to the power of the State to legislate against treason and sedition, and likewise I think there can be no theoretical limits to legislation against immorality."[48] Thus, he concludes, "the suppression of vice is as much the law's business as the suppression of subversive activities . . . . "[49]

Hart presents several criticisms of this argument. His major criticism is that it needs empirical support which is not forthcoming. If Devlin only claimed that those aspects of popular morality which seem to be required for *any* society to survive could be legislated, then his argument might be empirically supported. But he obviously wishes to maintain that society can legislate more than this moral minimum. As an empirical thesis, Devlin must maintain that a large part, but not all, of popular morality is essential for the existence of society. Support for this claim might come from historical evidence of the dissolution of societies or from social psychology about the effect of moral permissiveness or pluralism upon attitudes and behavior. However, such support is not available at present and seems unlikely.[50]

Hart further suggests that it is misleading to say, as Devlin does, that the moral minimum which all popular moralities contain is necessary for the existence of society; "[o]n the contrary," Hart asserts, "the preservation of any particular society is of value because among other things it secures for human beings some measure of these universal values."[51] Hence, the disintegration argument puts the cart before the horse by preserving morality for the sake of society instead of vice versa. Although Hart believes the moral minimum should be and usually is legislated, the reason for legislating it is not that it happens to be part of popular morality but that it proscribes conduct harmful to others.

Hart also suggests that Devlin sometimes confuses the disintegration and conformity arguments. Devlin defines a society, at least in part, as a set of shared ideas and beliefs. That is, he tends to identify a society with its morality and treat that morality "as a seamless web."[52] Thus, Hart

---

[48]*Id.* 14.

[49]*Id.* 13-14.

[50]Hart, *Social Solidarity and the Enforcement of Morality*, 35 U. CHI. L. REV. 1 (1967).

[51]H. L. A. HART, *supra* note 27, at 70.

[52]*Id.* 50-52. Devlin seems to be willing to accept this characterization of morality as a seamless web, but not the rest of Hart's argument. P. DEVLIN, *supra* note 5, at 13 n.1, 115.

claims, any change in popular morality involves a change in society. By definition, any deterioration in the popular morality will involve disintegration of society. Such an identification is absurd, for it denies the possibility of the morality of a society changing. Taken in this way, Devlin's view becomes another version of the conformity argument. He argues that the preservation of society is intrinsically valuable. Since a society's popular morality is identified with the society itself, it too is intrinsically valuable. Hence, a morality is legally enforced simply to preserve itself. However, for the most part Devlin does seem to defend a genuine disintegration argument rather than the conformity one.[53]

Hart does not provide a very sympathetic interpretation of Devlin's claim that a shared morality is essential to society. He does not allow much middle ground between the claim that practically the whole of morality is essential and that the moral minimum is essential. It does not seem possible to make sense of the claim that more than the moral minimum is essential to a society without claiming the whole of morality is. Different types of society exist, and part of the difference between them may be due to differences in shared moral beliefs in addition to the minimum required for any society. In this sense, some but not all elements of a popular morality may be essential to its being the *type* or *kind* of society it is.

Devlin's example of monogamous marriage provides a good example of this point. Involved in the ideal of monogamous marriage is what has been called the "Western Norm" of sexual morality. This norm "is that sexual relationships shall be exclusively heterosexual, and that no sexual activity shall take place outside monogamous unions which are, intentionally at least, life-long."[54] Although this norm may never have been realized in practice, it is the basis of popular morality. The abandonment of the Western Norm in the twentieth century can reasonably be said to involve a change in the way of life of society. This aspect of popular morality is essential to society viewed as a way of life. It is in this sense that Devlin holds that much, though not all, of morality is essential for the existence of society--the existence of a monogamous society.[55]

Thus, one may distinguish three interpretations of the claim that morality is essential for the existence of society. First, there are certain moral beliefs, the moral minimum, essential for the existence of any society. Second, there are certain moral beliefs essential for the existence

---

[53]*Id.* 91.

[54]R. ATKINSON, SEXUAL MORALITY 45 (1965).

[55]*Accord*, B. Mitchell, *supra* note 33, at 18-25, where the idea of a morality essential for a particular type of society is more fully developed. But *see* Ten, *Enforcing a Shared Morality*, 82 ETHICS 321 (1972).

of certain types of society--monogamous, polygynous, polyandrous, etc. Which beliefs are essential depend upon what type of society is involved. Third, the whole set of shared moral beliefs may be said to be essential for the particular society.

Hart, in the arguments considered above, correctly pointed out that neither the first not third interpretations of the claim that morality is essential for the existence of society will support Devlin's thesis. He did not argue against the second interpretation. This interpretation of the claim is open to the same kind of objection as was made to the conformity argument's premise that conformity to popular morality is intrinsically good. It is not an *a priori* truth that change in a society's characteristic institutions and practices (ways of life) is bad. This obviously depends upon evaluation of those practices and the effect of change. It is incorrect to maintain, as Devlin does, that any change of a society from one type to another is an evil to be avoided. Change from a slave owning to a non-slave owning type of society would not be bad. Even if conduct contrary to popular morality would change that society to one of another type, change alone is not necessarily a reason which a reasonable person can accept for legislating against it.

Further, Devlin's analogy with treason suffers from great weaknesses.[56] The differences between subversive and immoral activities are quite clear and provide a reasonable basis for distinguishing between them. The difference between treason, and, for example, homosexuality, rests upon a point Mill notes. He writes that for public interference with an individual's conduct to be justified "the conduct from which it is desired to deter him must be *calculated* to produce evil."[57] Treason and sedition are usually defined in terms of intending the violent overthrow or hatred of the government. By definition, these crimes are aimed against government. Sexual offenses are not defined in terms of intending the destruction of popular morality or the disintegration of society. Hence, the nature of treason and sedition is such that they are aimed against government, but it is not the nature of homosexuality to intend the destruction of popular morality or society. This major dissimilarity between treason and homosexuality as an example of immorality is sufficient to rob an analogy between them of any weight.

Finally, if one considers prohibiting conduct contrary to popular morality in order to protect society, one should consider what values one

---

[56]For a different criticism of this analogy, see Feinberg, "*Harmless immoralities" and Offensive Nuisances*, in ISSUES IN LAW AND MORALITY 91-93 (N. Care & T. Trelogan eds. 1973); J. FEINBERG, *supra* note 3, 38-39.

[57]J.S. MILL, *supra* note 1, at 13 (emphasis added).

would give up in so doing. For the sake of argument, it may be assumed that changes in popular morality would lead to the complete destruction of society. First, the harm is a very remote consequence of the actions to be legislated against. By most standards of causality in law, the morally deviant person does not "cause" the destruction of society. Rather, causal responsibility lies with those whose changing moral beliefs and conduct result in actions which harm others. Thus, one would give up the causation requirement of responsibility if one held a person who acted contrary to any part of popular morality responsible for the destruction of society.

Second, one would also abandon the requirement of *mens rea*. As noted above, a person engaging in conduct contrary to popular morality does not usually in the ordinary sense intend the destruction of society. Usually he will not intend it in any legal sense either, *i.e.*, foresee it as a consequence of his actions. Hence, one would be giving up the requirement of intention for responsibility. Of course, if the conduct were made illegal, then in engaging in it an actor would have the necessary intent for criminal responsibility, *i.e.*, to perform a legally proscribed act. But that is a long way from the intent to bring about the specific harm of the destruction of society. Usually the harm which the law seeks to avoid must itself be intended. Devlin emphasizes that sometimes the law may proscribe conduct which does not itself constitute the harm to be avoided but which may lead to it; the law builds an "outwork" to prevent conduct approaching the harm it seeks to avoid. But even he recognizes that conduct breaching these outworks is not really wrong.[58] To prohibit, say, homosexual conduct in order to prevent the destruction of society is to do more than to build an outwork far from the objective. It is to launch an attack into another territory. The casual nexus between homosexuality and the destruction of society has not been established[59] and is certainly more tenuous than that between minors purchasing alcoholic beverages and their becoming drunk.[60]

A reasonable person would not accept giving up the causal and *mens rea* requirements of responsibility. Such a person views himself as a reasonable, responsible person. To accept the disintegration argument for the legal moralist principle, he would have to cease viewing himself as such a person with respect to immoral conduct. There are no reasons for so doing.

Thus, the legal moralist principle is not one a reasonable person

---

[58] P. DEVLIN, *supra* note 5, at 28-30.

[59] Hart, *supra* note 50.

[60] One of Devlin's examples, P. DEVLIN, *supra* note 5, at 29.

can accept. It would involve the loss of liberty for no other benefit than the satisfaction of knowing that others act as one who shares the popular morality thinks proper. Nor is there evidence that immoralities which do not harm others lead to the disintegration of society. Even if they were apt to lead others to act in ways destructive of society, the prevention of harm provides sufficient justification for restricting this latter conduct and preserving society.

On Legal Reform: Legal Stability and Legislative Questions

The respective roles of courts and legislatures in reform of the common law is of continuing interest and importance. Philosophers, especially rule utilitarians,[1] frequently refer to the distinction between issues appropriate for judicial determination (judicial questions) and those more suitable for legislative resolution (legislative questions) as though it were clear, yet legal philosophers have not seriously examined the grounds for such a distinction. As used by philosophers and judges, the distinction frequently implies the discredited Blackstonian views that judges discover and apply law but do not make it. In his often cited statement of this distinction, even Justice Holmes, certainly no adherent to the Blackstonian view, employs the distinction:

> A judicial inquiry investigates, declares, and enforces liabilities as they stand on present or past facts and under laws supposed already to exist. That is its purpose and end. Legislation, on the other hand, looks to the future and changes existing conditions by making a new rule, to be applied thereafter to all or some part of those subject to its power.[2]

The question of the role of courts vis-à-vis legislatures in law reform has increased in practical importance during the last fifteen years. In the United States at least, there has been a noticeable increase in judicial activism in both the Supreme Court and state courts of final review. Although it has abated somewhat in recent years, there has been an increased tendency for courts to overrule prior decisions.[3] Yet, in many cases judges have insisted either that stare decisis prevents courts from making changes or that it is more appropriate for the legislature than the courts to make them. Judicial reluctance to depart from precedent is

---

[1]Rule utilitarians claim that acts are to be morally evaluated by their conformity to those rules which, if adopted, would produce more net utility (happiness) than the adoption of any other rules. For use of the distinction between judicial and legislative questions in this connection, *see* Rawls, *Two Concepts of Rules*, in UTILITARIANISM WITH CRITICAL ESSAYS 177 (S. Gorovitz ed. 1971).

[2]Prentis v. Atlantic Coast Line, 211 U.S. 210, 226 (1908).

[3]With respect to tort law, see R. KEETON, VENTURING TO DO JUSTICE 169-70 (1969).

W. L. Robison (ed.), The Legal Essays of Michael Bayles, 41–64.
© 2002 *Kluwer Law International. Printed in the Netherlands.*

illustrated in *Maki v. Frelk*,[4] a negligence action for personal injuries, in which the Supreme Court of Illinois had asked an appellate court to determine whether contributory negligence should continue to be recognized as a defense. The appellate court decided that it should not. Yet on rehearing, the Illinois Supreme Court reversed the judgment on the ground that abolition of the defense of contributory negligence should be left to the legislature.[5]

The main thesis of this article is that there is less reason for distinguishing between the proper roles of courts and legislatures in reform of the common law than is generally recognized. The doctrine of stare decisis has caused much confusion on this point. In particular, its use in cases raising the issue of overruling previous decisions often confuses two distinct questions: (1) Whether the law should be changed; and (2) who should change the law. The first section of this article analyzes stare decisis in order to clarify its status and to show how distinct considerations relevant to answering these two questions are confused in it. The second section analyzes the reasons for a principle against changing the law--the principle of stability--and demonstrates that it applies equally to both legislative and judicial change of the common law. The third section analyzes functional differences between courts and legislatures as a basis for a standard of legislative questions indicating which issues of change of the common law courts should leave to legislatures.

I. The Doctrine of Stare Decisis

The doctrine of stare decisis or precedent (rarely are the two clearly distinguished) may be construed in several different ways. First, the doctrine may be understood either as a doctrine which specifies the kind of reasons relevant to judicial decision-making, or as a specific reason in itself.[6] As a doctrine pertaining to the relevancy of reasons, stare decisis is the claim that the *only* relevant reasons for judicial decisions are precedents or analogies to precedents. So construed, stare decisis is a meta-doctrine

---

4 239 N.E.2d 445 (Ill. 1968).

5 Because a majority of states now have comparative rather than contributory negligence and three states adopted it by judicial decision, this controversy makes a good case study. Indeed, the courts in Florida and California adopted comparative negligence despite statutes arguably requiring contributory negligence. Kaatz v. State, 540 P.2d 1037 (Alas. 1975); Li v. Yellow Cab Co, 532 P.2d 1226, 119 Cal. Rptr. 858 (1975); Hoffman v. Jones, 280 So. 2d 431 (Fla. 1973).

6 *See* R. Wasserstrom, The Judicial Decision 53 (1961).

concerning the underlying reasons courts give for decisions and not itself a reason. More often, stare decisis is considered to be one among a number of reasons for judicial decisions. So interpreted, it states that courts ought to adhere to or follow precedents, but other reasons may be given for not following precedents. Thus, according to the first interpretation, wherein stare decisis is construed as a meta-doctrine, all arguments for decisions must be based on precedents, whether in accord with or contrary to them. The second interpretation of stare decisis, however, is that while good reasons exist for basing decisions on precedent, reasons other than precedent may also exist which justify deviation for precedent. It is this latter conception which is relevant here. Of course, it is a difficult and controversial task to determine the holding of a previous case. Herein it will be assumed that this task has been performed. One cannot sensibly ask whether a precedent ought to be followed until one has determined what it is.

Second, one may distinguish between the precedents stare decisis requires a court to follow. In one version, it only requires courts to follow the precedents of higher courts of the same jurisdiction. In another version, it requires courts to follow their own precedents as well. Since the present concern is with courts of final review, only the claim that courts ought to follow their own precedents is relevant to the present discussion, there being no higher courts in the jurisdiction. Moreover, the claim that courts ought to follow their own precedents may take two forms: strict or liberal.[7] The strict or English doctrine of stare decisis requires that courts always adhere to their own precedents, whereas the liberal or American doctrine permits departure from precedent in some cases. Although it is unclear whether any court ever really applied the strict doctrine, it has substantially been put to rest by a recent Practice Statement of the House of Lords which declared that courts may depart from precedent "when it appears right to do so."[8] Consequently, only the liberal version of the doctrine will be considered.

Third, one may distinguish the doctrine's application to different kinds of law. The justification for the doctrine of stare decisis and the strength of the reason it provides for adherence to precedent may vary depending upon the type of law involved. The most significant distinctions here are between (1) court-made rules (common law), (2) statutory interpretations, and (3) constitutional interpretations. The role of courts as

---

[7]*Id.* at 50; *see also* Wise, *The Doctrine of Stare Decisis*, 21 WAYNE L. REV. 1043, 1045 (1975).

[8][1966] 1 W.L.R. 1234, 3 All E.R. 77 (H.L.).

concerns their ability to decide constitutional matters largely depends upon considerations peculiar to specific forms of government, *e.g.*, whether there is a written constitution and judicial review. In statutory interpretation also, the respective roles of courts and legislatures are more clearly delineated than in common law. It is in the area of common law, the focus of this article, that the most difficult and general issues arise.[9]

Thus far, stare decisis has been referred to as a doctrine. In this context, the term "doctrine" has no clear meaning. It is thus useful to introduce the more precise terminology of standards, principles, and rules.[10] Standards such as good faith, due care, and fair rate provide a basis for evaluations which admit degrees and may be used to establish rankings. Such evaluations are frequently stated in terms of good, better, best, bad, worse, and worst. Principles, on the other hand, present the criteria (good- and bad-making characteristics) used in applying standards and may themselves refer to characteristics which admit degrees, *e.g.*, the ripeness of an apple in grading it. Rules are used in making evaluations which do not admit degrees; they are either complied with or not. Such evaluations are usually expressed in terms of right or wrong, correct or incorrect. Thus, rules apply in all or none fashion, whereas principles do not, since the various principles constituting a standard may be weighed against one another. For example, it is a rule that one who is contributorily negligent cannot recover for damages. The requirement that liability ought to be based on fault, on the other hand, is a principle because it may be balanced against other considerations.

Determining whether the law should be changed requires consideration of the factor of thc stability of the law. In particular, a decision to change the law cannot be made solely on the basis of the merits of the existing and the proposed rules but must also include consideration of the disadvantages or costs of legal change.[11] In this context, the liberal

---

[9]Moreover, within the common law, the weight of the reason provided against change by the doctrine of stare decisis may vary depending upon whether tort, contract, property, or criminal law is involved.

[10]On the difference between legal standards, principles, and rules, *see generally* Bayles, *Legal Principles, Rules and Standards*, 14 LOGIQUE ET ANALYSE 223 (1971). Dworkin, *The Model of Rules*, 35 CHI. L. REV. 14 (1967); and Dworkin, *Social Rules and Legal Theory*, 81 YALE L.J. 855, 822-90 (1972).

[11]R. Wasserstrom, *supra* note 6 at 173; *see also* W. SHAEFER, PRECEDENT AND POLICY 9 (1956).

doctrine of stare decisis cannot be treated as a rule.[12] This conclusion is predicated upon the theory that to be construed as a rule against change, it would be necessary for the liberal doctrine to consist of one of the following forms: (a) Precedents ought to be followed unless . . .; or (b) precedents ought usually or generally to be followed.

When given form (a), however, the doctrine often reduces to a tautology as in the House of Lords formulation that one ought to adhere to precedent unless it appears right to depart from it.[13] If, on the other hand, the "unless" clause is formulated so as not to reduce to a tautology, then the rule provides no reason at all against change whenever a case falls within the excepting "unless" clause. Yet, stare decisis always provides a reason for adhering to precedent, notwithstanding the fact that other factors may outweigh the factor of adherence to precedent. Consequently, stare decisis cannot be a rule of type (a).

Nor can stare decisis be treated as a rule of type (b). As such, stare decisis is a mere summarization of the results of considering the advantages and disadvantages of legal change in particular cases. Without explicitly so stating, Wasserstrom, in his utilitarian theory of judicial decision, treats stare decisis as a rule of this type.[14] He requires that to justify a judicial decision "the rule upon which its justification depends must be shown to be desirable, and its introduction into the legal system itself desirable."[15] This view considers only the disadvantages of change of the particular law in question.[16] Hence, whenever in a particular case the advantages of change outweigh the disadvantages, a new rule should be introduced. Yet in focusing upon the disadvantages of change of a particular rule, Wasserstrom has omitted consideration of the disadvantages of a practice of frequent change. However, as D. H. Hodgson has argued at length, Wasserstrom's view would make the law quite uncertain.[17] Lawyers would not be able to predict when a court might decide that it would be useful to change a rule. Yet certainty in the law (as discussed more fully in the next section) is one of the main reasons for stare decisis or stability. Thus, because it is essential to have one settled rule, a reason is provided for adhering to a previously settled rule although it is no better than another

---

[12]*Contra*, R. WASSERSTROM, supra note 6, at 53-54. On the basis of quite different considerations, Wise also claims stare decisis is not a rule. Wise, *supra* note 7, at 1043.

[13][1966] 1 W.L. R. 1234, 3 All E.R. 77 (H.L.).

[14]R. Wasserstrom, *supra* note 109.

[15]*Id.* at 173.

[16]In essence, this is an act utilitarianism view.

[17]D. HODGSON, CONSEQUENCES OF UTILITARIANISM 104-08 (1967).

one.

As it concerns the stability of law, stare decisis is a legal principle, the principle of stability. It is one of the principles constituting the standard of the appropriate rule to apply in a case and may be weighed against other relevant principles. As a principle, stability provides a reason in and of itself for applying an extant rather than a proposed rule. Basing the choice of a rule solely on a straightforward utilitarian calculation of the merits of the extant and proposed rules (a calculation which may include the disadvantages of change of the particular rule) is thereby foreclosed because of the failure to consider the principle of stability.[18]

As applied to the issue of whether courts should introduce legal change, stare decisis involves a standard. The standard is that of legislative questions, those which courts should leave to legislatures. The various principles which constitute this standard must be weighed against one another in particular cases to determine whether it is appropriate for a court to decide a question.

Thus, the doctrine of stare decisis consists of two elements: (1) A principle of stability; and (2) a standard of legislative questions. With respect to the proper role of courts in reform of the common law, two issues are presented: First, does the principle of stability apply more strongly with respect to judicial than to legislative reform? Second, what are the principles or criteria of the standard of legislative questions?

II. The Principle of Stability

One must examine the considerations which justify the principle of stability before determining whether it provides a reason against judicial change of common law rules. Five important considerations support the principle of stability: The need for certainty; fairness to those who have relied upon the extant rule; the efficiency of following precedent; the need for continuity in the law; and equality in treating similar cases similarly. Each of these considerations needs to be more fully elucidated.[19]

Certainty of the law is obviously a significant consideration. Essentially, it may be equated with the ability to predict the legal consequences of one's conduct. One must recognize the limits of this consideration. The argument for certainty may be pressed too far as in the

[18]However, consequentialist or utilitarian considerations may be relevant to the justification of principles. This view adds another level to rule utilitariansim. Instead of directly evaluating rules by their utility, rules are evaluated by principles which, in turn, may be justified by utility or other considerations.

[19]*See generally* R. WASSERSTROM, *supra* note 6, at 60-74.

following dissent of Chief Justice Bell of Pennsylvania:

> Unless the Courts establish and maintain certainty and stability in the law, businessmen cannot safely and wisely make contracts with their employees or with each other; the meaning of wills, bonds, contracts, deeds and leases will fluctuate and change with each change in the personnel or in the changing views of a Court; property interests will be jeopardized and frequently lost or changed; Government cannot adequately protect law-abiding persons or communities against criminals; private citizens will not know their rights and obligations; and public officials will not know from week to week or month to month the powers and limitations of government.[20]

Were there no predictability at all, the dire results Chief Justice Bell depicts would ensue. However, the fact that a complete lack of predictability would be disastrous does not justify the conclusion that some unpredictability would be so. One must balance the advantages of being able to change outmoded rules and predictability. The principle of stability occupies a middle ground between Bell's argument against all change and Wasserstrom's allowance of change whenever the advantages of change in a particular case outweigh the disadvantages.

Reliance is closely related to certainty. Although reliance is based upon predictability, the interest involved is somewhat different. Predictability refers to the ability to predict what the legal consequences of conduct will be, while reliance pertains to the effect a change of the law will have upon people who have acted on the basis of predictions. A subsequent change in the law involves unfairness to those who have relied upon a previously well-established rule even though the new rule may be a more just one. The concern is not, as Hodgson suggests, how long a rule has been relied upon but the extent to which it has been relied upon, *i.e.*, how many people, how often.[21] Moreover, the injustice or unfairness occasioned by changes in the law to those who have acted in reliance upon

---

[20]Reitmeyer v. Sprecher, 243 A.2d 395, 399 (Pa. 1968). This point is similar to Lon Fuller's argument that too rapid a change in laws would result in the absence of a legal system. L. FULLER, THE MORALITY OF LAW, 39, 79-81 (rev. ed. 1969).

[21]"The *longer* a rule has been relied upon by the profession and the public, the less willing a court will be to reject or qualify it." D. HODGSON, *supra* note 17, at 136 (emphasis added). Of course, the longer a rule has existed, the more people there are likely to be who have relied upon it, but the time is not the crucial point.

the law depends upon whether that reliance was justifiable.[22] To the extent that the existing rule is clearly contrary to community standards or where there are dicta and dissenting opinions indicating a desire to change it, reliance is less justified; that is, it is less justifiable to expect the rule to remain unchanged. This consideration, therefore, goes more to the pace of change than to the existence of change itself.

Considerations of efficiency relate to the allocation of judicial resources. A heavy burden would be placed upon courts if each case were to be treated as one of first impression. In the complete absence of the principle, each case could presumably be taken all the way to the court of final review--at least there would be no clear reason not to do so. Moreover, in each case courts would have to raise anew all the arguments for and against each rule, even though they would continually arrive at the same conclusion when one rule is clearly preferable over another.[23] When cases at the trial level clearly fall within the boundaries of a precedent, it saves time and money for all involved to follow precedent. Settlement rather than litigation is encouraged. As Mill recognized, even in ethics most situations need not be considered anew because rules have been worked out on the basis of previous experience.[24] Courts of final review can consider only a few of all the cases in their jurisdictions. Utilization of the principle of stability insures that few previously settled issues will be appealed to them, thereby enabling courts to devote their time and energy to issues of first impression and those involving rules which create serious injustice or disutility.

Continuity deals with the coherence or consistency of a body of rules.[25] A change in one rule may significantly affect a number of other rules which were made upon the assumption of the effectiveness of the extant rule. For example, change from a rule of contributory negligence to

---

[22]Alferitz v. Borgwardt, 58 P. 460, 462 (Cal. 1899); R. KEETON, *supra* note 3, at 41-43; Mishkin, *The Supreme Court 1964 Term, Foreward: The High Court, the Great Writ, and the Due Process of Time and Law*, 79 HARV. L. REV. 56, 70 (1965).

[23]Furthermore, rarely can an issue even be formulated without use of the principle of stability. For example, the issue of whether a restrictive covenant in a lease is enforceable presupposes a host of rules with respect to the nature and existence of various property rights. All of these various presuppositions involve rules based on precedents to which both parties agree. Were there no effect to precedent, all of these presuppositions would be open to question and there would be no formulable issue or issues short of justifying the bulk of property law.

[24]J.S. MILL, UTILITARIANISM WITH CRITICAL ESSAYS 29 (S. Gorovitz ed. 1971).

[25]*See* D. Hodgson, *supra* note 17 at 134-36.

one of comparative negligence would cast doubt upon the status of a last clear chance rule. A system of rules can be worked out by case law only on the assumption that previous rules are still valid.[26] Moreover, although a new rule may not directly affect other rules, it may rest upon a different principle than do the other rules and thus produce incoherence or discontinuity at the level of principles.[27]

The final consideration is equality. If courts were to decide each case afresh without regard to precedent, they might teach opposite conclusions in relevantly similar cases. When the justification for a rule is clear and it obviously applies to a case, the chances of disparate decisions may be relatively small. However, a decision as to which of two or more rules is the better is often a close one about which reasonable judges may disagree. In these cases, considerations of equality require that the same rule be applied to similarly situated litigants.

The considerations of certainty, reliance, efficiency, continuity, and equality provide adequate justification for a court's adherence to the principle of stability. These same factors are also relevant to legislative decisions to change the law. Too frequent legislative changes can have as serious an impact on certainty of the law as too frequent judicial changes. Considerations of reliance are also involved in legislative decision-making. Indeed, reliance is the primary factor in the general principle against retroactive legislation. However, since most legislation is prospective while most judicial decisions are retrospective, reliance is a more important check on judicial than on legislative change.[28] Continuity is also a legislative consideration. Legislators as well as judges ought to have regard for the orderly development of law, especially as it concerns consistency between laws. Considerations of equality and efficiency are involved in the principle that legislation should be general; that is, legislation should concern classes of persons and events rather than particular ones.

Thus, the only difference between the considerations supporting the principle of stability as it affects judicial as opposed to legislative

---

[26]There is a difference between the rules which must be presupposed to formulate an issue and the rules presupposed in considerations of coherence between laws. The latter presuppose the existence of the rule in question, but the rule in question does not necessarily presuppose the existence of the rules which compose the other laws.

[27]Discontinuity at the level of principles is a result of the rapid change of direction which overruling decisions may have. Such rapid change may additionally affect the considerations of certainty and reliance.

[28]Moreover, there is usually more warning of impending legislative change than of judicial change.

change of the common law is reliance and the retrospective character of judicial decisions. Overruling decisions are usually retroactive. For example, a decision invalidating a divorce obtained by a private legislative bill would ordinarily invalidate all previous such divorces as well as that in the instant case. In *Bingham v. Miller* the technique of prospective overruling was, however, used to avoid such a result; that is, the court held that past legislative divorces were valid, but that no valid divorces could be obtained by that method in the future.[29] The definitive feature of prospective overruling is, therefore, that the court limits the effect of the decision so that it does not apply to all previous cases. Since prospective overruling of precedents avoids the retrospective effect of judicial reform, the one difference in the relevance of the principle of stability as it applies to judicial and legislative change of the common law is eliminated.

Before prospective overruling may be justified, one must carefully consider the reliance factor upon which it is based, for in the absence of justifiable reliance on the existing state of the law, retroactive overruling is defensible. For example, reliance may not have been justified because of previous judicial warnings in dicta or dissents that the extant rule was in doubt. Moreover, ordinary citizens are often not aware of judicial opinions and may not have relied on them. Also, the impact of a retroactive decision may not be very great on any individual. For example, a change in tort liability may not have a serious impact upon the losing party because the damages he owes may be distributed amongst others via liability insurance rates.[30] Finally, the aspect of reliance may apply almost as strongly when courts do not utilize the device of prospective overruling, but, rather, distinguish an instant case from a previous one.[31] Of course, to the extent the instant case differed from previous ones, reliance upon the prior decisions was less justifiable. But to avoid the dead hand of precedent, courts have frequently distinguished cases on unpredictable grounds.

The major argument against prospective overruling is based upon equality. To see the force of this argument, one must consider the possible and actual variations in prospective overruling. In effect, courts set the date at which a new rule is to become effective. Very rarely do courts set a

---

[29]17 Ohio 445 (1848). Prospective overruling has also been used to ease the transition from contributory to comparative negligence. Li v. Yellow Cab. Co., 532 P.2d 1226, 119 Cal. Rptr. 858 (1975). For a brief discussion of prospective overruling, *see generally* S. MERMIN, LAW AND THE LEGAL SYSTEM--AN INTRODUCTION 263-66 (1973).

[30]R. KEETON, *supra* note 3, at 42-43.

[31]W. SHAEFER, *supra* note 11, at 15. Distinguishing an instant case from precedents may also decrease certainty and predictability. Wise, *supra* note 7, at 1056.

definite date in the future, such as forty days from the date of decision.[32] Courts more frequently use what has been called prospective-prospective overruling, *i.e.*, saying that the precedent will be overruled in the next case.[33] The variety of dates of effectiveness which are possible in overruling is made apparent by the decisions of the United States Supreme Court respecting the retroactive application of constitutional rules of criminal procedure. The Court has allowed retroactive application to (1) all cases; (2) all those in which direct review has not been completed; (3) all those which have not proceeded beyond a certain point in the trial; (4) all those in which trials have not yet commenced; and (5) the instant case and future cases in which the proscribed conduct has not occurred as of the date of the decision.[34] Cases of type (1) are the ordinary form of retroactive judicial decision, while those of types (2) through (5) involve limits on the retroactive effect of the decision and are thus versions of prospective overruling. Moreover, pure prospective overruling is that in which the new rule applies only to cases arising after the date of decision.[35]

Whatever date or point is used, some litigants may complain of inequality because their relative similar cases were decided differently. However, such inequality is always involved when the law is changed. Similar cases are decided differently before as well as after the change.[36] The relevant consideration is the number of temporal inequalities involved when the law is altered. For example, if court first changes from contributory negligence to limited comparative negligence, and then, two years later, changes to pure comparative negligence, within three years similar cases will have been treated in different ways more frequently than would have been the case had pure comparative negligence been adopted in the first instance. There will have been two temporal inequalities rather than one. This consideration applies equally to courts and legislatures.

The United States Supreme Court has justified temporal inequality by the impetus prospective overruling provides "for implementation of long overdue reforms, which otherwise could not be practicably

---

[32]Holytz v. City of Milwaukee, 115 N.W.2d 618 (Wis. 1962).

[33]Colby v. Carney Hosp., 254 N.E.2d 407 (Mass. 1969); Spaniel v. Mounds View School Dist. No. 621, 118 N.W.2d 795 (Minn. 1962).

[34]Ostrager, *Retroactivity and Prospectivity of Supreme Court Constitutional Interpretations*, 19 N.Y.L. FORUM 289, 294-95 (1973).

[35]The Supreme Court has rejected its use. Stoval v. Denno, 388 U.S. 293, 301 (1967).

[36]Keeton, *Law Reform and Legal Education,* 24 VAND. L. REV. 53, 57 (1970).

effected."[37] The Court's language is unfortunate in that it suggests that reforms are completely justified, the only problems being those of administration. While the Court has taken problems of administration into account as one factor among others justifying prospective overruling,[38] they are not the central reason for its use. Rather, the reason is more general in that unless a decision is prospective, the consideration of reliance, which is obviated by prospective overruling, would be sufficient to make the overruling unjustified. That is, unless some of the disadvantages of changing the law are avoided, the change is not justifiable.

With the availability of prospective overruling, therefore, the principle of stability provides no stronger reason against judicial than against legislative change of the common law.[39] Reliance is the only

---

[37]Jenkins v. Delaware, 395 U.S. 213, 218 (1969).

[38]Linkletter v. Walker, 381 U.S. 618, 636 (1965).

[39]Prospective overruling is not generally available to English courts. Lord Simon has indicated a desire to use it, but thinks that enabling legislation is required. Jones v. Secretary of State for Social Services, [1972] 1 All E.R. 145, 198-99. *But see* Connelly v. Director of Public Prosecutions, [1964] A.C. 1254 (H.L.), for a consideration of the effect of prospective overruling without enabling legislation.

Ronald Dworkin, however, suggests another reason for applying the principle of stability more strongly to courts than to legislatures. He distinguished between principles involving distributive values (rights or claims of individuals) and policies involving collective values (goals or claims of the community). His essential claim, the "rights" thesis, is that judicial arguments are and ought to be based on principles (rights of the parties), while legislative arguments are and may be based on policies as well as on principles. Dworkin, *Hard Cases*, 88 HARV. L. REV. 1057 (1975). The rights thesis thus has a descriptive version (how decisions are made) and a normative version (how decisions ought to be made).

The principle of stability would thus be less stringent upon legislatures than upon courts because the equality consideration is less strong for rules based upon policies than for those based upon principles. Since goals are not distributive, that a benefit to one class would further economic efficiency does not imply that other classes are entitled to a similar benefit. *Id.* at 1068. Similarly, since the economy may need stimulus at one time, yet may not later, temporal inequality would not be significant.

However, the rights thesis does not have this implication for common law rules which were originally adopted by courts. If the descriptive version of the rights thesis is correct, then the rules were adopted on the basis of arguments from principle. Consequently, the equality consideration for the principle of stability fully applies to the common law rules, and legislators would be as constrained by the principle as are judges. Moreover, cases of prospective overruling are prima facie counter-examples to

consideration underlying the principle of stability which may operate more strongly against judicial than against legislative legal change. Prospective overruling, however, eliminates any difference between courts and legislatures with respect to reliance. Consequently, if a court considers the possibility of prospective overruling, but correctly decides that the principle of stability militates against change, the law should not be changed by either a court or a legislature. Conversely, so far as the principle of stability is concerned, if it is appropriate for a legislature to change a common law rule, then it is also appropriate for a court to do so, at least by prospective overruling.[40]

---

the rights thesis. If courts are not willing to apply rights retrospectively, they seem either to be asserting that there is no right which the party had until the announcement of the new rule or to be allowing policy considerations to affect the application of the rule. Dworkin's only comment upon cases of prospective overruling adopts the former alternative. He considers the criminal case, Linkletter v. Walker, 381 U.S. 618 (1965), and claims that the rights thesis does not fully apply to criminal cases because the prosecution does not have a right to a conviction if the defendant is guilty, although the defendant does have a right to acquittal if innocent. In ordinary civil cases, he claims, one or the other of the parties does have a right to win. Dworkin, *supra* at 1077-78. Yet the use of prospective overruling in tort cases appears to falsify the descriptive version of the rights thesis.

[40]Thus far, the principle of stability has been treated as a principle presenting a reason against change which forecloses a straight-forward utilitarian calculation of the advantages and disadvantages of change in a particular case. No account has been given as to when this reason may be outweighed and overruling decisions justified. Such an account is not central to the point of this article; it suffices to show that the principle of stability provides no more reason against judicial than against legislative change. The best such an account could do would be to present other principles calling for change and to weigh them against the principle of stability. It should be noted that the merits of the proposed rule over the extant one is such a principle. In making this determination, the way in which a court construes the holding of the case relied upon as precedent may be of prime importance and open to consideration. See Stone, *The Lords at the Crossroads--When to "Depart" and How!*, 46 AUSTRALIAN L.J. 483, 488 (1972).

The principle of stability, however, prevents adoption of a proposed rule whenever it is preferable to the extant one, just as the obligation to keep promises prevents one from breaking a promise whenever doing so would have better consequences than keeping it. Yet, just as one may be justified in breaking a promise when the results of so doing are much better than those of keeping it, one may also be justified in introducing a new rule when it is clearly better than the extant one.

III. THE STANDARD OF LEGISLATIVE QUESTIONS

If the principle of stability does not provide a reason to prefer legislative to judicial reform of the common law, then the standard of legislative questions must bear that burden of preference. The principles which constitute the criteria used in the determination of legislative questions are based upon a combination of functional differences between courts and legislatures and also upon the considerations underlying the principles of stability.[41]

A. *Functional Differences Between Courts and Legislatures*

The most significant functional difference between courts and legislatures is that courts, unlike legislatures, are limited to deciding actual cases. The United States Constitution limits article III courts to deciding cases and controversies.[42] Although not necessarily constitutionally so limited, most common law courts are also restricted to deciding actual cases.[43] Such a limitation involves several elements. First, there must be a definite, concrete issue involving particular parties; courts do not decide general policy except in the context of a particular case. Second, the issue must be an actual one; courts do not generally decide hypothetical or moot cases.[44] Third, courts cannot decide an issue just because they think it an important one deserving resolution. The issue must be brought to them. However, this point must be qualified in two respects. Courts of final review frequently exercise much control over the issues they will decide. Moreover, they may sometimes decide a case on an issue other than that on which it is argued. For example, when the United States Supreme Court applied to the states the rule excluding material obtained in unconstitutional

---

[41]The various principles specifying criteria for legislative questions developed in this section rest on general functional differences between courts and legislatures, not on those limited to particular legal systems. *See generally* S. MERMIN, *supra* note 29, at 102-13.

[42]*See generally* C. WRIGHT, HANDBOOK OF THE LAW OF FEDERAL COURTS 34-38 (2d ed. 1970).

[43]S. MERMIN, *supra* note 29, at 175.

[44]Sometimes they do. For example, *M'Naghten's Case*, which set forth the famous tests of insanity, was not before the House of Lords in an actual case. [1843] 8 Eng. Rep. 718 (H.L.). The defendant had died before the United States Supreme Court's decision declaring unconstitutional those laws making the status of being a narcotic addict a crime. Robinson v. California, 370 U.S. 660 (1962).

searches and seizures from evidence at trail, the case had been granted certiorari and argued on an issue of obscenity.[45] Fourth, the plaintiff must state a cause of action or claim upon which relief may be granted. There must be a legal basis for the dispute before courts can take it up. But this limit is not absolute. At least in common law, courts do have the power to recognize new causes of action,[46] and so, theoretically, new issues can be recognized.

The functional limitation of courts to actual cases, therefore, significantly restricts their power as compared to that of a legislature. Courts are not as free as legislatures to choose the issues they wish to decide, and they must determine the specific legal situation of at least one legal person or entity. Legislatures, however, usually decide general issues without reference to the legal situation of any specific person.[47]

Another set of functional differences involves what may be called power over resources. Courts do not have a general taxing and spending power. So, for example, they could not institute a social security system. The federal courts have generally avoided issues of spending by determining that individual taxpayers do not have standing to sue with respect to Congressional spending decisions. Only when courts have the power to constitutionally review legislation may they restrict spending by legislatures, and even then they cannot say how money is to be spent, only how it is not to be spent. This sort of limitation does not imply that courts do not exercise functions similar to legislatures, but merely that they exercise fewer of them. A related and more significant aspect of courts' limited power over resources concerns the gathering of information. Unlike legislatures, courts generally cannot establish investigative bodies to obtain information relevant to issues. They must generally rely upon the information presented by the parties to the case.

A further functional difference between courts and legislatures relates to the acceptability of compromise. Legislatures are expected to compromise competing interests. Thus, the interests of charitable institutions and of victims of negligence may be compromised by a rule holding charitable institutions liable for negligent injuries, but only to the amount of $10,000. Courts do not compromise interests in this way;

---

[45]Mapp v. Ohio, 367 U.S. 643 (1961).

[46]The procedure is not to recognize an entirely new cause of action, but to recognize new claims for relief within a broad category such as negligence. *See e.g.*, Dillon v. Legg, 441 P.2d 912, 69 Cal. Rptr. 72 (1968); Henningsen v. Bloomfield Motors, Inc., 161 A.2d 69 (N.J. 1960). Eventually such decisions may lead to whole new bodies of law, such as that of products liability.

[47]S. MERMIN, *supra* note 29, at 104.

rather, judges are to determine the justice of a particular issue. Of course, in determining the just solution they are expected to weigh competing interests. However, it would be improper for a court to announce that since half the justices favor tort immunity for charitable institutions while half do not, the difference has been settled by determining that charitable institutions are liable for one half of the damages caused by their employees' negligence. Instead, when courts have evenly split decisions, the extant rule governs.

B. *Principles Constitutive of the Standard of Legislative Questions*

The combination of the functional differences between courts and legislatures, when taken in conjunction with the considerations underlying the principle of stability, provides certain principles constitutive of the standard of legislative questions. These principles concern: (1) The interrelation of the extent rule with other rules; (2) the complexity of the proposed rule; (3) the scope of the proposed rule; (4) the availability of information relevant to the relative desirability of the extant and proposed rules; and (5) the need for a bright line in a gray area.[48] Another consideration, alternative means of change, is relevant to differences in judicial activity in reform of constitutional, statutory, and common law. The ultimate basis of each of these principles is a functional limit on courts.

The interrelation between the extant rule and others is relevant to whether judges or legislators should change the existing rule. The greater a rule's relations and connections with other rules, the stronger the reason for leaving its change to the legislature. The reason for this principle is that since courts are limited to deciding actual cases, court decisions are binding only insofar as is necessary to decide the instant case. Since the relationship of a new rule to extant ones will not usually be at issue in a case, judges' comments upon related extant rules would be mere obiter dicta. The new rule would be a discontinuity in the law casting doubts upon many previously settled rules, and these doubts could not be resolved until many other cases had arisen and been decided. A legislature could settle many of these doubts at the same time it changed the existing rule in question because a statute need not be limited to as narrow an issue as a judicial decision.

The principle of interrelation should not be confused with that of complexity. Complexity refers to whether or not all elements of a proposed rule may be settled in one decision. For example, when the Supreme Court

[48]*See generally* R. KEETON, *supra* note 3, at 40-41; W. SHAEFER, *supra* note 11, at 10-13.

recognized an independent tort action for violation of fourth amendment constitutional rights, many issues, such as the elements of the damages, were left unsettled;[49] yet the decision did not disturb or affect prior rules. While a complex new rule cannot be completely fleshed out in a single court decision (due to the restriction on courts to deciding actual cases),[50] the rule may be fully developed in a statute, thereby avoiding uncertainty. It should be observed, however, that complexity is not always a strong reason for leaving a question to a legislature. Arguably, it is preferable to leave many details to be worked out in light of practical experience as cases arise rather than trying to foresee them in a legislative enactment.[51] Furthermore, when legislatures have acted, they have generally adopted a simple general rule and left the details to the courts to develop.[52] Whether courts or legislatures should work out the details depends primarily upon the foreseeability of the problems which may arise. To the extent the problems are not adequately foreseeable, they should be left to the courts to work out.[53] However, it should generally be left to legislators to initially determine whether they can foresee problems sufficiently to provide for them by statute.

---

[49]Bivens v. Six Unknown Agents of Fed. Bureau of Narcotics, 403 U.S. 388 (1971).

[50]"Our decision in this case is to be viewed as a first step in what we deem to be a proper and just direction, not as a compendium containing the answers to all questions that may be expected to arise." Liv v. Yellow Cab Co., 532 P.2d 1226, 1242, 119 Cal. Rptr. 858, 874 (1975).

> Our adoption of this new principle does not, of course, end our judicial tasks in this area. Subsidiary questions and problems concerning the relationship of the new rule to other doctrines of tort law must necessarily be adjudicated in the future. We must, for the most part, await future cases for the further development of law in this field.

Kaatz v. State, 540 P.2d 1037, 1049-50 (Alas. 1975). The court did, however, abolish the last clear chance rule.

[51]"We feel the trial judges of this State are capable of applying this comparative negligence rule without our setting guidelines in anticipation of expected problems. The problems are more appropriately resolved at the trial level in a practical manner instead of a theoretical level at the appellate level." Hoffman v. Jones, 280 So. 2d 431, 439-40 (Fla. 1973); *accord*, Li v. Yellow Cab Co., 532 P.2d 1226, 1242, 119 Cal. Rptr. 858, 874 (1975).

[52]R. KEETON, *supra* note 3, at 50-51; Leflar, *Comment on Maki v. Frelk*, 21 VAND. L. REV. 918, 923 (1968).

[53]K. DIPLOCK, THE COURTS AS LEGISLATORS 13 (1965).

The third principle, the scope of the proposed rule, is closely related to its complexity. Scope and complexity are, however, distinguishable in that complexity, as previously mentioned, refers to whether or not all elements of a proposed rule may be stated in one decision; scope relates to a court's power to make a change regardless of whether all elements of the change may be stated in the same decision. Simply stated, the principle of scope rests upon the limits on courts' personal jurisdiction and power over resources. An illustration of scope considerations is found in the dissent of Chief Justice Burger in *Bivens v. Six Unknown Agents of Federal Bureau of Narcotics* in which it was suggested that a special court be instituted to handle tort claims for violation of constitutional rights.[54] No court, however, has the power to establish another court. Also, due to the considerations of scope, courts should not undertake to develop a workmen's compensation type system for automobile accidents.[55] Moreover, no court has adopted a no fault insurance system by decision. Part of the reason for such a limitation rests upon the power of courts. They do not have the power to require people generally to obtain insurance or to set the limits of such insurance. On the other hand, the setting of schedules and the like is not an issue of the scope of a law but of its complexity, the availability of information, and the need for a bright line.

A court's lack of information on which to evaluate the merits of rules is yet an additional reason for leaving questions to legislatures. For example, one reason courts should not set schedules of damages is their lack of information about the general costs of accidents. A court's inability to obtain adequate information pertaining to a particular subject is ultimately founded on the court's lack of power over resources.[56] Courts cannot instigate or conduct detailed social scientific investigations into problems, nor can the litigants in a case usually afford to do so. Legislatures, on the other hand, do possess power over resources. If, therefore, a court lacks the information needed for making a reasonable judgment, the issues under consideration should be deferred to the legislature, provided it

---

[54]403 U.S. 388, 422-23 (1971).

[55]R. KEETON, *supra* note 3, at 43.

[56]Gray, *Judicial Legislation: Judicial Constructs and Societal Facts*, 31 U. TORONTO FACULTY L. REV. 75, 84-87 (1973); Hall, *Law Reform and the Judiciary's Role*, 10 OSGOODE HALL L.J. 399, 409 (1972). Note the inappropriateness of the adversary procedure for determining legislative facts, *i.e.*, those needed for evaluating rules as opposed to those needed for deciding cases under rules.

is better able to obtain the needed information.[57]

The fifth principle is that issues requiring the drawing of a bright line through a gray area are best left to legislatures. Any issue which, in justice, requires a rule setting a maximum dollar amount of damages would be such. Likewise, statutes of limitations set bright temporal lines. To some extent, the drawing of such lines is arbitrary. There is a range in which a line appropriately belongs, but no particular point can be justified vis-à-vis others nearby. Consequently, the drawing of such lines involves a process of compromise between conflicting interests and no justification by means of neutral principles may be given for drawing it though one part of the gray area rather than through another. Since these bright line issues are the sort open to compromise, they are apt to be surrounded with political activity. So the rather arbitrary drawing of a bright line by the judiciary may provoke attacks upon the court. For example, the Supreme Court decision establishing a constitutional right to abortions during the first two trimesters of pregnancy essentially permitted state prohibition of abortion after the fetus is viable.[58] But Justice Blackmun's suggestion that the time of viability is twenty-four to twenty-eight weeks has provoked

---

[57]One must be careful not to confuse the availability of information with the kind of information involved. Hodgson contends that courts work reasonably well without hearing sociological information or evidence and that it is not desirable for them to receive it since judges are not specially trained to evaluate it. D. HODGSON, *supra* note 17, at 137, 149. However, he tends to confuse the valid point that courts are not empowered to conduct investigations with the invalid one concerning the ability of judges to make policy decisions on the basis of sociological evidence. The judges would not primarily be assessing the reliability and accuracy of such evidence, but making policy decisions on the basis of it. Legislators are no more qualified than are judges to evaluate the scientific validity of sociological evidence. Moreover, as other correctly argue, at least in cases of first impression, if judges are to make reasonable decisions they must consider empirical evidence bearing upon the desirability of alternative rules. R. WASSERSTROM, *supra* note 6, at 156-57; Gray, *supra* note 56, at 82, 87; Hall, *supra* note 56, at 405. In cases which are not of first impression, judges do not have to decide which of two rules is the more desirable. If they lack information needed for making a reasonable judgment on the matter, they should defer it to the legislature provided it is better able to obtain the needed inforamtion.

[58]Roe v. Wade, 410 U.S. 113 (1973). During the first trimester of pregnancy, abortion decisions are left to the medical judgment of the attending physician; after the first trimester, the state may regulate the abortion procedure in ways reasonably related to maternal health.

criticism for opponents of abortion.[59] It would undoubtedly have been better to allow state legislatures to define the time of viability, subject to judicial review for reasonableness.

Yet another frequently suggested principle for determining a legislative question is the availability of alternative means for changing the extant rule. For example, Shaefer suggests that one reason courts are more likely to overrule previous constitutional interpretations than they are to overrule statutory ones is the difficulty involved in otherwise changing a constitution.[60] Although this consideration is not as significant when directed to the subject of change of common law rules, such a principle might be relevant in two respects. First, if a court is uncertain that it wants to fully reconsider a rule, the likelihood of soon having another chance to do so might be taken into account. However, if a court does want to reconsider a rule, it usually will have no difficulty in finding a case in which to do so. Second, this principle may also be relevant when the legislature is actively engaged in considering the issue. If the legislature is soon likely to make a change, it may be appropriate for a court to defer it.

This raises a consideration much discussed in the cases, namely, the significance to be attached to legislative inaction. Sometimes legislative inaction is taken to indicate satisfaction with the law. However, it can also be interpreted as indicative of a legislative desire for courts to assume the responsibility of making any needed changes. If a legislature has voted on a bill proposing a change, then it may seem more reasonable to construe its failure to change the law as indicating satisfaction with it. However, there are extreme difficulties in knowing why a legislature has not passed a bill.[61] Moreover, the pressure upon legislatures to act in various areas has increased during this century, making it extremely difficult for legislators to devote time to law reform, especially when there are no pressure groups pushing for change in certain areas of private law.[62] Rupert Cross suggests that the system of case law is workable only on the assumption that when it breaks down under the dead weight of precedent, amending legislation will be available.[63] Assuming this to be true, courts will have to

---

[59]Horan, Gorby, and Hilgers, *Abortion and the Supreme Court: Death Becomes a Way of Life*, in ABORTION AND SOCIAL JUSTICE 301, 315 (1972).

[60]W. SHAEFER, *supra* note 11, at 11; *see also* S. MERMIN, *supra* note 29, at 262.

[61]*See* Berry v. Branner, 421 P.2d 996, 998 (Ore. 1966).

[62]R. KEETON, *supra* note 3, at 16-17; Leflar, *supra* note 52, at 928. For an extensive analysis of reasons for legislative inaction, *see* Peck, *The Role of the Courts and Legislatures in the Reform of Tort Law*, 48 MINN. L. REV. 265, 268-85 (1963).

[63]R. CROSS, PRECEDENT IN ENGLISH LAW 218 (2d ed. 1968).

overrule more decisions than previously to keep the legal system viable when legislatures are unable to act. Consequently, courts must decide on the basis of a realistic appraisal of the situation when to make changes themselves and when to leave them to legislatures.

The issue of legislative inaction is frequently thought to be most perplexing when in earlier decisions a court has expressed a preference for a new rule, but has declined to overrule precedents. The issue in this context, however, is spurious. If the court considered prospective overruling and declined to overrule precedent because of the principle of stability, then it should not prefer, everything considered, a change in the rule. If it failed to consider prospective overruling, then it should do so in the next appropriate case. If the court declined to overrule precedent because, when considered in light of the appropriate principles, the issue was determined to be a legislative question, then the issue should still be left to the legislature. In short, legislative inaction should not be a special bar to judicial change: Either the principle of stability militates against the change and only the legislature should make it; or the court was wrong not to have made the change previously.

Thus far, five principles have been considered as constituting a standard to be utilized in a determination as to which types of issues are more appropriately resolved by legislatures than by courts.[64] However, there is a general argument that since the common law rules were originally promulgated by courts, not legislatures, courts are the only bodies competent to consider the proposed changes. Change of the common law, therefore, could never be a legislative question. This argument, however, overlooks the probability of changed circumstances. A rule's interrelations with other rules may have developed over time, so that a current change in it may have much wider ramifications in the legal system than did its original adoption. Similar considerations apply when the principle of complexity is regarded. Moreover, the availability of information may be

---

[64]One might contend that Dworkin's distinction between arguments based on principles and those based on policies should be a sixth principle, since only legislatures should make decisions involving policy considerations. *See* Dworkin, *supra* note 39. However, even if one accepts the distinction of the rights thesis between principle and policy, it has little relevance to common law rules. Since, if the descriptive version of Dworkin's rights thesis is correct, that rules were adopted on the basis of rights, it is likely that such considerations, rather than policies, would be the ground for changing them. For example, the standard argument in favor of a comparative rather than a contributory negligence is based upon a more just application of the principle of fault. A legislative question would be involved only if policy considerations had arisen for changing a rule; for example, limiting damages in medical malpractice suits.

much more crucial now than it was at the time of the rule's initial adoption. The development of sociology and economics has made it possible to obtain information not obtainable in the nineteenth century. Also, the proposed rule may require such information for an evaluation of its merits, while alternative rules considered when the existing rule was originally promulgated did not. Hence, the fact that an extant rule is a court made one is not dispositive in a determination of whether its change is a legislative question. At best, a basis is provided for skepticism of the claim that courts should not alter common law rules. Thus, the basic principles which constitute the standard of a legislative question should be applied in each case.

Conclusion

The proper role of courts in reform of the common law has been neglected by legal philosophers. The confusions inherent in the doctrine of stare decisis have generally prevented courts from developing a clearly articulated rationale for their action or inaction in reform of the common law. In particular, the doctrine of stare decisis confuses the principle of stability with the standard of legislative questions. Such a confusion is natural, for if courts decide that the law should not be changed (principle of stability), change must emanate from the legislature (legislative question). However, if courts may engage in prospective overruling, then the principle of stability provides no stronger a reason against judicial than against legislative change.[65] The standard of legislative questions does

---

[65]At this point it should be noted that there is a general argument that courts should not overrule precedents or at least should be very cautious in so doing because courts, as compared to legislatures, are undemocratic institutions. Legislators must frequently stand for reelection, whereas some judges are not elected and those who are generally have long terms of office. Consequently, it is claimed that courts do not reflect the will of the people as well as legislatures and should not be involved in lawmaking.

Since a complete consideration of this argument would require a complex analysis of political theory, only a few brief points may be made here. First, historically, the law developed primarily by judicial decision rather than by legislative enactment. The discussion herein has been explicitly restricted to judicially created common law. If judges were historically competent to make law, then they may be presumed to be competent to do so now absent a showing that changed social circumstances render the matter a legislative question. Second, the value of public representation is greatest when various competing interests need to be compromised. The principle of a need for a bright line covers many of these situations. Such compromise is also important in decisions about governmental spending, but courts do

provide a basis for distinguishing rules which courts ought not undertake to change from those which they may. If the change of a rule is a legislative question, then courts are not qualified to determine the relative merits of proposed and extant rules. Consequently, it is inappropriate for courts to declare that although a particular common law rule should be changed, it is a legislative question.

The proper role of courts of final review in reform of the common law is greater than most of them seem to realize. If the standard of legislative questions is applied realistically, few issues of change of the common law will be found to be legislative questions. If the common law is arcane and inadequate for social conditions, the blame will frequently be placed upon the nonfeasance or malfeasance of contemporary judges. The blame can rarely be passed to legislatures under the guise of the issue being a legislative question.

Legal philosophers cannot reform the law, but they may help by sorting out the distinct considerations involved in deciding to overrule precedent. The courts must still apply these considerations to actual cases. There is considerable evidence that judges on courts of final review in the United Stated are becoming aware of their responsibilities in reform of the common law. A well considered judicial activism in common law reform will benefit the public at large.

---

not make such decisions. Third, and most significantly, the argument that courts, as undemocratic institutions, should not overrule precedents is not directly relevant either to the principle of stability or to the standard of legislative questions. The principle of stability provides a reason against change of the law which is applicable to both courts and legislatures. Furthermore, even if the general argument provides a good but not conclusive reason against judicial change of the law, it does not help in distinguishing between those questions which courts should handle and those which are legislative questions. Consequently, unless the argument proves that courts should never overrule precedents, it at best provides a principle against judicial change which is distinct from the principle of stability and the standard of legislative questions.

OBEDIENCE TO LAWFUL AUTHORITY

During the past decade and a half, we in the United States have been forced by civil rights and anti-war demonstrations, the slaughter at Mai Lai, and the Watergate break-in to reconsider the reasons for, and limits to, obedience to lawful authority. What is the justification for such obedience? What are its limits?

The life of Sir Thomas More makes us realize how perennial these issues are. More confronted them when King Henry VIII demanded that he accept the Act of Succession, repudiate papal supremacy over the Church of England, and swear loyalty to Henry. In the course of this talk I shall try to make clear that it would be misleading to say More refused to obey a person having lawful authority. However, I will not primarily discuss More's problems. Nor can I, in the brief time available, provide a philosophically satisfactory and detailed discussion of the whole issue. Rather than present a detailed argument on a small aspect of it, I shall provide a thumbnail sketch of a general approach.[1]

The expression "obedience to lawful authority" may be misleading. It suggests that one has a duty to a person in authority rather than an obligation to comply with legal norms. Some political philosophers write of people in authority having a right to command and of subjects having a correlative duty to obey. A simple example illustrates a difficulty with this account. Suppose Abernathy negligently injures Baker and that under the tort law of the jurisdiction he owes compensation to Baker. Abernathy then has a duty to Baker to compensate him; but if subjects have a duty to obey people in authority, Abernathy has two duties--one to Baker and another to some person (it is unclear who) in authority. However, it is unnecessary to claim Abernathy has a duty to someone in authority, for it adds nothing to his duty to Baker. The same act would fulfill both duties. It is more perspicuous to say that Abernathy has a duty to Baker and that someone is authorized to enforce that one duty.

On Hohfeld's analysis of legal relations,[2] positions of authority chiefly consist of legal powers to establish and to enforce norms. People subject to the norms may find their legal positions thus regulated. In

---

[1]For a detailed discussion of the various concepts presented in this speech, see M. BAYLES, PRINCIPLES OF LEGISLATION (1978).

[2]W. HOHFELD, FUNDAMENTAL LEGAL CONCEPTIONS AS APPLIED IN JUDICIAL REASONING (1919).

W. L. Robison (ed.), The Legal Essays of Michael Bayles, 65–72.
© 2002 *Kluwer Law International. Printed in the Netherlands.*

H.L.A. Hart's terms,[3] positions of authority are constituted by power-conferring rules rather than by duty-imposing ones. The general form of such a power-conferring rule or set of rules is as follows: Person X, with qualification Q, may establish or enforce norms N, in a manner or procedure M, for persons Y, concerning topics T, for purposes P. Each of the various elements of the general form of a power-conferring rule is important. For example, a judge occupies a position of authority constituted by such rules. A judge must meet certain qualifications and must apply law in accordance with due process for people and for topics within the court's personal and subject matter jurisdiction in order to resolve disputes peaceably and justly. Only when a judge acts in conformity to the rules specifying these conditions are his orders lawful.

A major consequence of this account of positions of authority is that any obligation to comply with laws and lawful order depends upon the justifiability of the power-conferring rule and not upon allegiance to the persons who occupy the positions of authority. Some of the protagonists in Watergate failed to appreciate this point and thought their allegiance to Richard Nixon was greater than that to the rules constituting the office he occupied.

If the power-conferring rules constituting a legal system are justifiable, then there is a prima facie obligation to comply with norms established in accordance with system. A legal system is a decision procedure; it is a method for deciding what is to be done and how people should act. In modern legal systems, the procedures for reaching decisions are quite complex. Nonetheless, the system of legislative enactment and executive and judicial enforcement is to decide certain matters of common policy and conduct.

One cannot consistently accept a decision procedure yet claim that decisions in accordance with it make no difference as to how one should act. It would be like agreeing to settle a dispute by tossing a coin yet claiming what whether it came up heads or tails would be irrelevant to what one would do. The difference that decisions made by acceptable procedures make may be small, merely a willingness to forgo proscribed actions when doing so is inconvenient.[4] Nonetheless, that norms established in accordance with a justifiable decision procedure require conduct must carry some weight in deciding how to act. This weight may be called a procedural prima facie obligation to comply with laws and lawful orders. It pertains to all properly established laws and orders of a

---

[3]H. HART, THE CONCEPT OF LAW 27-33 (1961).

[4]Wasserstrom, *The Obligation to Obey the Law*, 10 U.C.L.A. L. REV. 780, 799-800 (1963).

justifiable system.

However, Barry Smith objects that even if there is a prima facie obligation to comply with laws, it is so weak that one should "refuse to count an act wrong merely because it violates some law."[5] His argument for this claim is as follows: An obligation is serious if, and only if, either an act which violates it and no other obligation is seriously wrong, or an act which violates another obligation is made considerably worse if it also violates the obligation in question.[6] According to these tests, the obligation to comply with laws is not a serious one. It is not seriously wrong to run a stop light late at night when one has clear vision in all directions and no traffic is coming. Nor is it seriously worse to defraud a person if it is illegal than if it is not.

Smith's argument, however, confuses the wrongness of an act with the harm which it causes or with the mental state with which it is done.[7] There are no degrees of being wrong; there are no comparative expressions of "wrongest." Yet one may speak of the seriousness or gravity of the wrong done--depending on either the resulting harm or the mental state of the actor. These distinctions are clear in tort and contract law. It is one element of a plaintiff's case to prove that the defendant acted negligently or defaulted on a contract and another element to prove damages. Intentionally hitting another person is more serious than negligently bumping him, and battery becomes more serious if the victim dies. Some instances of disobeying the law, such as running a stop light in the circumstances mentioned above, are not serious, while others, such as running a stop light when many pedestrians are crossing, are serious.

Some obligations are basically content neutral; that is, within broad limits they are independent of the subject matter. Almost all voluntarily assumed obligations, such as those to keep promises and to perform contracts, are of this sort. If Smith's argument for the weakness and the dispensability of a prima facie obligation to comply with laws were sound, it would also show that each of these obligations is weak and dispensable. Suppose Carver promises to meet Duff at noon sharp for lunch. If Carver is five minutes late, the fact that he broke a promise does not make his lateness seriously wrong. Suppose Carver cheats Duff. The fact that Carver had promised Finney he would not do so does not make his act seriously worse. Thus, by Smith's tests, the obligation to keep promises also turns out to be weak.

---

[5]Smith, *Is there a Prima Facie Obligation to Obey the Law?*, 82 YALE L.J. 950, 971 (1973).

[6]*Id.* at 970.

[7]A. DONAGAN, THE THEORY OF MORALITY 152 (1977).

Nonetheless, there are cases in which the fact that one promised to do something makes all the difference between a serious wrong and no wrong. In *Hamer v. Sidway*,[8] for example, an uncle promised that if his nephew refrained from drinking, smoking, swearing, and playing cards or billiards for money until he was twenty-one years old, the uncle would pay him $5,000. Such restraint by the nephew would not seriously harm him; indeed, many people would believe that such restraint would be good for him. In the absence of such a promise, the uncle would do no wrong in not giving his nephew $5,000. Yet, his uncle having so promised, the court recognized that because the nephew complied, it would have been a serious wrong for him not to have received the money. Likewise, there are cases in which failure to comply with a law makes all the difference between serious wrong and no wrong at all--for example, compromise jury verdicts, housing rental in violation of a building code to an informed and willing tenant, and admission of hearsay evidence in a trial. Many wrong acts are not mala in se (wrong in themselves) but mala prohibita (wrongs because they are prohibited).

However, even if the prima facie obligation to comply with laws and lawful orders is significant, there are limits to it. The obligation is a procedural one because it rests upon a law or order being established by a justifiable procedure. As the obligation to comply depends upon the justifiability of the procedure, if this procedure is not followed, there is no prima facie obligation to comply. In particular, if a person is not qualified under the power-conferring rules to occupy the position of authority, or he does not follow the prescribed procedures in establishing or enforcing forms, or he attempts to apply them to people not within the scope of his authority, or he establishes or enforces norms on topics beyond his authority, then there is no prima facie obligation to comply. In short, the procedural obligation to comply does not pertain to ultra vires acts.

Some procedurally defective rules or orders may be void ab initio, and others may be voidable. It is useful to distinguish between rules made by legislative or quasi-legislative bodies and orders made by enforcement officials. Procedurally defective rules are void ab initio; they are not norms of the system and create no prima facie procedural obligation to comply.[9] Orders and decisions of courts are voidable, valid until invalidated.[10] A good reason for this difference is to permit people to test the validity of

---

[8]124 N.Y. 538, 27 N.E. 256, 11 N.Y.S. 182 (1891).

[9]Shuttleworth v. Birmingham, 394 U.S. 147, 151 (1969). *See also* Strasser v. Doorley, 432 F.2d 567, 568 (1st Cir. 1970).

[10]Walker v. Birmingham, 388 U.S. 307 (1967).

rules by noncompliance. However, if people were also permitted to resist orders of those in authority who were engaged in the process of determining the validity of the rule, the entire process would break down. The legal system makes the final determination of the validity of rules.

Even if a law or order is in accordance with proper procedures and thus creates a prima facie obligation to comply, it does not follow that one's obligation, everything considered, is to comply. Valid laws and orders may be bad or unjust. The purposes for which the law is enacted may be inappropriate ones, or the law or order may be badly designed to promote these purposes--it may even thwart them. Here the substantive merits of law or order are in question. When a law or order promotes appropriate purposes, even if it does not do so as well as is possible, then it is not bad. There are then two reasons for compliance--the procedural obligation and the substantive merits of the rule. When, however, a law or order is substantively bad, its badness needs to be weighed against the procedural obligation to comply and may outweigh it.

It is, of course, one thing to say that there is no prima facie obligation to comply with an invalid rule or order; it is another to know whether a particular rule or order is valid. The same applies to valid rules or orders which are so bad that the procedural obligation to comply is outweighed. No one can provide a certain guide to these situations. The best one can do is obtain all the relevant available information and make the best decision one can. Recognizing one's fallibility, one may be cautious and comply with rules or orders when one doubts there is an overall obligation to do so. However, one's reasons for caution are most likely prudential rather than moral or legal.

Tax laws provide a good illustration of how a justifiable decision procedure produces an obligation to perform an act. Assume the state of Upaymia has a justifiable political/legal system. As the system is justifiable, one has a procedural obligation to comply with laws the legislature validly enacts, just as one has an obligation to do what one promises. Suppose the Upaymian legislature validly enacts a law annually taxing all financial holdings outside the state at one one-thousandth of their net value. Before the law was adopted, a person with financial holdings outside the state had no obligation to send the state treasurer a payment each year, but now he does.

Similarly, one may have no obligation to perform an act before one promises to do so. The tax may not be a wise one, but one does not always make wise promises. Yet once the promise is made or the law enacted, there is an obligation to perform the promised act or to pay the tax. Failure to do so may not be a serious wrong. Whether it is depends on the resulting harm or on the mental state of the actor. Nonpayment of five dollars due in taxes would not cause a serious harm. Intentional evasion of the tax might be a serious wrong. However, a deliberate intention not to pay the money could not be a serious wrong without a law requiring its payment, for it would not be wrong at all.

At this point, one can see why it would be misleading to say that Thomas More refused to obey a person having lawful authority. The argument so far has assumed that the power-conferring rules constituting the positions of legal authority are justifiable. In More's case, this is precisely what King Henry wanted him to acknowledge and what he refused to acknowledge. More was willing to accept the new rule of succession but not Henry's claim, as head of the Church of England, that the Church would now be independent of papal authority.[11] Thus, More refused to acknowledge a power-conferring rule which gave Henry ultimate authority in religious matters. Consequently, he did not refuse to obey a person he acknowledged to be in a justifiable position of authority concerning religion. He did not refuse to comply with a lawful order in a justifiable system.

More's stand was not based on religious toleration or liberty, although his account in *Utopia* suggests he accepted religious toleration for all but atheists;[12] nor was it based on separation of church and state. Instead, his stand was against the King's claim to ultimate authority in religious matters. Some of us would find him more saintly had he taken a stand on one of the first two bases before he ordered Protestants burned at the stake. Nevertheless, his was a courageous refusal to acknowledge any obligation to comply with unjustifiable authority.

In conclusion, a few comments are appropriate about how one may show that a power-conferring rule establishing a position of ultimate legal authority is or is not justifiable. Essentially, such a rule is justifiable if reasonable people subject to such authority have good reasons to accept it. They will have good reasons if the powers of the position are exercised to promote their secular well-being--physical, psychological, economic, and social. This view is basically that expressed in More's *Utopia*. The virtue of the government of Utopia is that it promotes its subjects' secular well-being--or pleasure, as More calls it--far better than do the governments of existing states.

When governments and laws fail to promote the well-being of subjects and even decrease it, the ultimate power-conferring rules on which their authority rests are not justifiable. Consequently, there is no prima facie obligation to comply with their laws and lawful orders. More

[11] Thomas More also refused to accept other elements of the Act of Succession.

[12] T. MORE, UTOPIA 70 (H. Ogden trans. 1949).

described such a situation in *Utopia*. Hythloday states:

> So when I weigh in my mind all the other states which flourish today, so help me God, I can discover nothing but a conspiracy of the rich, who pursue their own aggrandizement under the name and title of the Commonwealth. They devise ways and means to keep safely what they have unjustly acquired, and to buy up the toil and labor of the poor as cheaply as possible and oppress them. When these schemes of the rich become established by the government, which is meant to protect the poor as well as the rich, then they are law.[13]

Although such schemes may be law, because the purposes of governmental authority and law have been perverted, the poor and oppressed have no good reasons to accept the power-conferring rules of such states. Consequently, they have no prima facie obligation to comply with such states' laws and lawful orders. Members of the legal profession, as exemplified by Thomas More, have a special obligation to prevent such perversion of the law's purposes and thereby preserve the justifiability of the legal system and the prima facie obligation to comply with laws and lawful orders.

[13]*Id*. at 81.

Morality and the Constitution

Besides clauses specifying the various offices, methods of election, etc., the United States Constitution contains clauses which require that valid laws conform to certain moral norms. Most of these norms, which may be called "moral clauses," protect persons from governmental actions and are to be found in the amendments. Some of them are fairly specific, such as the fifth amendment's guarantees of a public trial and confrontation of witnesses. Others are more general, such as the due process clauses of the fifth and fourteenth amendments and the equal protection clause of the fourteenth amendment.

The specific and general moral clauses pose rather different problems of interpretation. Although one may have to decide whether provisions such as double jeopardy apply to states, the specific clauses give rather explicit directions as to what is required or prohibited. The general moral clauses allow more leeway for the use of different secondary norms to interpret them. Supreme Court justices and commentators disagree widely as to what specific norms are required for due process. Interpretation involves choosing between different moral norms of due process, equal protection, and so on, and this seems to involve arguments for one moral theory over another. How does one decide what moral theory to use? Does one use that of the authors of the clauses or may one use whatever moral theory one believes is correct? Are all moral theories compatible with the Constitution?

The problems do not pose an issue of natural law versus legal positivism. Positivists have never denied that moral requirements may be written into specific laws or constitutions. These clauses do not establish any necessary connection between law and morality, because the legal system could exist without them. The constitutional framers could have omitted them.

The issue to be considered here is whether these moral clauses impose a particular morality or kind of morality. Several grounds exist for claiming that they do require a particular morality. The most pervasive view of this sort is the historical school of interpretation. According to it, the Supreme Court should interpret the clauses as their drafters meant them; the Courts should be faithful to the intentions of the Founding Fathers. Although arguments of this sort occur in many court opinions and commentaries, the difficulties with this view are well-known. Besides undesirably locking-in the opinions of the authors of the Constitution and its amendments, this view provides little guidance for new cases which

W. L. Robison (ed.), The Legal Essays of Michael Bayles, 73–84.
© 2002 *Kluwer Law International. Printed in the Netherlands.*

constitutional drafters could not have foreseen.[1] One may always ask how the framers would have decided cases had they thought of or confronted them, but that leaves considerable room for the importation of interpreters' views without having to argue directly for their merits. Moreover, the historical view does not justify the conclusion that a particular morality was interred in the moral clauses. Jefferson, Madison, and Adams, for example, hardly shared the same principles of free speech and due process.

Much the same problems confront the interpretation of statutes, but they become more serious at the constitutional level. Statutes may be more easily revised than the Constitution. Constitutional provisions are not open to change by a mere majority and the moral clauses restrain majoritarian rule. Consequently, being bound by past constitutional mistakes is less desirable and judicial interpretation plays a more significant role in keeping the Constitution consonant with contemporary social conditions and thought. Thus, many commentators have tried to develop theories which give weight to the views of the authors of the Constitution without being completely bound to them.

Two very capable contemporary commentators, David A. J. Richards and Ronald Dworkin, have argued that the moral clauses of the Constitution enact a particular morality or at least a specific kind of morality. In neither case is the morality necessarily identical to that held by those who authored or adopted the clauses. David A. J. Richards has developed the most explicit form of this theory.[2] He contends that a particular contractarian theory of morality must be used to interpret the moral clauses. Richards' view is developed from that of Ronald Dworkin, who in some places appears to argue that the Constitution imposes a specific kind of morality, namely, one based on rights, and is therefore incompatible with a utilitarian approach to constitutional issues.[3] Dworkin certainly does not restrict the range of moral views which might be used to interpret the Constitution as much as Richards does. He contends only that any adequate theory must be a rights theory; it need not be a contractarian theory let along the specific version Richards propounds. Dworkin does,

---

[1]*See* Munzer & Nickel, *Does the Constitution Mean What It Always Meant?* 77 COLUM. L. REV. 1029, 1030-33 (1977).

[2]D. Richards, THE MORAL CRITICISM OF LAW (1977).

[3]R. Dworkin, TAKING RIGHTS SERIOUSLY (1977). As discussed later, see text accompanying notes 32-33 infra, other remarks by Dworkin appear to allow at least utilitarian rights theories to be used.

however, partially explicate the particular moral theory he believes best.[4] Thus, in many respects Richards' view is a more confining version of the general position which Dworkin seems to adopt occasionally.

Richards presents his view of constitutional interpretation as both a descriptive and a critical or normative one.[5] The founders of the Constitution, he claims, wrote it on the basis of a contractarian view derived from Hobbes and Locke. This is the descriptive part of Richards' theory. Regardless of the correctness of contractarianism, it is the theory of the Constitution and must be employed to understand and interpret it. The choice to adopt a contractarian theory of constitutional interpretation is not an open one in the United States.[6]

Adoption of the contractarian view does not, according to Richards, necessarily commit one to the particular opinions of the Founding Fathers. One must distinguish between concepts and particular conceptions.[7] The concept of justice does not imply any particular conception, which is an explicit norm for concrete situations in historical periods. While the Constitution commits one to the concept of a contractarian morality, it does not commit one to the particular conceptions of contractarian morality held by the Founding Fathers or the Supreme Court. Those conceptions may be criticized on the basis of a more adequate account of contractarian morality. This is the critical or normative part of Richards' position.

Contractarianism is superior to other forms of constitutional interpretation, Richards claims, because it explains both judicial review and the moral rights implicit in the Constitution.[8] Given a contractarian view, which is strongly countermajoritarian, a written constitution protects minorities by entrenching certain moral rights. The contractarian method of analysis provides a basis for deciding which rights (such as privacy) should be entrenched in the Constitution and for interpreting those entrenched in explicit clauses. Judicial review is an appropriate technique to preserve these rights against encroachment by legislative majorities. Richards illustrates his approach by developing a Rawlsian contractarian morality which he applies to particular problems of constitutional decision

---

[4]*Id.* at 259-78. *See also* Dworkin, *Liberalism*, in PUBLIC AND PRIVATE MORALITY (Hampshire ed. 1978).

[5]D. Richards, *supra* note 2, at 33.

[6]*Id.* at 44, 51.

[7]*Id.* at 52-53; R. DWORKIN, *supra* note 3, at 134-36.

[8]D. RICHARDS, *supra* note 2, at 50-51.

such as obscenity[9] and equality of school funding.[10] These particulars are not at issue here.

Richards' view is intuitively suspect simply because it elaborately argues that, with some emendations, the Constitution mandates John Rawls's theory of justice.[11] The supposition that the Constitution incorporates Rawls's *A Theory of Justice* or Richards' *A Theory of Reasons for Action*[12] is no more plausible than that it incorporates Herbert Spencer's *Social Statics*.[13]

If Richards is right that regardless of its correctness, the use of contractarian morality for constitutional interpretation is not an open question, then the Supreme Court is committed to working out that theory regardless of the morality of the results. Because he does not believe the contractarian theory is false, Richards does not confront the full force of this claim. Imagining the moral dilemma confronting a judge in Nazi Germany of fascist Italy illustrates the force of the claim. The constitution or political-legal system fundamentally rests upon the concept of naziism or fascism. A conscientious judge would thus be committed to the concept of naziism or fascism, but not the particular conceptions of the founders. His criticism would be restricted to claims that previous judicial interpretations and decisions had used an inappropriate concept of naziism or fascism and the substitution of his own conception. The law would be working itself to a pure naziism or fascism.

The point of this example is not merely that a moral person cannot be a "good" judge in a corrupt political-legal system.[14] Rather, Richards (as well as Dworkin) is trying to free the legal system from commitment to moral mistakes of the authors of the Constitution. He believes he is successful only because he believes they basically had the right approach. One who believes the entire contractarian approach to be mistaken, such as a utilitarian, will find Richards' theory very conservative. Richards can free the Constitution from only comparatively minor moral mistakes, not major ones. No reason is given, nor does it seem plausible that one can be given, why one should follow the Founding Fathers in gross but not petty

---

[9]*Id.* at 56-77.

[10]*Id.* at 138-61.

[11]J. RAWLS, A THEORY OF JUSTICE (1971).

[12]D. RICHARDS, A THEORY OF REASONS FOR ACTION (1971).

[13]Lochner v. New York, 198 U.S. 45, 75 (1905) (Holmes, J., dissenting). *See also* L. TRIBE, AMERICAN CONSTITUTIONAL LAW 890 n.3 (1978).

[14]Dworkin's solution of this problem is that a moral judge should lie about what the law is. Dworkin, *Seven Critics*, 11 GA. L. REV. 1201, 1240 (1977).

immoralities.

The underlying theoretical defect is that Richards, like Dworkin in another context,[15] attempts to develop a doctrine which is simultaneously descriptive and critical (normative). This is an attempt to bridge the so-called is-ought gap, the gap between the law as it is and as it ought to be. Natural law theory attempts to bridge this gap at the level of the foundation of moral theory, basing morality upon human inclinations and the purposiveness of nature. Although natural law theory may have either radical or conservative implications,[16] it never commits one to grossly immoral rules, such as some of those of Nazi Germany, being valid laws.

The views of Richards and Dworkin do so commit one because they attempt to bridge the is-ought gap at the level of legal theory. The examples of Nazi Germany or apartheid South Africa bring out the tension between the descriptive and normative aspects of such theories. To the extent a theory is descriptive of a legal system, it cannot be critical; to the extent it is critical, it cannot be descriptive. If a theory accounts for previous decisions, then it provides no grounds for criticizing them. If a theory provides grounds for criticizing previous decisions, it can be only because those decisions do not flow from the theory.[17] For example, a theory which describes and explains decisions limiting the first amendment to restraints upon governmental interference with the press cannot also interpret it as allowing states to require newspapers to provide space for replies by political candidates criticized in editorials.[18]

Richards might contend that this criticism mistakes the descriptive element of his theory. It does not pretend to describe decisions interpreting the Constitution. Instead, the descriptive element is simply the general empirical observation that the Constitution was written from a contractarian perspective. But the criticism only relies upon the claim that a Nazi constitution is written from a Nazi perspective. Moreover, that a constitu-

---

[15]Dworkin contends as both a descriptive and normative thesis that courts decide cases on the basis of principles (rights) but not policies. R. DWORKIN, *supra* note 3, at 84.

[16]D. RICHARDS, *supra* note 2, at 9-11.

[17]Dworkin does allow judges to reject precedents as mistaken. However, he recognizes that sometimes immoral principles may be so clearly embedded in law that they cannot be rejected as mistakes, and thus the problem of the Nazi or South African judge arises. *See* R. DWORKIN, *supra* note 3, at 118-23. If all mistakes could be rejected, then no descriptive element would be left; the results in particular cases would be the same as simply applying the moral theory to each case, i.e., a straight-forward natural law theory.

[18]Miami Herald Publishing Co. v. Tornillo, 418 U.S. 241 (1974).

tion was written from a contractarian or Nazi perspective would be completely irrelevant if it did not help describe and interpret some previous decisions.

This possible defense leads to another difficulty in Richards' view. He contends that a contractarian concept must be used to interpret the Constitution because the Founding Fathers were contractarians, but their particular contractarian conception need not be used. Richards does not provide a reason why one must follow the Founding Fathers at one level but not another. Three positions may be taken about the Founding Fathers' view. (1) One must comply with their particular conception of the Constitution and their intentions about particular moral clauses. This is the historical view. (2) One is committed to the concept of contractarian interpretation because the Founding Fathers were contractarians, but one is not committed to their particular conception. This is Richards' view. (3) One may reject both the Founding Fathers' conception and the very concept of contractarianism as a basis of interpretation.

Richards contends that one should not be locked into the Founding Fathers' conception simply because they had it.[19] The moral views of people two hundred years ago should not bind the present court. Historical evidence of their conception is often lacking or inadequate to decide particular cases.[20] Yet most of the reasons he gives may also be given for rejecting a general contractarian interpretation. Why should not the use of a concept of contractarianism for constitutional interpretation be open to question if particular conceptions of contractarianism are? Granted, if one wishes to describe constitutional interpretation in the nearly two hundred years since the Constitution was adopted, one cannot be restricted to the conceptions of the Founding Fathers. One must consider the conceptions of the various Supreme Court justices over the whole period of time. For this descriptive enterprise neither Richards' nor Rawls's conception is appropriate, because they are not conceptions held by many if any Supreme court justices.

This point may be made more specific. Although the contract conception which the Founding Fathers held was closer to Locke's than to Kant's, Richards proceeds with a Rawlsian contractarian conception which is more in the Kantian than the Lockean tradition. Robert Nozick has recently developed a contemporary version of the Lockean theory.[21] Nozick's theory is based on natural rights and is certainly closer to that of

---

[19]D. RICHARDS, *supra* note 2, at 51-52

[20]*Id.* at 52.

[21]R. NOZICK, ANARCHY, STATE, AND UTOPIA (1974).

the Founding Fathers than Richards'. Richards contends that one need not be committed to the Founding Fathers' conception and thus, in modern times, a Nozickian form of contractarianism. Yet, he maintains that one must use a contractarian theory and thus rules out any utilitarian constitutional interpretation.[22] Richards' decision to follow the Founding Fathers' to the extent of rejecting utilitarianism but not to the extent of following Locke-cum-Nozick is arbitrary.

Finally, contractarian theory does not explain judicial review better than any other theory which holds that certain rights are to be protected and maintained against legislative majorities. To the extent judicial review is required, it is on the basis of institutional considerations.[23] Legislatures, being more responsive to the desires and wishes of the majority than courts, are less likely than courts to preserve such rights. This defense of judicial review for protecting rights has nothing to do with contra ctarianism.[24] This argument is an instrumental one, and anyone wishing to protect some rights against legislative majorities may offer it for judicial review.

Richards derives his views from Ronald Dworkin's analysis of the moral basis of constitutional interpretation. Although Dworkin does not hold a contractarian position,[25] he does view constitutional moral clauses as general moral concepts establishing individual rights against legislative majorities. Dworkin considers the particular clauses to be moral concepts to be interpreted by judicial conceptions.[26] Dworkin thus uses the concept/conception distinction at a more particular level than does

---

[22]D. RICHARDS, *supra* note 183, at 247. This claim ignores the fact that with suitable interpretation a contractarian view may yield utilitarianism. *See* J. RAWLS, *supra* note 11, at 161-66; Kavka, *Rawls on Average and Total Utility*, 27 PHIL. STUD. 237 (1975).

[23]"The suggestion here is that the judiciary and legislatures differ in their competencies to consider the kinds of issues involved...[T]he proper application of the equal liberty principle is well within the competence of the judiciary to assess in a reasoned way, whereas the application of the principle of justified inequality involves complex assessments of social and economic facts and theories which should in general be left to legislatures." D. RICHARDS, *supra* note 2, at 54-55. *See also* Bayles, *On Legal Reform: Legal Stability and Legislative Questions*, 65 KY. L.J. 631, 647-54 (1977).

[24]*Cf.* D. RICHARDS, *supra* note 183.

[25]He does view Rawlsian contractarianism as a specific form of a rights based theory, but Dworkin himself argues directly from an underlying abstract right to treatment as an equal rather than by a hypothetical contract. R. DWORKIN, *supra* note 3, at 173, 272-78.

[26]*Id.* at 135, 226.

Richards.[27] Dworkin reads the constitutional moral clauses as countermajoritarian rights which must be upheld even when doing so prevents the pursuit of policies in the general interest.[28]

At one point (or time) Dworkin implies that certain moral theories, in particular, utilitarianism, cannot be used for constitutional interpretation. Constitutionalism, the view that the majority must be restrained to protect individual rights, he claims, simply is the theory adopted in the United States.[29] The Constitution protects individual moral rights against the state, and such rights are claims that "the state would do wrong to treat him [an individual] in a certain way, even though it would be in the general interest to do so."[30] He cites utilitarianism as a theory which a critic of this view might hold.[31] Dworkin's theory appears to rule out some moral theories as a basis for interpreting the moral clauses.

These contentions are incompatible with other aspects of Dworkin's view. Consequently, either he is mistaken or his view does not in fact rule out use of any moral theory for constitutional interpretation. Dworkin allows that a rights theory might be based on utilitarianism, although he does not think it provides a plausible account of rights in extant law.[32] Indeed, he chiefly argues for constitutional rights as necessary to permit a pure utilitarian calculus.[33] Constitutional rights in the moral clauses exclude extraneous factors which would sully utilitarian calculations. Courts defend individual rights in the Constitution (and case law), while legislatures perform utilitarian calculations within that rights framework.

The moral clauses of the Constitution are undeniably countermajoritarian restraints. As noted above, Dworkin claims that they restrain majority decisions which "would be in the general interest."[34] This contention is ambiguous between particular acts being in the short-term general interest and general policies which are in the long-term general interest. Only if a majority decision would be in the long-term general

---

[27]Richards also employs it at the level of constitutional clauses. D. RICHARDS, *supra* note 2, at 92-93. His crucial use of it, however, is at the level of contractarian interpretation.

[28]R. DWORKIN, *supra* note 3, at 191-92.

[29]*Id.* at 142.

[30]*Id.* at 139 (emphasis added).

[31]*Id.*

[32]Dworkin, *supra* note 14 at 1225-27, 1229.

[33]R. DWORKIN, *supra* note 3, at 276.

[34]*See* text accompanying note 30 *supra*.

interest is a constitutional restraint contrary to utilitarianism. Otherwise, one may contend that a constitutional countermajoritarian moral clause is in the long-term general interest. The Founding Fathers may well have believed the moral clauses were in the long-term general interest. They were well aware that momentary passions and actions, even of a majority, might in the long term be detrimental to the general interest of the body politic.

The first amendment's freedom of speech clause provides a good example of how a utilitarian interpretation can be offered. One of the hallowed justifications for freedom of speech given in many Supreme Court decisions is the marketplace of ideas.[35] Even though on particular occasions speech may be disruptive and contrary to the momentary public good, in the long-term a free marketplace of ideas is in the general interest. The point here is not that this justification is necessarily adequate, but that it (1) is a common non-contractarian constitutional interpretation, (2) does support countermajoritarian rights, (3) does not claim that such restraint on the majority is contrary to the long-term general interest, and thus (4) does not rest on a moral theory ultimately based on rights.

Indeed, it is puzzling how anyone can believe utilitarian doctrine cannot possibly justify countermajoritarian conditions. John Stuart Mill's *On Liberty*[36] is probably the most classic defense of countermajoritarian restraints on government and yet is clearly in the utilitarian tradition. While commentators have noted a non-utilitarian element in Mill's account of the individual's well-being[37], the bulk of the book, especially the argument for freedom of speech, is based on utilitarian considerations. Whether or not a utilitarian view generally or even of constitutional interpretation is ultimately correct, acceptance of utilitarianism is not necessarily incompatible with countermajoritarian constitutional moral clauses.

Two major considerations are open to utilitarians and others who do not use contractarian or rights based theories to support constitutional moral clauses restraining majoritarianism. These considerations are (1) a distinction between ethical and political "moral" norms and (2) skepticism of legislative wisdom. Ethical norms are those which apply to everyone

---

[35]"It is the purpose of the First Amendment to preserve an uninhibited marketplace of ideas in which truth will ultimately prevail. . . " Red Lion Broadcasting Co. v. FCC, 395 U.S. 367, 390 (1969); Abrams v. United States, 250 U.S. 616, 630 (1919) (Holmes, J., dissenting).

[36]J.S. MILL, ON LIBERTY (Shields ed. 1956), cited in Red Lion Broadcasting Co. v. FCC, 395 U.S. 367, 392 n.18 (1969).

[37]Levi, *The Value of Freedom: Mill's Liberty (1859-1959)*, in LIMITS OF LIBERTY 6 (Radcliff ed. 1966).

and are typically enforced by praise and blame.[38] An individual may make his own judgments about the ethics of his conduct subject to praise and blame by others. Political norms, including those of a legal system, concern the organization and subject matter of a coercive order. Not all laws and political norms are coercive ones, but failure to comply with power-conferring and other rules may result in judgments backed by the coercive power of the state.[39] One does not decide how political norms apply to oneself; rather, others--legislators and judges--do so. Thus, when one asks what ethical norms are appropriate, one is asking what norms the general populace should accept to guide their conduct subject to praise and blame by others. When one asks what political norms (especially substantive ones) are appropriate, one is asking what norms one is willing to allow others to apply to one and back by the use of coercion when they think appropriate.[40]

One may well be willing to accept others using norms applying to a broader range of conduct when the norms are backed only by praise and blame (ethics) than when they may be backed by coercion (political norms). Mill was well aware of this distinction, and it plays a key role in his argument to restrain majorities and protect liberty. He believed that state coercion was justifiable only to prevent people causing harm to others,[41] but he did not think that only conduct which harms others is morally wrong. "The acts of an individual may be hurtful to others or wanting in due consideration for their welfare," he wrote, "without going to the length of violating any of their constituted rights. The offender may then be justly punished by opinion, though *not by law*."[42]

Dworkin and Richards do not consider this distinction between ethical and political norms as a reason for countermajoritarian constitutional rights because they conflate ethcial and political norms. Dworkin interchangeably uses the expressions "morality" and "political morality" as though they were identical.[43] Richards explicitly identifies moral obligations and duties as those norms which may be coercively en-

---

[38]H.L.A. HART, THE CONCEPT OF LAW 175-76 (1961).

[39]M. BAYLES, PRINCIPLES OF LEGISLATION 69-70 (1978).

[40]*Id.* at 50.

[41]J.S. MILL, *supra* note 3, at 136.

[42]Id. at 91-92 (emphasis added). Mill further distinguishes unfavorable judgments of others for their self-regarding faults and for moral faults affecting others, only some of which should be subject to law. *Id.* at 93, 96).

[43]*E.g.* R. DWORKIN, *supra* note 3, at 136.

forced.[44] He develops this view from an analysis of legal obligation and uses it to distinguish when a person may be required to aid another in distress and when he need not (supererogatory action).[45] One need not use the concept of coercion to distinguish morally obligatory actions from supererogatory ones. An action is morally obligatory if a person is appropriately blamed for failure to perform it. An action is morally supererogatory if a person is not appropriately blamed for failing to perform it but is appropriately praised for performing it. This distinction makes no reference to coercion.

Skepticism provides non-contractarian and non-rights based theories another reason for countermajoritarian constitutional moral clauses. Both Dworkin and Richards criticize a skeptical approach to constitutional rights as exemplified by Learned Hand and Oliver Wendell Holmes.[46] The skepticism of Holmes and Hand concerned the objectivity of morality. Such skepticism does lead to a simple majoritarian conception of the polity. Another, more limited skepticism, has the opposite implications. Citizens have certain basic values. If legislative majorities were always correct in determining the policies which would best promote and protect those values, no justification would exist for constitutional restraints upon the majority. Unfortunately, even the best willed legislatures are not always correct. Legislatures do not always have the best will in the world; they are often prejudiced and corrupt. This is a skepticism of legislative wisdom, not of the objectivity of ethics or political morality.

The countermajoritarian moral clauses are built upon this basic skepticism of legislative wisdom. They are restraints against momentary majoritarian mistakes. Supreme Court justices are more insulated than legislatures from the momentary passions of the majority. The Constitution is difficult to amend so that provisions will not be imposed without adequate reflection. If upon reflection, after the momentary crisis and passion have dissipated, norms still appear to be correct, they can be incorporated into the Constitution by amendment or judicial interpretation.

Again, Mill was partially aware of this reason as a basis for limited political norms. He uses it as a reason for not interfering in self-regarding conduct.[47] Mill failed to realize that the same reason applies to some conduct which affects others. He assumed that the majority in society

---

[44]D. RICHARDS, *supra* note 2, at 197, 239-40; D. RICHARDS, *supra* note 12, at 98-99, 103.

[45]D. RICHARDS, *supra* note 2, at 222-23.

[46]R. DWORKIN, *supra* note 2, at 138-139; D. RICHARDS, *supra* note 2, at 42-43.

[47]J.S. MILL, *supra* note 36, at 102.

makes decisions about political issues. However, it is the legislatures and courts which do so, and even representative legislatures and popular majorities are subject to momentary passions and mistaken judgments. A moral theory may hold some values, such as freedom of speech, privacy, and equal protection of the law, so basic as to wish to protect them from the mistakes and momentary passions of majorities. These values may be either central to maximizing happiness or independently justified. In any case, a theory need not be contractarian or ultimately based on rights in order to justify countermajoritarian constitutional moral clauses.

This skepticism is not restricted to legislatures but extends to the judiciary as well. The elements of judicial constitutional interpretation--reference to the intent of the authors, fixed written expressions, restriction to cases and controversies, and consistency with precedent--restrain the Supreme Court from sudden and radical breaks with precedent. Radical innovation from the bench is as suspect as radical innovation by a legislative majority, as witnessed by the frequent criticism of the Warren Court for innovative constitutional decisions. Consideration of the intent of the authors of constitutional measures often provides guidance as to the values a qualified majority upon reflection deemed worthy of constitutional protection. Yet changing social conditions or reconsideration of the arguments may justify deviance from their views. Such deviance is restrained by having to conform to a written Constitution. Only a limited number of doctrines may plausibly come under the expressions "due process" or "equal protection." The most expedient method for determining cases is not plausibly due process. The restriction to cases and controversies prevents the Supreme Court from taking up any matter its members happen to think important, although discretionary review allows considerable latitude. Consistency is a desideratum for any rational system that is to guide human conduct, and, therefore, supported by any plausible political morality.

The point herein is not to sketch a theory of constitutional interpretation but simply to show that Richards and Dworkin have not demonstrated that the Constitution must be interpreted by a particular moral theory or a specific kind of theory. The instrumentalist considerations mentioned simply indicate the kinds of arguments utilitarians or holders of other non-contractarian, non-rights based theories may give for counter-majoritarian constitutional moral clauses. The development of an alternative positive theory is a major task for another occasion or another person.

Hercules or Proteus?
The Many Theses of Ronald Dworkin

For over a decade, Ronald Dworkin has been developing a theory of law as an alternative to positivism and natural law theories. He has primarily developed his theory by criticism of positivistic doctrines. Four of Dworkin's theses form the core of his view and provide a basis for many of his criticisms of positivism. First, contrary to the positivists' insistence upon judicial discretion in hard cases, Dworkin claims that in those cases there is nearly always a right legal answer, although which it is may be controversial. Second, the right answer is that determined by the best legal theory. The best theory is distinct from both positivism and natural law. Third, the legally correct answer must be based on the pre-existing rights of the parties to the dispute. This rights thesis holds that courts do and should decide cases only on the basis of pre-existing rights. Fourth, courts do not and ought not decide cases on the basis of policies. Rights are justified by principles, not policies, and because courts decide rights, they should base their decisions only on principles. Policy considerations are for legislatures.

Although these four theses are not the whole of Dworkin's theory, they are its central elements. If these claims cannot be sustained, the heart of his jurisprudence fails. Although the four claims are interrelated, and consideration of any one spills over to the others, we shall basically criticize each in turn.

1. The Logical Completeness Thesis

Perhaps Dworkin's most controversial claim is that even in hard cases there is nearly always a right answer. The claim directly contradicts the legal realist and positivist theory of judicial discretion in hard cases. In a recent article, Dworkin attacks the logical coherence of the no right answer view. If he is correct, he has presented a mortal blow to many versions of positivism.[1]

Dworkin formulates the problem as one of the relation of dispositive concepts such as valid contract, civil liability, and crime to judges' duties to decide legal claims.[2] He describes the issue and possible

[1]But he has not dealt a mortal blow to *all* versions of positivism. See note 21.
[2]"No right Answer?" in *Law, Morality, and Society*, ed. by P. M. S. Hacker and J. Raz, (Oxford: Clarendon Press, 1977), p. 59.

W. L. Robison (ed.), The Legal Essays of Michael Bayles, 85–116.
© 2002 *Kluwer Law International. Printed in the Netherlands.*

positions in the following way.[3]

Let p = df. Tom's contract is valid.
non-p = df. Tom's contract is not valid.

(A) Dworkin's right answer thesis is that *non-p* is identical to $\sim p$. Because p or $\sim p$, there is always only one correct answer, although it may be controversial whether it is p or $\sim p$. In contrast, there are two versions of the claim that there is no right answer. (B1) The first version denies that *non-p* is identical to $\sim p$ and contends *non-p* should be represented by some other symbol, r. As p and r may both be false, a judge in a hard case has discretion. It is as though the judge were asked, "Is the plaintiff old or young?" and could reply "Neither, he is middleaged."[4] (B2) The second version does not deny that *non-p* is identical to $\sim p$; rather, it holds that in some cases neither p nor $\sim p$ is true.

Dworkin contends that the second version (B2) of the no right answer claim is incoherent. Positivists hold that legal propositions are true if and only if some set of facts obtains such as the sovereign having commanded that certain types of contracts are valid.

Let $S(p)$ = df. The sovereign commands p.
1. $S(p) \equiv p$
2. $\sim S(p) \equiv \sim p$
3. $S(p)$ or $\sim S(p)$
4. *Therefore*, p or $\sim p$.

But 4 is Dworkin's right answer thesis. Hence, the positivist has no logical alternative.

Positivists, Dworkin contends, often mistakenly confuse internal and external negations.[5] They are inclined to argue that because $S(p) \equiv p$, then $S(\sim p) \equiv \sim p$. However, that view leads to a false conclusion. Because $\sim S(p) \equiv \sim p$, $S(\sim p) \equiv \sim S(p)$. Yet, "The sovereign commands $\sim p$" is obviously not equivalent to "It is not the case that the sovereign commands p."

The same difficulty, however, appears to confront Dworkin's right answer thesis. He claims that dispositive concepts bridge between certain events and conclusory claims about right and duties.[6]

---

[3]Ibid., p. 61.
[4]Ibid., p. 60.
[5]Ibid., pp. 71-72.
[6]Ibid., p. 65.

Let $Oj(q)$ = df. The judge is obligated to enforce the contract.
and $Oj(\sim q)$ = df. The judge is obligated not to enforce the contract.

If, as Dworkin claims, the validity of a contract determines a judge's obligation to enforce it, then the following argument obtains.

5. $Oj(q) \equiv p$
6. $Oj(\sim q) \equiv \sim p$
7. $\sim Oj(q) \equiv \sim p$
8. $Oj(\sim q) \equiv \sim Oj(q)$

But 8 is as false as 4, because "The judge is obligated not to enforce the contract" is not equivalent to "It is not the case that the judge is obligated to enforce the contract."

The first version (B1) of the no right answer claim seizes upon this fact and contends that corresponding to $\sim Oj(q)$ there must be a third alternative between the contract's being valid and not being valid. However, Dworkin denies that because the concept of duty has three possibilities, the dispositive concepts used to define the occasion of duty must have three possibilities. In logical terms, Dworkin denies that equivalence holds between a judge's obligation and a contract's being valid. In short, he denies 5 and 6. What he must hold is the following:

5. $'p \supset Oj(q)$
6. $'\sim p \supset Oj(\sim q)$

It appears open to positivists to take a similar way out of their problem. They certainly hold the following:

1. $'S(p) \supset p$
9. $S(\sim p) \supset \sim p$.

These two propositions alone do not get them into any logical difficulty, because "$S(p)$ or $S(\sim p)$" is not logically true.

The difficulty arises from the cases in which the sovereign has not commanded anything, $\sim S(p)$ & $\sim S(\sim p)$. There are three logically possible approaches to this situation. (a) One is to adopt the principle that all such contracts are valid; (b) another is to contend they are all invalid; and (c) the third is to say the situation is indeterminate and one must decide whether to treat the contract as valid. Dworkin takes the second approach, in effect adopting a completeness rule so that the system provides an answer for all situations. Positivists adopt the third approach and contend that prior to a judicial determination the answer is open. However, they do generally subscribe to the view that courts must decide cases and thus provide an answer. Judges, Austin claimed, have delegated or tacit authority to act for the sovereign. If they determine $\sim p$, then it is also the case that $S(\sim p)$. However, prior to the judges' decision, there was no basis for deducing $\sim p$ and $Oj(\sim q)$.

This conclusion appears to commit positivists to the first version of the no right answer claim. Yet, it is not the first no right answer position Dworkin describes. As an illustration of the first view, Dworkin considers a statute providing indeterminate sentences of three to five years.[7] In such a case, however, one has the following sort of logical relations.

Let s = df. The defendant has committed a crime.
and t = df. The sentence is between 3 and 5 years.
10. $S(s)\ \&\ S(s \supset t)$
11. $s \supset Oj(t)$

In this illustration, the sovereign has commanded that the judge exercise discretion. However, positivists argue for discretion and claim there is no right answer when the sovereign has not commanded anything at all.

Moreover, the positivist could consistently adopt Dworkin's completeness thesis for cases in which the sovereign has not commanded anything. He could hold the following:

12. $\sim S(p) \supset \sim p$.

Moreover, if 9 and 12 together exhaust the possibilities for $\sim p$, the positivist would be committed to the following:

13. $[\sim S(p) \vee S(\sim p)] = \sim p$[8]

However, from 13 it does not follow that $\sim S(p) = S(\sim p)$.

---

[7]Ibid., p. 62.

[8]Dworkin has not addressed this form of positivist view, although he has recently discussed a related one. Dworkin, "No Right Answer," *N.Y.U. Law Review* 53 (1978): 18-19 n. 4. He contends such a view must be able to distinguish all legal propositions into positive and negative ones and to reduce them all to statement of duty or permission. His argument, however, assumes that (1) no cases arise in which a decision cannot be based on dispositive concepts, and (2) the conditions for the application of dispositive concepts are completely given.

Thus, Dworkin has not shown that the positivist's claim of discretion is logically incoherent. At best, he has shown that the logic of dispositive concepts requires that when they apply a judge is obligated to decide a certain way. He and the positivists agree that the concepts either apply or not. But Dworkin assumes that the conditions for their application are completely given before the case reaches court, whereas positivists claim that in hard cases judges decide the conditions of application. Dworkin assumes that a principle of logical completeness is part of the rules of the legal system, but obviously it need not be. He has tried to formulate the principle as a logical requirement of a legal system using dispositive concepts. But a deeper analysis brings out the positivists' point, namely, that the conditions for the application of dispositive concepts need not be given in all cases.

Dworkin makes this same assumption in different forms in other arguments for the right answer thesis.[9] For example, he contends that if the plaintiff does not have a pre-existing right, then the defendant has a special defendant's right to win. The contention amounts to saying that if the sovereign has not commanded *p*, then ~*p*. It assimilates cases in which the legal system has a rule specifying that the defendant win with cases in which there is no such rule nor a rule giving the plaintiff a right to what he claims. Yet, he has not shown the positivists are wrong to claim the latter cases are indeterminate.

As Dworkin's logical arguments against the positivist's claim of discretion begs the question by assuming logical completeness, he must establish the right answer thesis on other grounds. If he can provide a theory of legal decision such that an answer may be found for every legal issue, then he will establish the right answer thesis. However, he cannot use the right answer thesis as a premise for his theory of legal decision; it must be a consequence of that theory.

2. The Best Theory Thesis

In order to establish the right answer thesis, Dworkin needs a theory of law and judicial decision which will provide a right answer for all cases. He attempts to provide such a theory as an alternative to positivism and natural law. In this section, we show that his view either collapses into the natural lawyer's concept or faces crucial moral objections which both positivism and natural law avoid.[10] No morally defensible space exists between the positivist's and natural lawyer's conceptions of law; they

---

[9]Dworkin, "Seven Critics," *Georgia Law Review* 11 (1977): 1215-19.
[10]Ibid., pp. 1253-4.

basically agree about what morally ought to be done but because of their different conceptions of law describe it differently.[11] Although we believe the positivist conception is superior to that of natural law, either is morally preferable to Dworkin's.

Some assumptions provide a backdrop for the Dworkin-positivist-natural lawyer dispute. Suppose that a society possesses a "true" political morality, whether truth in such matters means correspondence to an objective moral order or internal coherence.[12] Because of human finitude and fallibility, translating the abstract norms of the political morality into clear, predictable directives in concrete situations requires rulemaking and rule-applying institutions (with rules defining the institutions).[13] The rules promulgated by the institutions define institutional (legal) rights and duties.

Sometimes institutional rights and duties conflict with moral rights and duties derived directly from the principles of the political morality. In some cases, the morally correct course of action, all things considered, is to act in accordance with the strictures of the political morality and disregard the rules. In other cases, however, the morally correct course of action, all things considered, is to follow the rules. In both sets of cases, the wrong (unjust) rules and the institutions which promulgated them are facts which must be taken into account in determining what is the morally best course of action to take overall.[14]

We call someone a "sophisticated natural lawyer" if he equates the term "law" with the morally best course of action all things considered, including the rules, good and bad, generated by legal institutions. (A simplistic natural lawyer equates "law" with the requirements of the norms of political morality unaffected by the existence of legal institutions and their products.) This view is a version of natural law because all legal rights and duties are ultimately derivable from the background norms of political morality. Those norms, however, can be correctly applied only by taking account of the need for clear, determinate rules, the reliance of

[11]See also Norman E. Bowie and Robert L. Simon, *The Individual and the Political Order* (Englewood Cliffs, N.J.: Prentice-Hall, Inc., 1977), p. 220.

[12]See Ronald Dworkin, *Taking Rights Seriously* (Cambridge, Mass.: Harvard University Press, 1977) Ch. 6, for the distinction between correspondence and coherence theories of moral reasoning. See also Nickel, "Dworkin on the Nature and Consequences of Rights," *Georgia Law Review* 11 (1977): 1121.

[13]For critical studies of the role of clear but rigid rules in legal theory, see Kennedy, "Form and Substance in Private Law Adjudication," *Harvard Law Review* 89 (1976): 1685-1778, and Kennedy, "Legal Formality," *Journal of Legal Studies* 2 (1973): 351-398.

[14]See also Nickel, "Dworkin of the Nature and Consequences of Right," p. 1141. Cf. Dworkin, "Seven Critics," pp. 1259-60.

people on such rules, the need to support rulemaking and rule-applying institutions, past decisions of those institutions, the likely responses of those institutions and the public to particular decisions, and so forth.[15] (Reasoning by analogy in judicial opinions can be justified morally as a means of taking account of the likely institutional and public reaction to a decision.) Such a sophisticated natural lawyer might hold that one should comply with an institutional rule that should not, according to the political morality, have been originally enacted, and thus call it "law." We call someone a "positivist" if he reserves the term "law" for the norms generated by the legal institutions. For most positivists, therefore, the fact that the "law" requires an action does not settle the question of whether, all things considered, the action is morally required or permissible.

In an easy case, one in which the legal rules and the course of action they require are clear, a positivist and a sophisticated natural lawyer may disagree about what course of action is legally required but agree about what is morally required, especially if they share the same political morality. In a hard case, one in which the rules are either unclear, conflicting, or silent, a sophisticated natural lawyer again calls "law" the course of action morally required, all things considered. The existing rules and institutions are factors he considers, but in the hard case they are less weighty considerations than they are in the easy case. A positivist says that in a hard case the "law" does not determine any particular decision, and a judge therefore has strong legal discretion regarding how to decide the case. A morally responsible judge, a positivist claims, should look to the same factors a sophisticated natural lawyer suggests, the difference being that the positivist denies there is "law" prior to the judge's decisions being rendered.

Thus, the dispute between sophisticated natural lawyers and positivists who are agreed on moral norms and the factors to consider in applying those norms concerns the concept of law, not what is to be done.[16] And thus, if they share the same political morality, there is no

---

[15]See Bayles, "On Legal Reform: Legal Stability and Legislative Questions," *Kentucky Law Review* 65 (1977): 636-7; Soper "Legal Theory and the Obligation of a Judge: The Hart/Dworkin Dispute," *Michigan Law Review* 75 (1977): 512 n. 129.

It is not clear, however, whether the typical paradoxes of consequentialism can be avoided by sophisticated natural lawyers who view the moral necessity of law in consequentialist terms. See Devine, "The Conscious Acceptance of Guilt in the Necessary Murder," *Ethics* 89 (1979): 221. See also N. MacCormick, *Legal Reasoning and Legal Theory* (Oxford: Clarendon Press, 1978), p. 116.

[16]The terminology of positivism, with its provision for such items as "unjust laws," is most felicitous in hard cases in which the controversy is focused on lower level legal norms (e.g., on whether a case is governed by one statute or another). The terminology of sophisticated

necessary reason in any case for a positivist and a sophisticated natural law judge to reach different decisions regarding their moral obligations.

Dworkin's enterprise appears to assume that there is space between the natural lawyers and the positivists for a third jurisprudential position. However, it should already be clear that if his view requires judges to act differently from how positivists and sophisticated natural lawyers recommend, the judges will not act in the morally best way. Dworkin rejects both the positivist's contention that often the law does not provide a right answer, and the sophisticated natural lawyer's contention that the law is that which is morally required, all things considered. He wishes to accept both the natural lawyer's claim that there is a legally correct answer to every legal dispute and the positivist's claim that what is legally required is not necessarily what is morally required. He is thus committed to there always being a legally right answer in hard cases which may be morally wrong to enforce, a result which both positivists and natural lawyers avoid.

In the rest of this part we consider in more detail three concepts of law which would have the above implications. We do not suggest that Dworkin holds or even appears to hold two of these. They are presented to help show the problems with his concept and locate it within a range of views.

A. The Theory Which Best "Fits" All of the Legal Materials

One concept of law which might imply Dworkin's "right answer" thesis is that law is the product of the theory which accounts for all existing rules, decisions, institutional designs, and institutional practices. Even though these legal materials are the products of different people acting at different times with different goals and moral views, they should be treated as though they were authored by one person pursuing one consistent set of aims over time. It is the "will" of this Author of Legal Materials which is

natural law, with its equation of legal and moral terms, is most felicitous in those hard cases in which the controversy lies in the open texture of basic constitutional or metaconstitutional forms (e.g., on the meaning of the Rule of Recognition, or the correct weight to be given precedent). See N. MacCormick, Legal Reasoning and Legal Theory, p. 241; Tur, "Positivism Principles and Rules," in *Perspectives in Jurisprudence*, ed. E. Attwooll, (Glasgow: University of Glasgow Press, 1977), pp. 42-78; Levinson, "Taking Law Seriously: Reflections on 'Thinking Like a Lawyer,' " *Stanford Law Review* 30 (1978): 1103-4; Coleman, Review of *Taking Rights Seriously, California Law Review* 66 (1978): 894-902; Griffiths, "Legal Reasoning from the External and Internal Perspectives," *N.Y.U. Law Review* 53 (1978): 1134 n 42.

represented by the theory constructed and the right answers deduced from it. This one author is assumed to have consistent aims, just as is the author of *David Copperfield*, and this allows meaningful arguments about character traits and incidents which are not clearly described in the book.[17]

There are two fatal flaws in such a concept of law. First, the legal materials themselves are inadequate for constructing a theory which will answer all questions not already answered by the materials.[18] There is an indefinite number of theories or Authors of Legal materials which could account for any set of legal materials, no matter how extensive. Further principles not necessarily from within the legal materials must be resorted to in order to choose among the theories which fit the legal materials. The Author of Legal Materials must be endowed with the particular set of goals and principles, consistent with, but not necessarily entailed by, what he has authored, to extrapolate from what he has authored to what he would author.

Second, it is difficult to imagine why any society would want its judges to reach decisions in hard cases by extrapolation from materials authored by different people at different times with different aims and principles. Such decisions will surely not be easily predictable, non-controversial ones, and, therefore, will lack the advantage of clear rules over vague background moral norms. Nor will they necessarily be what is morally best, all things considered. They will not even possess the Hegelian virtue of manifesting the spirit of one Author of the Legal Materials working them pure and rational over time. Judges make mistakes and legislatures change their course, and these mistakes and changes may be part of the legal materials.[19] The theory which accounts for all legal materials will have all these mistakes and changes embedded in it. Moreover, each judicial mistake about such a theory, by virtue of becoming part of the legal materials when made, itself requires adoption of a new theory.

Happily, Dworkin rejects such a concept of law.[20] Nor does

---

[17]Cf. Dworkin, "No Right Answer?," p. 73.

[18]See also Steiner, "Judicial Discretion and the Concept of Law," *Cambridge Law Journal* 35 (1976): 154-7; Sandalow, "Judicial Protection of Minorities," *Michigan Law Review 75* (1977): 1168-9.

[19]See Levinson, "Taking Law Seriously: Reflections on 'Thinking Like a Lawyer,'" p. 1083. Cf. Winston, "Taking Dworkin Seriously," *Harvard Civil Rights-Civil Liberties Law Review* (1978).

[20]He does so in the context of rejecting Rolf Sartorius' claim in *Individual Conduct and Social Norms* (Encino, Cal.: Dickenson Pub. Co., 1975), Ch. 10, that positivism can account for all the materials which Dworkin claims to be part of "the law." Dworkin, *Taking Rights*

Dworkin adopt such variants as "decide all cases as you would predict the present legislature, or the community at large, would decide by majority vote," a variant which is compatible with positivism.[21]

B. The "Best" Theory Which "Fits" All of the Legal Materials

A variant of the preceding concept of law might support Dworkin's "right answer" thesis. According to this concept, the answer to an issue of law is the product of the morally best of those theories which account for all existing legal materials. Again, law is viewed as if all legal materials had a single author. This time, however, that author has the best set of moral principles consistent with what he has done.

This concept does not necessarily suffer from the first of the two flaws found in the preceding concept. There may be one of the indefinite number of theories which *is* morally superior. Yet, because there is an indefinite number of theories consistent with all existing legal materials, it may be impossible to show conclusively that the one selected is the morally best among them. Moreover, there may not be any one best theory; two or more may be equally good.

The second flaw does infect this concept, however. Why should a society wish to restrict judges in hard cases to doing the morally best consistent with *all* existing legal materials? Such a restriction will not avoid uncertainty, unpredictability, controversiality--the drawbacks of reasoning from abstract moral norms rather than from clear rules in particular cases. Nor will it produce decisions which are morally best all things considered, because the morally best decisions may imply part of the existing legal materials are mistaken. There may be a "best" *David Copperfield*, a fictitious person with a set of character traits consistent with Dickens' description but morally superior to the traits of any other possible David. But why be ruled by him?

Seriously, pp. 64-8.

[21]See *Taking Rights Seriously* p. 109, for Dworkin's rejection of these variants. See also Greenawalt, "Policy, Rights, and Judicial Decision," *Georgia Law Review* 11 (1977): 995, 1035-6. For the position that positivism is formally consistent with incorporations of natural law injunctions at the level of master rules or general rules regarding the application of more specific rules, see Coval and Smith, "The Casual Theory of Law," *Cambridge Law Journal* 36 (1977): 110-151; Kearns, "Rules, Principles, and the Law," *American Journal of Jurisprudence* 18 (1973): 114-35; Soper, "Legal Theory and the Obligation of a Judge: The Hart/Dworkin Dispute," 513-6; N. MacCormick, *Legal Reasoning and Legal Theory*, pp. 229-46; Coleman, Review of *Taking Rights Seriously*, pp. 894,912. Cf. Greenawalt, "Discretion and Judicial Decision: The Elusive Quest for the Fetters That Bind Judges, " *Columbia Law Journal* 75 (1975): 380-1. See also Johnson, "Toward a Cautious Return to Natural Law: Some Comments on Moral and Legal Obligation," *Western Ontario Law Review* 14 (1975): 43-7.

C. The "Best" Theory Among Those With a Certain Measure of "Fit"

Recognizing the defects of the above two concepts, Dworkin has adopted a concept of law as based on the morally best of those theories which account for some, but not all, of the legal materials.[22] There are two coordinates, a coordinate of "fit" and a coordinate of moral acceptability.[23] Each theory of political morality fits directly with part of the legal materials. Each fits with another part of the legal materials only by reinterpreting them.[24] And each fails to fit with part of the legal materials, which are regarded as the product of mistaken moral beliefs.[25] The law is the product of that theory which is at the highest point on the moral acceptability axis among those beyond a threshold point on the "fit" axis.

The crucial weakness of this concept lies in choosing the threshold point along the "fit" axis. The threshold may either be determined by the theory itself or on some independent basis. Each theory will fit fully, partially, or not at all with different portions of the legal materials.

1. Suppose each theory, because it is a theory of morality, dictates the degree of fit which is the threshold for acceptability. Such degree of fit will always be one actually produced by application of the theory! In other words, each theory will deem whatever degree of fit it results in to be acceptable. In choosing a theory, one chooses not only the degree and specifics of fit but also the threshold of fit required for the acceptability of the theory. Consequently, the only real choice is along the moral acceptability axis.[26]

The morally best theory will take account of existing legal materials as factors to be considered, but it will reject those which, everything considered, do not lead to the morally best result. In short, one is led to the sophisticated natural lawyer's position of always taking the morally correct course, all things considered, including the existing legal materials and the moral constraints they dictate--constraints regarding predictability, past treatment of other persons, institutional and public acceptance of decisions, institutional limitations, reliance, and so forth.

2. Suppose the threshold of fit is somehow independent of the

---

22Dworkin, "Seven Critics," p. 1252.

23Ibid.

24Dworkin, *Taking Rights Seriously*, pp. 110-23

25*Ibid.*, pp. 119-23. See also Nickel, "Dworkin on the Nature and Consequences of Rights." See Note 12, pp. 1121-3.

26Cf. N. MacCormick, "Dworkin as Pre-Benthamite," *The Philosophical Review*: 87 (1978): 596.

theory adopted.[27] Then it may be that accounting for the legal materials

---

[27]Dworkin apparently believes that there *are* criteria which determine the adequacy of a legal theory's account of particular legal judgments and which are themselves independent of the theory. Perhaps any theory of the physical world must satisfy certain theory-independent criteria of "fit" with particular observations. Indeed, it is plausible that to be deemed adequate any normative theory must satisfy theory-independent criteria of "fit" with considered moral judgments. Thus, even a coherence theory of the proper background political morality would require that the principles of that morality display a certain degree of fit with particular moral judgments. See Dworkin, *Taking Rights Seriously*, pp. 159-168. However, once the principles of the political morality are ascertained, it would seem that it should be those principles which determine the degree of fit particular legal decisions must display with other legal materials, at least if the legal order is conceived of as part of the moral order. Dworkin obviously does so conceive of the legal order, which explains the axis of moral acceptability. But he fails to explain how independent criteria of "fit," which might have operated at the level of choosing the best political morality, continue to operate at the level of choosing the best legal theory which fits sufficiently with the legal materials. Either those criteria operate only in choosing the best political morality, in which case choosing the best political morality and choosing the best legal theory are really the same thing. Or they operate at both levels, resulting in a concept of the legal order which is autonomous from the correct moral order.

(John Griffiths has recently argued that Dworkin holds law to be tied to the positive or conventional morality of the community, not to critical morality. Griffiths, "Legal Reasoning from the External and Internal Perspectives," pp. 1139-49. If Griffiths is correct, Dworkin's position is even harder to defend than we have made out. Positive morality, like positive law but unlike critical morality, will contain gaps, hard cases, which cannot be handled without recourse either to critical morality or to discretion. And hard cases within positive law may be cases which are also hard cases within positive morality, rendering positive morality incapable of resolving hard cases within the law. In this issue of *Social Theory and Practice*, see Levenbook, "D-Theories, Discretion, and the Justification of Adjudication," n 5. Moreover, a judge's recourse to positive morality rather than to critical morality in hard cases lacks normative force if the parties do not accept the positive morality. A hard case under Nazi law, decided by recourse to Nazi morality, surely is of no normative solace to antipositivists like Dworkin. Griffiths suggests a contractarian obligation to abide by positive morality. But this obligation either is part of positive morality, in which case it is no independent justification for the obligations of that morality, or else it springs from critical morality, in which case it is critical morality which ultimately determines our obligations under both positive morality and positive law. Of course, Dworkin might be offering only a description of legal reasoning, i.e., that judges often appeal to principles of positive, not critical, morality in hard cases. But such a description, even if accurate, does not support the theses that there are right answers in every case and that such answers are based on pre-existing rights.)

In what sense could a legal system be a moral system and generate real moral rights and duties and yet remain autonomous from the correct moral order? Dworkin sometimes speaks of institutional rights as being partially autonomous: *Taking Rights Seriously*, pp.

involves such constraints that the theory will not be capable of being that of the sophisticated natural lawyer. Indeed, Dworkin does reject the natural lawyer's view.[28] This theory will generate a legally right answer to all hard cases. However, unlike the sophisticated natural law theory, the legally right answer may not be morally right.

Thus, Dworkin must envision the possibility of a judge in a corrupt regime--say, South Africa--confronting an exceedingly hard case, laboring like Hercules to arrive at the "right answer," and then finding the "right answer" to be morally obnoxious. A positivist avoids this dilemma by denying there is a legally right answer. Thus, if he believes there is a morally right answer, he may use it to decide the case.

In summary, Dworkin's view either collapses to sophisticated natural law or allows the possibility that in hard cases the legally right answer is morally obnoxious. In easy or clear cases, the positivist may be committed to asserting that the legally correct answer is morally obnoxious. However, in hard cases, where he claims there is no legally right answer, he may give the morally best answer, all things considered. Dworkin either is driven to the sophisticated natural law view that in clear cases the decision implied by the legal materials is not in fact the legally right answer, or he is denied the opportunity to provide the morally best answer, all things considered, even in hard cases. Thus, Dworkin's theory

101-5. However, the most plausible account of institutional rights as a species of moral rights is that institutional rights themselves derived from a background political morality as a consequence of the vagueness of the demands of the political morality and the need of fallible, finite persons to translate those demands into clear, predictable rules. Therefore, only when the rules *are* clear--that is, only in easy cases--are distinct, "autonomous" institutional rights generated. In hard cases, the institutional rights merge with the rights generated by applying the background political morality directly but taking into account institutional practices and constraints. That is, in hard cases, the independent moral force of institutional rights is exhausted, and all that institutional rights demand is that we follow the course of action which is morally superior, all things considered. Cf. Soper, "Legal Theory and the Obligation of a Judge: The Hart/Dworkin Dispute," p. 506; Levinson, "Taking Law Seriously: Some Reflections on 'Thinking Like a Lawyer,'" p. 1100 n. 117. Dworkin explicitly rejects the idea that the moral force of autonomous institutional rights is exhausted in hard cases, but he offers no argument for the continued moral force of such "rights." "Seven Critics," p. 1238. Nor can we see how such force can be supported beyond taking into consideration, in determining the morally superior course of action, such institutional constraints as part decisions, future responses, and settled expectations. In short, the "best" theory of institutional rights is itself derived from the "best" theory of political morality, and thus once again one cannot choose a threshold of "fit" prior to choosing a political morality.

[28]Dworkin, "Seven Critics," pp. 1239-41, 1254-5. See also Soper, "Legal Theory and the Obligation of a Judge: The Hart/Dworkin Dispute," pp. 513, 516-9; Greenawalt, "Policy, Rights, and Judicial Decision," pp. 1035, 1042, 1051-2.

may be an alternative to sophisticated natural law and positivism; but as a normative view it is surely less acceptable than either of them.

3. The Rights Thesis

A central component of Dworkin's jurisprudence is his contention that in every legal dispute brought before a court one party or the other has a pre-existing legal right which the court must vindicate.[29] It is never possible for a court to say, "Neither the relief requested by the plaintiff nor that requested by the defendant need be granted as a matter of legal right, so we are free to choose the relief on other grounds." Intimately related to this thesis is his distinction between principles, which support claims of right, and policies, which prescribe means towards collective aims. As courts are restricted to claims of pre-existing legal rights, they are also restricted to arguments of principle. Legislatures, however, are not restricted to deciding on the basis of pre-existing legal rights and so may consider arguments of policy.

Dworkin's rights thesis is clearly a natural outgrowth of his position on logical completeness and his right answer thesis. In this part, we examine the rights thesis in detail and certain problems it raises about legislation. In the next part, we examine the principle/policy distinction and the motivation for the rights thesis.

A. The Rights Thesis: Analytic, Descriptive or Normative?

At times Dworkin seems to regard the rights thesis as an analytic truth.[30] If a court's *conclusion* is that the plaintiff has a right to a certain kind of relief, or that the defendant has a right to be free of the imposition of such relief, then its *premises* must have contained an imputation of such a right. Of course, this argument begs the question of whether the proper premises are those concerning *pre-existing, legal* rights.

Dworkin does not generally imply that the rights thesis is analytic. More commonly he makes the more limited and interesting claim that it is descriptive of adjudication in Anglo-American legal systems.[31] Although many commentators have challenged the descriptive version of the rights thesis by invoking various practices which apparently contradict it, we limit our discussion to two such practices. The first, limited prospective overruling, has been raised by other critics of Dworkin. The second, that

---

[29]*Taking Rights Seriously*, p. 81.
[30]See text at note 58.
[31]Dworkin, *Taking Rights Seriously*, p. 123.

of lawmaking by legislatures, has not been seized upon by the critics in attacking the rights thesis. However, we think that the rights thesis creates a difficulty in accounting for the justice of legislation.

1. Limited Prospective Overruling

Any descriptive version of the rights thesis must account for the following not infrequent type of case. The court decides a precedent should be overruled. However, it determines that there is no reason to apply the new rule generally to transactions arising before the new rule is announced, because the new rule is justified by forward-looking concerns and/or the old rule was relied upon by many persons. Therefore, the court holds that the rule of the precedent is replaced by the new rule, which will govern all transactions from the date of the decision forward but only the prior transaction involving the parties before the court.[32]

What were the legal rights in existence at the time of the transaction involving these parties? Dworkin must say either that the plaintiff had a legal right to the relief he subsequently sought and was granted, or that the defendant had a legal right to denial of the relief sought. If he says the former, then he cannot explain why the court's ruling is generally prospective. There is nothing which distinguishes this plaintiff from other plaintiffs and transactions to which the new rule is not applied. If he says the latter, then he cannot explain the ruling in favor of the plaintiff.

Of course, Dworkin may criticize limited prospective overruling on

[32]In Linkletter v. Walker, 381 U.S. 618 (1965), the Supreme Court held that its decision in Mapp v. Ohio, 367 U.S. 643 (1961), applying the exclusionary rule for evidence illegally seized to the states, was not retroactive, except, of course, in the case of Mrs. Mapp herself. In Li v. Yellow Cab, 13 Cal.3d 804 (1975), the California Supreme Court announced a new rule of comparative negligence in torts, which it said would be prospective only, except for Li. Dworkin attempts to account for *Linkletter* on the ground that in criminal cases the rights thesis does not hold because the prosecution has no right to win even when the defendant also has not right to win. *Taking Rights Seriously*, p. 100. This defense is unable to square the rights thesis with limited prospective overruling in civil cases (see Bayles, "On Legal Reform: Legal Stability and Legislative Questions," pp. 643-4 n. 39); and Dworkin's claim that in criminal cases the government has no right on behalf of the citizens it represents to the conviction of guilty defendants appears to be an unsupported, *ad hoc* assertion. See Nickel, "Dworkin on the Nature and Consequences of Rights," p. 1137. See also Oakley, "Taking Wright Seriously: Of Judicial Discretion, Jurisprudence, and the Chief Justice," *Hastings Constitutional Law Quarterly* 4 (1977): 814-5.

moral grounds,[33] but he cannot maintain the descriptive version of the rights thesis without explaining how limited prospective overruling is consistent with it.

2. Special Defendants' Rights: Rights in Court Versus Rights in the Legislature

If there are always pre-existing legal rights on one side or the other in every case which comes before a court, then those legal rights should also be present if the dispute is taken to the legislature.[34] Yet Dworkin acknowledges that legislatures are not always bound by and often do not honor pre-existing legal rights. Indeed, quite often legislatures change rights through retroactive legislation. Other times legislatures change rights through legislation which is prospective in form but which upsets expectation based on legal rights arising from past transactions. Of course, in the United States there are various federal and state constitutional provisions which limit the legislature's ability to disturb pre-existing rights and expectations. Some disturbances are considered takings of property, or impairments of the obligations of contract, or deprivations of vested rights constituting denials of due process of law. But within these limitations, legislatures regularly modify or extinguish pre-existing legal rights.

---

[33]There is one other possible tack for Dworkin. He may claim that a second-order legal rule prescribing limited prospective overrule in certain cases is already in existence. Under such a rule only the successful challenger of the overruled precedent gets the benefit of the new rule's application to transactions arising prior to the overrule. The secondary rule is justified by forward-looking considerations, i.e., encouraging challenges to unwise or unjust precedents, which considerations outweigh the reliance interests of defendants singly but not collectively. However, because such challenges will vindicate rights, encouraging them may be viewed as supporting the secondary rule on the basis of principle rather than of policy. Such a tack is one that the sophisticated natural lawyer might take to justify limited prospective overruling, although he would not, like Dworkin, need to distinguish principles from policies. Cf. Nickel, "Dworkin on the Nature and Consequences of Rights," p. 641. And such a tack is open to Dworkin if he is willing to abandon his rigid distinctions between courts and legislatures and between considerations of principle and policy, and to allow courts as well as legislatures to take into account the effects of actions on persons other than the parties before them. See *Taking Rights Seriously*, pp. 99-100.

[34]Soper, "Legal Theory and the Obligation of a Judge: The Hart/Dworkin Dispute," pp. 508-9; Steiner, "Judicial Discretion and the Concept of Law," p. 149. Cf. Bayles, "On Legal Reform: Legal Stability and Legislative Questions," pp. 643-4. See also Greenawalt, "Policy, Rights, and Judicial Decision," p. 1048; Greenawalt, "Discretion and Judicial Decision: The Elusive Quest for the Fetters That Bind Judges," pp. 380-1.

Dworkin needs to explain how legislatures, despite appearances to the contrary, avoid upsetting pre-existing legal rights, or alternatively, why it is permissible for legislatures but not courts to override them.[35] We consider the first alternative in the rest of this section and the second in the next section and the last part. Dworkin could view legislation as basically illegitimate in that it can contribute nothing to the legal rights people have except to clarify them by codification. In all other respects, the relation between legislation and legal rights is purely contingent; legal rights are not the product of legislature will.

Dworkin does not seize upon this extreme view of legislation to give an account of it consistent with the rights thesis.[36] Nor does he seize upon another alternative available to him, which is to focus on the differences in structures of courts and legislatures and to conclude from those differences that some legal rights are rights warranting judicial but not legislative protection. This approach is the familiar one of the legal process analysts about when courts should overrule precedent as opposed to await legislative overrule, or what kinds of decrees a legislature might issue that a court should not, and so forth.[37]

---

[35]If rights may be legislatively overridden for trivial policy reasons, they can no longer be considered the meaningful restraints on the furtherance of policies that Dworkin claims them to be. They cannot be taken seriously.

[36]The sophisticated natural lawyer would view legislation as essentially similar to adjudication in that both are attempts to produce the morally optimal social order. Cf. Soper, "Legal Theory and the Obligation of a Judge: The Hart/Dworkin Dispute," pp. 508-9; Greenawalt, "Discretion and Judicial Decision: The Elusive Quest for the Fetters That Bind Judges," pp. 380-1. Both can change persons' moral rights by affecting factors which are relevant to the existence of those rights, such as by giving notice of a change in the law or clarifying the law, awarding benefits to or imposing burdens on specific individuals (thereby affecting comparative justice), or establishing new conventions. Neither legislation nor adjudication, however, can alter rights in the sense of altering the principles of the background political morality. Legislation differs from adjudication only to the extent that institutional differences between them are relevant to their moral assessment. Among such institutional differences are not only facts about resources and personnel, but also specific, well-settled norms such as those relating to legislative supremacy and jurisdiction. Dworkin cannot take this explanation of legislation because he wishes to maintain a radical moral distinction between courts and legislatures. Cf. Griffiths, "Legal Reasoning from the External and Internal Perspectives," pp. 1133 n. 40, 1143-4; Coleman, Review of *Taking Rights Seriously*, p. 909; Levenbook, "D-Theories, Discretion and the Justification of Adjudication."

[37]Of relevance here would be the democratic make-up of the legislature versus the nondemocratic make-up of the court, the doctrine of legislative supremacy, the breadth of the legislature's jurisdiction compared to that of the court, the fact finding capability of the legislature compared to that of the court, the vagueness of precision of the relevant standards

The problem with this alternative as a way of squaring Dworkin's rights thesis with legislation is that there are probably no differences between courts and legislatures which would justify the claim that courts may never upset pre-existing legal rights, but legislatures often may (or, what for Dworkin amounts to the same thing, courts may never consider policy, but legislatures often may). Institutional differences between courts and legislatures do have normative implications, but those implications are not nearly strong enough to support the rights thesis.

There is a third alternative for squaring the rights thesis with legislation. Dworkin has said[38] that there is a special legal right parties possess in disputes before courts but not before legislatures. This special legal right is defendants' right to win (in court) when plaintiffs have no right. Legislation can be squared with the rights thesis if one accepts the existence of this special defendants' rights. Thus, when legislatures change the rules in ways which do not amount to takings of property and so forth, the parties who benefitted from the old rules may not have previously had any primary legal rights which have been upset legislatively. What they had was the benefit of rules under which other parties, for example, those who benefitted from the new rules, had no primary legal rights against them. Had they been sued by these other parties under the old rules, neither they nor their plaintiffs would have had any primary legal rights. The absence of primary legal rights in the plaintiffs would have brought into play the special defendants' right, which would have shielded them from liability. That special defendants' right is all that the legislation has deprived them of.

The following example will illustrate the role of Dworkin's special defendants' right. Suppose company *A* is polluting air. Homeowner *B*, who breathes the polluted air, sues to enjoin *A*'s operation as a nuisance. The court concludes that under the relevant statutes and precedents, *B* has no legal right to enjoin *A*. *B* then brings his case to the city council, which passes an ordinance forbidding the pollution. If the ordinance is valid, it

of decision, and myriad other factors. See H. Hart and A. Sacks, *The Legal Process* (tent. ed. 1958); Bayles, "On Legal Reform: Legal Stability and Legislative Questions," pp. 637, 645-54; Griffiths, "Legal Reasoning from the External and the Internal Perspectives," pp. 1143-4. See also Greenawalt, "Policy, Rights, and Judicial Decision," pp. 1045-7, 1053; Richards, "Rules, Policies, and Neutral Principle: The Search for Legitimacy in Common Law and Constitutional Adjudication," *Georgia Law Review* 11 (1977): 1099-1103. Sartorius attempts to justify a radical distinction between courts and legislatures based on utilitarian considerations, but he fails to note that legislative change, even if prospective in form, can upset expectations just as much as judicial overrule. Compare Sartorius, *Individual Conduct and Social Norms*, pp. 175-9, with Bayles, "On Legal Reform: Legal Stability and Legislative Questions," p. 640.

[38]Dworkin, "Seven Critics," pp. 1215-6.

must be because *A* has no primary legal right to continue to pollute. His legal right in the prior adjudication was a special defendants' right to be immune from liability since the plaintiff had no legal right.[39]

This special defendants' right will not work for Dworkin for two reasons. First, much legislation affects primary rights, rights which would provide a basis for recovery as a plaintiff, not merely special defendants' rights.[40] The special defendants' right can at most square only a portion of legislation with the rights thesis.

Second, the special defendants' right is incoherent because there is no necessary connection between the side of an issue a person is on and whether he is a plaintiff or a defendant. Consider the following hypothetical. *A* and *B* are landowners of the opposite side of a stream. *A*, according to his deed, owns the stream-bed. The stream shifts course towards *A*'s land and there is accretion to *B*'s land. Both *A* and *B* claim the accretion. The legal issue in their dispute is one of first impression in the jurisdiction, and there are thus no controlling precedents. Moreover, there are no other factors which would lead us to say that if either *A* or *B* were plaintiff in a suit, he would have a primary legal right to the accretion. Thus, if the legislature passed a statute awarding the accretion to either one, the other would not be able to say the legislation infringed his legal rights.

Suppose now that *A* sues *B*, who has occupied the accretion, seeking ejectment. According to Dworkin, because *A* has no primary legal right, *B* can invoke the special defendants' right and defeat *A*. However,

---

[39]Dworkin might quarrel with this example because it involves seeking an injunction, a forward-looking judicial decree, and not damages, which are backward-looking. See Dworkin, "Seven Critics," pp. 1214-5. However, if the city council not only forbids the pollution in the future, but also awards B compensation from A for past pollution, the ordinance will either involve a legislative override of A's primary legal rights, or else A's right to be free of a damage award must be one of Dworkin's special defendants' legal rights. Cf. Greenawalt, "Policy, Rights, and Judicial Decision," pp. 1005-7.

Consider an example suggested by the famous case of Lochner v. New York, 198 U.S. 45 (1905). A bakery employee sues his employer seeking a declaratory judgment that their contract, which calls for 70 hours of labor per week by the employee, is void. The court determines after considering all relevant legal principles that the contract is valid, but before it renders it decision the New York legislature passes a law forbidding contracts with bakery employees requiring more than 60 hours of labor per week and voiding all prior contracts calling for more than 60 hours. If the statute is constitutional, then the employer's right, which the court was prepared to vindicate, must have been a special defendants' right.

[40]In the Lochner example in note 39, suppose the suit for declaratory relief had been brought by the employer, and the court determined that the contract was valid. The legislation upsetting the employer's right would thus have affected a plaintiff's right, not a special defendants' right. See also Greenawalt, "Policy, Rights, and Judicial Decision," pp. 1006-7.

suppose also that there are two other landowners, *C* and *D*, with a similar dispute, except that *C*, the stream bed owner, has occupied the accretion and is being sued by *D* in ejectment. According to Dworkin, *C* should win, because *D* has no primary legal right and *C* therefore can invoke the special defendants' right. Yet the court could not consistently side with both *B* and *C*. Unless the court is prepared to say that no one has any judicially protectible rights in the accretion, or that rights go to the first occupier, or something of the sort, it cannot decide in favor of both *B* and *C*. In short, if the court wants to say (1) that accretion should go to either the owner of the land to which it is attached or to the owner of the streambed; (2) that it should not go on the basis of first occupation; but (3) that a legislative rule awarding it to one party or the other would not be wrong in the sense of violating pre-existing, primary legal rights, then the court cannot decide on the basis of Dworkin's special defendants' right.[41]

To summarize this section, Dworkin cannot preserve legal rights from changes by legislatures based upon trivial policies (and thus take rights seriously) unless he contends that certain rights exist in courts that do not exist in legislatures. This contention might be analytic, in which case it reduces to "a court is defined as that institution within which parties have certain legal rights that they do not have within legislatures."[42] Such an analytic contention obviously begs all of the interesting and important questions. The contention may also be descriptive, in which case it reduces to "people (lawyers, parties) act as though one party or the other always has a pre-existing legal right in court but not in the legislature." However, people urge courts to overrule precedent or create new rules on the same grounds as they urge legislatures to legislate. Moreover, courts do appear to act like legislatures when they engage in prospective overruling, and legislatures often enact rules which change the legal effects of past transactions. Finally, the contention may be a normative one which rests on the normative implications of the institutional differences between courts and legislatures. Those differences do not support a position from which one can argue justifiably that one party or the other always has a pre-existing legal right before a court, which the court *must* honor but which a legislature is often warranted in overriding.

B. Retroactive Judicial Legislation

---

[41]A similar analysis applies to the Lochner example in note 39, if we imagine the validity of the employment contract is litigated simultaneously in two suits: one in which the employer is plaintiff, the other in which the employee is plaintiff.

[42]Soper, "Legal Theory and the Obligation of a Judge: The Hart/Dworkin Dispute," p. 505. Cf Griffiths, "Legal Reasoning from the External and the Internal Perspectives," p. 1133 n. 40.

There is a normative argument for the rights thesis which Dworkin advances and which is distinct from the normative argument derived from institutional features of courts. An underlying theme throughout Dworkin's work has been that a concession that courts decide cases in which there are no pre-existing legal rights, no right answers, amounts to a concession that the decisions in those cases are instances of retroactive legislation.[43] Because retroactive legislation is morally objectionable, so, too, are judicial decisions not premised on pre-existing legal rights.

There are three related responses to this argument. First, as Steven Munzer has pointed out, the evil of retroactivity--upsetting legitimate expectations--is, by hypothesis, absent in hard cases.[44] Hard cases are those in which the legal materials do not give clear guidance and in which the "right answers" are inherently controversial. Thus, retroactive, judicial legislation could not upset legitimate expectations of citizens.[45]

Second, the retroactive elimination and creation of legal rights as the positivist would define legal rights is both commonplace and morally unobjectionable. Legislatures often pass retroactive statutes. As mentioned previously, in the United States there are constitutional limits on the power to enact retroactive legislation, for example, the takings clause. Within these limits, legislatures may and do enact retroactive laws. Moreover, much legislation that is prospective in form has no less (or more) effect on expectations than much retroactive legislation. To the average person who loses or find a billfold, the effective date of a new statue governing the

---

[43]Dworkin, *Taking Rights Seriously* pp. 30, 44, 84.

[44]Munzer, "Right Answers, Preexisting Rights, and Fairness," *Georgia Law Review* 11 (1977): 1060-5. See also Note, "Dworkin's 'Rights Thesis', " *Michigan Law Review* 74 (1976): 1178; Brilmayer and Nickel, "Book Review," *Columbia Law Review* 77 (1977): pp. 823-4.

[45]Dworkin's response to Munzer completely misses Munzer's point. Dworkin asserts that the existence of a legal right in one party to a dispute implies that it is fairer to enforce it than not to do so, even though the right is exceedingly controversial and neither party could have been at all sure about its existence. However, that assertion does not touch Munzer's point, which can be made in the following manner: Legislatures may change people's rights prospectively, for reasons of policy as well as reason of principle. Why can they not change people's rights retroactively for reasons of policy? Because in enacting retroactive policy-based rules legislatures trample upon expectations to a greater degree than when they enact policy-based prospective legislation. But where there are no firm expectations, if a legislature can enact prospective policy-based rules and thereby use policy to override whatever principles support the overturned right, why cannot it enact retroactive policy-based rules? What considerations other than expectations could be relevant to the prospective/retroactive distinction? Dworkin has given no answer.

rights of losers and finders is irrelevant: whatever that date is, it did not affect his behavior, nor would we have expected him constantly to monitor legislation of this sort. Finally, some legal rights in the positivist's sense are morally obnoxious, so morally obnoxious that the morally best course of action, all things considered, is to repudiate them and extinguish their effects by making the repudiation retroactive.[46] In those cases where the rules are both clear and obnoxious there is nothing morally wrong in acting retroactively and benefiting the parties who until the decision was announced clearly had no legal right at all. *A fortiori* there is nothing morally objectionable in acting retroactively in hard cases so long as all of the morally relevant factors have been weighed.

This last point brings us to a third response to Dworkin's argument against retroactive judicial legislation. If one denies that there are pre-existing legal rights in hard cases, as the positivists do, then one may deny as a consequence that judicial decisions in those cases are retroactive in one basic sense. No decision can undo the past. At most it can affect the future effects of past acts. Retroactive legislation changes the legal rights arising from past transactions.[47] But if, as positivists maintain, neither party in a hard case has a legal right at the time of a transaction, neither party's legal rights arising from that transaction can be altered retroactively. Nor can any party's expectations, if any, be premised on actual possession of a legal right. Therefore Dworkin's argument against positivism is circular on this point. It assumes that there are always pre-existing legal rights for its moral force (that it would be wrong for judges to upset retroactively those legal rights that exist in hard cases); and the positivists' denial of the pre-existing legal rights eliminates the logical possibility of such retroactivity and dissipates whatever little moral force there is in Dworkin's argu-

---

[46]See Greenawalt, "Policy, Rights, and Judicial decision," p. 1007. Cf. Dworkin, *Taking Rights Seriously*, p. 108, where Dworkin maintains that "it is inconsistent with any plausible theory of the constitution that judges have the power retroactively to make conduct criminal." Although the circumstances would surely have to be unusual in which it would be morally, as opposed to constitutionally, proper to impose criminal penalties retroactively, the Nuremberg trials suggest that they are conceivable. Moreover, if criminal legislation were to be deemed invalid for some petty technical reason, and a defendant were to disobey the legislative command proscribing a heinous act unaware of the technical defect, it is not absolutely certain that a retroactive application of the legislation, amended to avoid the technical defect, would be constitutionally infirm. In any event, whatever the objections to retroactive criminal legislation, they are inapplicable to many instances of retroactivity outside the area of criminal law.

[47]For an excellent discussion of the concept of retroactivity in the law, see Munzer, "Retroactive Law," *Journal of Legal Studies* 6 (1977): pp. 373-94.

ment.[48]

If the positivist account of hard cases is correct, then a court in such a case need not fear upsetting pre-existing legal rights retroactively. Neither party has a legal right prior to the court's decision. The court should look, of course, to the moral claims of the parties, to which the parties' actual expectations and the bases of those expectations will frequently be relevant. Whichever party has the stronger moral claim should be granted the legal right. His stronger moral claim places him in a position to demand legal vindication from both courts and legislatures, not merely to beg for it as Dworkin fears. The conversion of claims of political morality into legal rights is, in fact, how we conceive of what happens in hard cases. By hypothesis, such conversion cannot be morally wrong. Indeed, upsetting clear but morally obnoxious legal rights in what would otherwise be easy cases is often morally required despite reliance.

In summary, courts should look to expectations as one ingredient, sometimes the most important one, that goes into the calculus of decision. To fail to do so would be unfair. But courts are not different in this respect from legislatures.[49] The injunction to consider expectations does not make the case for the existence of pre-existing legal rights (as opposed to moral rights) in hard cases. If anything, it defeats it. Dworkin's normative argument for the rights thesis will fail so long as he wishes to distinguish his position from the sophisticated natural lawyer's position. Only on the sophisticated natural lawyer's account is it coherent to maintain that there are always pre-existing legal rights and that these rights should never be upset by *either* courts or legislatures.[50]

Even if we have misread Dworkin and he accepts the sophisticated

---

[48]See Coleman, Review of *Taking Rights Seriously*, pp. 908-9.

[49]Perhaps Dworkin's whole point with respect to retroactivity is that neither courts nor legislatures should attempt to alter the legal consequences of past transactions solely for policy reasons, but that both courts and legislatures may change rules retroactively for reasons of principle such as fairness, vindication of moral rights, etc. But if the point is anything more than a general repudiation of the use of policy justification by both courts and legislatures, it must be the more limited point that the adoption of a rule for policy reasons renders its retroactive application *per se* unjustifiable. This point is surely wrong; for example, there are reasons fairness--i.e., comparative justice--for attempting to place the parties to past transactions in the positions they would be in had the present rules been in existence at the time of the past transactions even if the present rules are based on policy considerations. Compare *Taking Rights Seriously*, p. 88, with Lyons, "Principles, Positivism, and Legal Theory," *Yale Law Journal* 87 (1977): 430. See also Oakley, "Taking Wright Seriously: Of Judicial Discretion, Jurisprudence, and the Chief Justice," pp. 806-7, 815-7. Dworkin recognizes those reasons in his treatment of precedent.

[50]See note 36.

natural law position, nothing in the sophisticated natural law account of legal rights warrants Dworkin's strong distinction between legislatures and courts either in terms of when rights may be altered or what considerations--principles or policies--are proper. It is to this last subject--the distinction between principles and policies and Dworkin's contention that courts, but not legislatures, are limited to considering only principles--that we now turn.

4. Principles, Policies, and Legislation

Because he believes courts are to decide cases on the basis of pre-existing legal rights of the parties, Dworkin contends that the reasons for the courts' decisions must be reasons of principle, not policy. Principles but not policies, he contends, are capable of supporting claims of rights. If courts determine rights, their arguments must be of principle. Only legislatures may consider arguments of policy to override rights. If, as argued in the previous section, the rights thesis is false, Dworkin's claim that courts are limited to arguments of principle becomes weaker. Nevertheless, even if courts do not always decide on the basis of pre-existing rights, they might still be limited to arguments of principle.

Like the rights thesis, this principles thesis is both a descriptive and normative one. We shall not canvass the large number of cases in which courts appear to consider policy arguments and say that they are so doing. Instead, we shall focus upon what the principle/policy distinction is, the difficulties in using it to describe judicial conduct, and the normative reasons for restricting courts to arguments of principle.

A. The Principle/Policy Distinctions

Over the last decade or so, Dworkin has offered somewhat different if not incompatible accounts of the distinction between principles and policies. Both principles and policies differ from rules in not applying in an all-or-nothing fashion and in allowing for considerations of weight. That is, different principles and policies may apply to a case and have to be balanced against one another.[51] It is the difference between principles and policies which appears to have varied.

1. Moral requirements vs. desirable goals. Dworkin's first distinction between principles and policies was that principles are standards to be observed because they are requirements of justice, fairness, or some other dimension of morality, while policies present goals

[51]Dworkin, *Taking Rights Seriously*, pp. 24-27.

or desirable economic, political, or social situations to be reached.[52] By itself, however, this distinction is unworkable. Securing adequate health care may be a political goal and requirement of justice. Rawls' difference principle of making the least advantaged as well off as possible may be a political and economic goal and a requirement of justice of fairness.[53] Dworkin's distinction comes close to that between teleological and deontological norms. However, in his later wrings Dworkin clearly allows arguments of principle to involve consequentialist considerations. Since Dworkin's subsequent distinctions are more developed, it is best to turn to them.

2. Individual vs. collective aims. Political aims, Dworkin claims, present states of affairs the promotion and protection or the retarding and endangering of which provide reasons for or against decisions. Rights are individuated political aims that assign opportunities, resources, or liberties to individuals, while goals are non-individuated political aims that do not require particular opportunities, resources, or liberties to be assigned to particular individuals.[54] Principles state rights and policies state goals.

One can, of course, distinguish between distributive and aggregative aims.[55] However, it follows neither that aggregative aims cannot be the basis or rights nor that courts cannot consider them. For example, a clean environment may be an aggregative aim, but individual citizens may have a right to sue to protect the environment. A court might well permit, as an efficient way of preserving that aim, individual citizens to sue polluters either as individuals or on behalf of the class of affected citizens.

Dworkin would object to the preceding argument that even though courts might grant rights to individuals as an effective or efficient way of pursuing collective goals, the individuals cannot make claims of right to such benefits. Courts might have decided that another method of preserving collective goals in which the individuals did not have these rights was preferable. Consequently, because according to the rights thesis courts must decide on the basis of the preexisting rights of the parties to a dispute, such decisions would be inappropriate and based on policies.

The expression "claim of right" is ambiguous between (a) a claim based on a right and (b) a claim to a right. Obviously, within the rights thesis, Dworkin means to assert that only claims of right in sense (a) are relevant. However, it still does not follow that policy considerations are irrelevant. In hard cases, courts try to decide what concrete, institutional

[52] *Ibid.*, p. 22.

[53] John Rawls, *A Theory of Justice* (Cambridge: Harvard University Press, 1971), p. 303.

[54] *Taking Rights Seriously*, p. 91.

[55] Brian Barry, *Political Argument* (London: Routledge & Kegan Paul, 1965), pp. 43-44.

rights the parties to a dispute have. Each party claims a concrete, institutional right based on an abstract right and tries to show that his abstract right should be recognized as a concrete, institutional one. In doing so, he may appeal to the advantages for collective goals in recognizing his right rather than that of the opposing party.[56] Moreover, Dworkin admits that any collective goals will suggest a particular distribution given particular facts.[57] As courts are confronted with particular fact situations, there is no reason why they cannot use collective goals to determine the rights of parties based on the particular facts of the case.

3. Questions of right vs. questions of policy. Dworkin's third distinction between principles and policies appears to be based on the second sense of "claim of right," i.e., claim to a right; thus it rests not upon any inherent difference between principles and policies but upon the uses to which they are put. "The difference between an argument of principle and an argument of policy, then, is a difference between two kinds of questions that a political institution might put to itself, not a difference in the kinds of facts that can figure in an answer."[58] Arguments of principle are all those which may be advanced for someone having a right, while arguments of policy are all those which may be advanced when the question is not whether someone has a right but what would be the best course of action.

With this distinction, there is no restriction on the kinds of arguments which courts may consider, except their relevance to the question at hand. The same considerations may be raised in courts as in legislatures. There may be a few considerations which could never be given for someone's having a right; however, most considerations could be relevant to answering either questions of right or questions of the best course of action. Consequently, there is no hard distinction between what courts may consider and what legislatures may consider. The same considerations which lead a legislature to decide that a course of action is the best may lead a court to decide that a party to a dispute has a right. This point is detailed further in the next section.

B. Converting Policies into Principles

Even if Dworkin provided a clear distinction between principles and

---

[56]See John Mackie, "The Third Theory of Law," *Philosophy & Public Affairs* 7 (1977): p. 8; Coleman, Review of *Taking Rights Seriously*, pp. 908-9.
[57]Dworkin, *Taking Rights Seriously*, p. 91.
[58]Dworkin, "Seven Critics," p. 1207.

policies, much of its significance is vitiated by his tendency to convert policies into principles. One aspect of this convertibility results from his distinction between abstract and concrete rights. Concrete rights must take account of competing abstract rights. Thus, what appears to be a policy argument is really a basis for balancing abstract rights. For example, Learned Hand's test of the reasonableness of a defendant's action in a negligence case was roughly whether he could have avoided the action at less cost than the expectable loss to the plaintiff. Although this test appears to be an obvious instance of a rule based on furthering a collective aim of economic efficiency, Dworkin claims it is merely a test for balancing competing abstract rights.[59] However, it is exceedingly difficult to distinguish determining which abstract right is weightier and deciding on one because of the support of a policy consideration.

Second, principles of right become so general that they encompass nearly all considerations one might wish to advance for any rule. Dworkin suggests as a principle that each person has right that others accord him the minimal respect due a human being.[60] This principle is close to Kant's categorical imperative in the formulation of ends, which Kant thought encompassed the whole of morality. Dworkin's own preferred principle is that each person has a right to treatment as an equal.[61] Moreover, if courts consider public safety, resource scarcity, or court congestion, these too may be considered appeals to competing abstract rights. Indeed, the act-utilitarian principle could be a foundation of rights, although Dworkin believes it incredible any court would consider it the best theory of existing law.[62]

The key to Dworkin's claim that arguments of principle and policy do not collapse into one another is that all policy arguments are consequentialist, but not all arguments of principle are.[63] There are consequentialist theories of right, and to the extent a judge operates solely on utilitarian views he will approach the same results he would achieve solely on the basis of utilitarian policy considerations. Yet, Dworkin maintains, even on a utilitarian theory, the question of what one may in fairness demand of others differs from what a legislature should require of everyone in order to promote utility. Dworkin thinks these differ because the legislature has powers of publicity and enforcement which an individual lacks. Even if there is such a difference, it does not show a

---

[59]Dworkin, *Taking Rights Seriously*, p. 99.
[60]Ibid., p. 98.
[61]Ibid., p. 273.
[62]Dworkin, "Seven Critics," pp. 1218-19, 1225.
[63]Ibid., pp. 1228-29.

difference between arguments of policy and principle in civil court cases and legislatures. The question is not what individual *A* can require of individual *B*; rather, it is what a court should require of individual *B*. In deciding the case, a court will establish a rule for all such persons and other courts will enforce it.

Here likes the heart of the difficulty of denying courts arguments of policy. In deciding cases, courts establish concrete, institutional rights on the basis of the rule of their decision. The rule establishes an institutional right, even if the court is wrong in so deciding. Dworkin believes that such rules may be adopted only if the arguments for them are in terms of abstract rights and the gravitational force of rights established in precedents. However, policics may also be the basis for concrete, institutional rights. If the legislature adopts a rule (law) based upon policy considerations--for example, providing loans to defense industries--it nonetheless establishes institutional rights. Both courts and legislatures are asking what institutional rights people in certain kinds of situations should have.

The right answer thesis does not require courts to forgo policy considerations. The right answer thesis is primarily a claim of objectivity. Dworkin must assume objectivity in political morality, for without it he cannot develop the best theory. Moreover, for the best theory to go beyond the legal materials, it must supplement them with principles of political morality. If, however, there is an objective political morality, then there is a right answer for policy questions. Consequently, there is a right answer as to what rule a legislature should adopt. If there is a right answer, then in Dworkin's Pickwickian terminology the people who would have rights under that rule already have such rights, i.e., the rights are pre-existing. Thus, given Dworkin's assumption of an objective political morality, legislatures should also base decisions on the pre-existing rights of citizens. Of course, some legislative decisions, such as funding the Department of Health, Education and Welfare, may not establish rights in anyone. Nevertheless, for all the sorts of legislative issues which courts as well are institutionally allowed to take--cases and controversies--policies also provide a basis for pre-existing rights on which decisions may be based.[64]

---

[64]Dworkin apparently recognizes that if policy decisions are objectively based, then the argument can be made that they can be demanded as a matter of pre-existing right and are subject to the constraints of consistency. But he denies that in fact policy decisions are constrained beyond a prohibition of gross unfairness or gross arbitrariness. Dworkin, *Taking Rights Seriously*, pp. 113-14. Indeed, he posits the distinction between the consistency restraint on principles and the not-grossly-inconsistent restraint on policies as the correct explanation of the distinction between strict and minimal review in equal protection

The only feasible way for Dworkin to avoid this conclusion is to claim that principles are objective but policies are not. Yet, he has little basis for doing so. He cannot appeal to the controversiality of what the right policy is, for he disallows that as a reason for principles not providing right answers.[65] Nor can he appeal to the dependence of policy considerations on changing factual conditions; for the concrete, institutional rights required by abstract rights also depend on changing factual conditions. Thus, as arguments of policy may support rules granting citizens rights and there may be a correct answer even though it is controversial, policies may also support rights of parties in court cases. Consequently, there is no reason to exclude arguments of policy from court decisions, assuming they could be distinguished from arguments of principle.

C. Dworkin's baseless fears

In conclusion, it is useful to consider the motivations for Dworkin's theory. Two motivations are paramount.[66] First, courts are non-democratic institutions unrepresentative of the interests of the community at large. If they were to decide cases on the basis of policies, various interests might not be adequately considered. Second, if it deciding cases judges were to adopt new rules and rights, then defendants might be unjustly held liable for violating duties they did not have at the time they acted.

Dworkin's theory is an attempt to avoid these difficulties. The logical completeness thesis ensures that there is always a basis for deciding a case. The best theory provides a foundation for the right answer even though people may disagree as to what it is. The rights thesis ensures that no defendant is ever held to a duty he did not objectively have when he acted. The principles thesis excludes policy considerations pertaining to unrepresented interests and thus prevents the unrepresentative character of courts significantly influencing decisions.

However, Dworkin's solution does not solve the problems. The

jurisprudence. Ibid., pp. 113-14 n. 1. However, the latter distinction is better explained by factors such as (1) the likelihood of legislative prejudice, (2) the importance of the benefit at issue, and (3) the ability of the courts to second-guess the legislative determination, rather than by the principle/policy distinction. And if, as Dworkin concedes, the legislature cannot be grossly unfair or inconsistent in its policy determinations, why can it be unfair or inconsistent at all? To call a policy determination a "little unfair" or "a little arbitrary" is like calling a woman "a little pregnant": it is a concession which is not minimized by minimizing adjectives.

[65] Dworkin, *Taking Rights Seriously*, Ch. 13.

[66] Ibid., pp. 84-85.

alleged problem of retrospective judicial decisions is not alleviated in hard cases; indeed, it may be exacerbated. By definition, in hard cases it is unclear whether the plaintiff had a pre-existing right. As there is a right answer, a losing defendant may complain that the court made a mistake, so he is still being treated unjustly. Moreover, even if the decision is right, he may always complain that he is being held to a duty which he could not reasonably have known at the time he acted.

The traditional account does as well by the defendant in hard cases. Rather than settle their difference by force, the plaintiff and defendant come to a court. The legal materials do not determine the answer. The court considers the claims of each in light of consistency with previous decisions, promoting the aims of the community, and a multitude of other moral considerations. It then says that everything considered, it is best for the plaintiff to win. The defendant need not feel guilty about having violated the plaintiff's pre-existing right, for plaintiff had none. While the defendant may doubt the wisdom of the court's decision, he cannot contend it was a simple mistake by which he was unjustly deprived of property. He may say that he reasonably thought it should have been decided the other way. However, he can recognize that there is a need for a clear, definite rule and that it is better to have a peaceable settlement of the dispute than a fight with the other party. Moreover, he can recognize that the court decided what, everything considered, it thought was morally best. On Dworkin's view, the best theory may not dictate the morally best solution. Thus, the defendant may believe that the court thought he was morally right but that, even in the absence of clear precedent, it had to decide in a morally wrong way.

Finally, allowing courts to base decisions on policy considerations will not be a disaster. If there is an objective political morality as Dworkin assumes, then there is a right answer to policy questions. There is no reason to assume representative legislatures are better at determining that answer than courts. Even if there is no objective political morality which always determines a correct decision, there are limits to the goals and policies which even legislatures may justifiably pursue.[67] Neither legislatures nor courts can justifiably pursue policies intentionally contrary to the public interest or destructive of public institutions. The justifiable goals and policies are as much a part of the background political morality as abstract rights. Moreover, courts are restricted to the cases brought to them and are not free, as legislatures are, to roam over all the possible issues in society. The structural differences between courts and legislatures

---

[67]See Michael D. Bayles, *Principles of Legislation* (Detroit: Wayne State University Press, 1978).

and the principle of legislative supremacy are adequate to restrain courts from rampant, wrongheaded lawmaking.

It may be useful to encourage courts to take rights seriously, but it is a positive disservice to encourage them to ignore social goals and policies. In jurisprudence as well as ordinary life, tunnel vision is a defect, not a virtue.[68]

---

[68]Two significant articles on Dworkin relevant to our arguments were not available when this paper was originally written. Relevant to the text between footnotes 18 and 22 is Ten, "The Soundest Theory of Law," *Mind* 88 (1979): 530-7. Relevant to footnotes 33, 64 and 65 are Regan, "Glosses on Dworkin: Rights, Principles, and Policies," *Michigan Law Review* 76 (1978): 1213-64.

CHARACTER, PURPOSE, AND CRIMINAL RESPONSIBILITY

ABSTRACT. This paper explores analyzing criminal responsibility from the Humean position that blame is for character traits. If untoward acts indicate undesirable character traits, then the agent is blameworthy; if they do not, then the actor is not blameworthy--he has an excuse. A distinctive feature of this approach is that the voluntariness of acts is irrelevant to determining blameworthiness.

This analysis is then applied to a variety of issues in criminal law. Mens rea supports inferences to character traits, and the Humean approach provides a reason for rejecting strict criminal liability. The Humean approach also helps resolve a number of issues about attempts, such as punishment for impossible attempts and the defense of abandonment. It also supports the broad outlines of the defense of mistake and provides a third alternative in the Wooton-Hart debate over punishment and treatment.

This paper explores criminal responsibility--mens rea and excuses--from a perspective quite different from that in most recent writing. Philosophical literature provides three general theories of blame and excuses largely stemming from Bentham, Kant, and Hume. The Kantian type of view predominates in recent literature, with the utilitarian view being the only other one usually considered. This paper explores a Humean theory of blame and excuses for criminal responsibility. Although a more detailed analysis would be necessary for a complete justification of the Humean approach, this paper argues for its plausibility and general compatibility with the current law.

The utilitarian theory of criminal responsibility stems from Bentham. His rationale for excuses, as opposed to other reasons for not punishing, is that punishment would be inefficacious, that is, could not deter.[1] This general rationale, he thought, would support several sets of excuses. Ignorance of insufficiently promulgated laws, infancy, insanity and intoxication excuse, because the penal law could not have an effect on persons committing crimes in such conditions. Excuses of lack of mens rea and mistake are justified, because the law could not deter the individual act. Finally, because the penal law is not the dominant influence on the actor, duress excuses. Bentham's utilitarian theory of criminal excuses has been rejected by a number of contemporary writers, because even though punishment may have no deterrent effect on the punished individual

[1]Jeremy Bentham, *An Introduction to the Principles of Morals and Legislation* (New York: Hafner publishing co., 1948), chap. 13, sec. 3, pp. 172-75.

W. L. Robison (ed.), The Legal Essays of Michael Bayles, 117–128.
© 2002 *Kluwer Law International. Printed in the Netherlands.*

(specific deterrence), it may have a deterrent effect on others (general deterrence).[2] For example, although punishing an insane person might not deter him, it might deter others who would otherwise think they could feign insanity or who would not interpret the case as one of punishing an insane person.

The predominant theory of criminal responsibility is a form of Kantian theory. People should be excused if they could not have avoided performing a criminal act. This claim is reminiscent of Kant' dictum that 'ought' implies 'can'. The Kantian dictum does not, however, apply to excuses. Excuses differ from justifications precisely in that with them what a person did was wrong (ought not to have been done) even though he is excused from blame or punishment, whereas if a person has a justification, what he did was not wrong. Excuses defeat blame or punishment of the particular individual but not the wrongness of his conduct. Nevertheless, the underlying moral force is the same, namely, that a person should not be punished if he could not have reasonably avoided violating the law.

H.L.A. Hart is the most prominent recent exponent of this type of view. To punish someone is unjust and unfair, he claims, unless the person had the capacity and a fair opportunity to conform to the law.[3] Although Hart's argument for this principle is perhaps more utilitarian than Kantian, the principle remains one stemming from the Kantian retributivist tradition. This principle of responsibility is also adopted by Hyman Gross in his recent book on criminal law.[4] It grounds excuses such as mental abnormality, compulsion, ignorance of the law, and a lack of mens rea. Individuals who act in these conditions either cannot conform to the law or do not have a fair opportunity to do so.

Although the arguments for the dominant Kantian view of criminal responsibility are strong, it is worth exploring an alternative stemming from David Hume.[5] This theory is based on character. Blame and punishment are not directly for acts but for character traits. On this view,

---

[2]H.L.A. Hart, *Punishment and Responsibility* (New York: Oxford University Press, 1968), pp. 40-43; George P. Fletcher, *Rethinking Criminal Law* (Toronto: Little, Brown and Co., 1978), pp. 813-17. See also Hyman Gross, *A Theory of Criminal Justice* (New York: Oxford University Press, 1979), pp. 302-04.

[3]Hart, *Punishment and Responsibility*, pp. 181-82, 201, and 22-23.

[4]Gross, *Criminal Justice*, p. 137.

[5]*Treatise of Human Nature*, ed. L.A. Selby-Bigge (Oxford: Clarendon Press, 1888), pp. 477, 575; see also Michael D. Bayles, 'Hume on Blame and Excuse,' *Hume Studies* 2,1 (1976): 17-35.

'character trait' is not, as in the Aristotelian view,[6] restricted to traits which people can voluntarily control possessing or manifesting in behaviour. Instead, it refers to any socially desirable or undesirable disposition of a person. Acts may or may not indicate character traits. If an act does indicate an undesirable character trait, then blame is appropriate; if it does not, then blame is inappropriate although measures to prevent such conduct in the future might be taken. For example, if a person accidentally kills another, his conduct does not indicate an undesirable character trait. However, to try to prevent similar accidents in the future, one might take measures such as keeping guns away from people.

One must distinguish blame, expressions of blame, and punishment. Blame is a negative attitude towards a person for a character trait; it is appropriate if the person is blameworthy. Even if a person is blameworthy, one may or may not express blame verbally. Finally, punishment is more than an individual expression of blame; it is a particular social response to blameworthy conduct--that exhibiting an undesirable character trait. Because legal punishment is a particular social response, it is not always appropriate for blameworthy conduct. Considerations other than blameworthiness are needed to justify punishment. However, the assumptions in this paper are that blameworthiness (or blame) is a necessary condition for justifiable punishment and that justified excuses render individuals blameless and thus punishment inappropriate.

1. MENS REA AND CHARACTER

On the outset, this character trait view confronts a powerful objection. Single acts do not necessarily indicate dispositions. As Gross puts it, from a single dangerous act one cannot infer that the actor is a dangerous person.[7] This objection may be defeated if other elements of criminal law aid in making the inference from an act to a disposition. In particular, the law's emphasis upon mens rea--whether an act is committed purposely, knowingly, recklessly, or negligently--may greatly strengthen the warrant for inferring an undesirable character trait. If a person kills purposely, his act reflects more undesirably on his character than if he merely kills another negligently. Even this line of thought, however, confronts Gross's

---

[6]The Aristotelian view emphasizes that one is responsible for one's character traits because one could have avoided developing them. For an application of this view to the criminal law, see Edmund L. Pincoffs, 'Legal Responsibility and Moral Character,' *Wayne Law Review* 19 (1973): 905-23.

[7]Gross, *Criminal Justice*, pp. 340, 386.

further claim that the distinctions among degrees (or kinds) of mens rea are based on dangerousness rather than a particular mental element. Thus, an analysis of the various states of mens rea is necessary.

The distinction between purposely and knowingly bringing about a harm cannot be made simply by the dangerousness of the acts. Gross contends that acting purposely involves a harmful act in which the occurrence of harm is imminent and avoided only by chance.[8] Acting knowingly involves only an imminently dangerous act in which the harm will almost certainly occur in the normal course of events and failure to take steps to avoid it is irrational. This basis for the distinction will not suffice, however, for a purposeful act may not create as great a risk of harm as one done knowingly. Gross fails to see this because he always uses examples of the same type of conduct, such as fumigating a ship with a sailor below deck. If one compares different forms of conduct, then it is clear that some purposeful acts are not as dangerous as some done knowingly. Sticking to homicide, in which the harm is the death of another person, purposely cutting the brake hose on someone's car in the hope that it will cause a fatal accident is not as dangerous as blowing up a building knowing someone is inside it. To act knowingly with respect to some harm is to be practically certain that the harm will result, yet purposely to try to bring about a harm, one need not be practically certain, or even very sure at all, that one will succeed.

In contrast, the distinction between acting knowingly and recklessly does require a difference in the risk of a harm's occurrence. Whereas to act knowingly, the actor must be practically certain a result will occur, to act recklessly, he need only consciously disregard a substantial and unjustifiable risk of its occurrence.[9] The major difference is thus the degree--practical certainty or substantial--of risk.

Nevertheless, each of these distinctions indicates something about an actor's character which is plausibly the reason for distinguishing them. They each indicate something about an actor's attitude toward the occurrence of a harm. A person who acts purposely desires or wants a harm to occur. A person who acts knowingly displays a less undesirable attitude towards a harm, because although he does not care whether it occurs, he does not desire it occurrence. Nevertheless, he displays a more undesirable attitude than one who acts recklessly. Indifference to a substantial risk of a harm is different from indifference to its practical certainty. A person who operates a factory recklessly, indifferent to a

---

[8]Ibid., pp. 84, 87, 429.

[9]*Model Penal Code: Proposed Official Draft* (Philadelphia: American Law Institute, 1962), sec. 2.02 (2) (b) and (c).

substantial risk of pollution, does not have as undesirable an attitude as one who is practically certain his factory pollutes but does not care. A reckless person, such as a reckless driver, will usually try to avoid a harm at the last moment, whereas someone who knowingly causes harm, simply not caring, will not.

The requirement of one of these mental elements supports the inference of an undesirable character trait and conforms to the Humean analysis of blame and excuses. The claim that a dangerous act may not indicate a dangerous person sounds plausible because it does not consider these mental conditions. Discharging a gun in a crowded room is a dangerous act, but it may not indicate a dangerous or undesirable character trait. If the discharge was accidental, then it does not. But if the gun was discharged purposely, knowingly, or recklessly, then, a justification being absent, the act does warrant inferring an undesirable character trait. The various mental states indicate different attitudes towards harm. Blame is greater the more undesirable the attitude. The behaviour plus the attitude evidence an undesirable disposition. While attitudes may be fleeting, the law uses a general presumption that the combination of behaviour and attitude indicates an undesirable character trait, and excuses are designed to show that the normal inference is not warranted.

Considering negligence only strengthens this analysis. One who acts negligently is unaware, but should be aware, of a substantial and unjustifiable risk of harm.[10] On the predominant Kantian view, negligence is punishable only if the actor had a fair opportunity to become aware of the risk. On the Humean character view, all that matters is whether the conduct indicates an undesirable character trait. As the actor is unaware of the harm, the act does not indicate as undesirable a trait as the other mental states. Moreover, on the basis of one careless act, the inference to a careless attitude is less valid. Failure to conform to a standard of care on one occasion does not indicate an attitude of indifference to standards of care. Consequently, the basis for blame is much less sure. This may account for the qualms most people have about punishing negligent conduct. On the predominant view, these qualms do not find a purchase, because even though an actor was unaware of the risk of harm, he may have had as great a capacity and as fair an opportunity to become so as one who was aware of the risk and disregard it--acted recklessly. One might try to avoid this criticism by claiming that awareness of a risk is part of the degree of opportunity to avoid harm. However, this conflates avoidable and unavoidable ignorance the distinction in which depends upon the opportunity to know, and it also rewards carelessness.

---

[10]Ibid., sec. 2.02 (2) (d).

Finally, the Humean view provides a reason for rejecting strict criminal liability. With strict liability, no inquiry is made into an actor's state of mind. As no attitude to the harm is shown, the basis for inferring an undesirable character trait is undermined. Thus, blame and punishment become inappropriate. This conclusion does not, however, rule out an alternative rationale and method for dealing with strict liability offences, but it does support the widespread judgment that punishment for them is inappropriate.

2. ATTEMPTS

If a Humean character approach draws strength from the mens rea requirements for criminal acts making inferences to undesirable character traits more reliable, then it may provide a good account of liability for criminal attempts. It is widely recognized that the contemporary law of attempts emphasizes the intent to commit a crime over the dangerousness of acts, and certainly over the occurrence of harm. Less widely recognized is that the law of attempts requires acting purposely, not merely knowingly. (The failure to realize the significance of this requirement of purpose may stem either from the fact that much criminal law fails to distinguish between knowingly and purposely--lumping them together as intentionally--or the obviousness of the point.) To attempt a crime involves more than simply knowing that harm will result; it involves striving to bring it about, making its occurrence an aim in acting.

If punishment is a response to undesirable character traits rather than dangerous acts, then punishment for impossible attempts seems to make more sense. One may approach this point by considering the now classic hypothetical umbrella examples.[11] In the first case, *D* finds an umbrella left in his house after a party. Thinking it belongs to someone else and hoping to keep it for himself, he puts it away. However, the umbrella was left by one of his guests as a gift, with a note inside to that effect. Presumably *D* is not guilty of an attempt. In the second case, *D* sees a celebrity put his umbrella in a stand at a club. When no one is looking, *D* goes to the stand and takes the umbrella in the rack where the celebrity has left his. However, someone has since moved the umbrellas, and *D* in fact takes his own. Presumably *D* is guilty of an attempt.

In both cases, *D* takes his own umbrella and, therefore, does not take possession of anyone else's and so cannot commit theft. In each case, however, he mistakenly believes he is taking possession of someone else's umbrella. Consequently, the questions arise whether these cases should be

---

[11]See Gross, *Criminal Justice,* pp. 204-7.

treated differently, and if so, why they should. At bottom is the question of when mistakes are relevant to attempt liability.

George Fletcher persuasively argues for the thesis that "mistaken beliefs are relevant to what the actor is trying to do if they affect his incentive in acting. They affect his incentive if knowing of the mistake would give him a good reason for changing his course of conduct."[12] This he calls the rational motivation test. If this test is applied to the umbrella cases, then the presumed results can be justified. In the first case, if *D* knew that the umbrella was left as a gift, he would still have kept it. In the second case, had *D* known he was taking his own umbrella rather than the celebrity's, he would have not take it but would have tried to find the celebrity's.

As the rational motivation test determines whether a fact was relevant to an actor's motivation, it picks out elements of an actor's purpose. In the first case, the actor was not purposely but, had the facts been as he supposed, only knowingly taking or keeping another's umbrella. In the second case, his purpose was to take another's umbrella; he wanted it *because* it belonged to someone else. Thus, his conduct gives evidence of a more undesirable character trait than does the conduct in the first case.

As Fletcher recognizes, the rational motivation test has difficulty with one class of cases, namely, those in which the attempt is obviously impossible, such as trying to kill someone by sticking pins in a doll replica of him.[13] As only part of a Humean character approach, the rational motivation test fares better in these cases. Punishment is a social response to undesirable character traits and requires more for its justification than mere blameworthiness. Although people who hope to kill others by sticking pins in dolls may not have admirable characters, they are more a nuisance than a harm. For punishment, one must look not simply to whether their intent or purpose indicates an undesirable trait, but also to whether this trait is likely to produce criminal harm. The criminal law should be restricted to those undesirable dispositions which may result in criminal harm. As long as the person's disposition is manifested only in ways which obviously cannot produce harm, such as sticking pins in dolls, the character trait is not one with which the criminal law should be concerned, and a social response is not appropriate. However, should the person be disposed to change methods in light of the ineffectiveness of his current one, then a social response is appropriate.

The Humean character trait approach also fits well with the

---

[12]Fletcher, *Rethinking Criminal Law*, p. 161.

[13]Ibid., pp. 165-66.

affirmative defense of abandonment. This defense requires a voluntary and sincere renunciation of an attempt.[14] Ceasing the attempt for fear of being apprehended will not suffice. Most discussion of the voluntariness of abandonment is concerned with factors other than coercive threats and only brought under the rubric of 'voluntariness' by a weak analogy. In some borderline cases, such as the intended victim of a potential robbery not having enough money[15] or that of a potential victim of rape being pregnant, desisting has been held insufficient to provide a defense of abandonment. A character approach may help explain these cases. If a person ceases an attempt only because the circumstances make it appear less desirable than it did, then there is no rebuttal of his having a disposition to commit the crime should the circumstances be more attractive, e.g., he espies an attractive woman who is not pregnant. What is needed is proof that the defendant gave up his purpose in such a way as to prevent the inference of an undesirable character trait. As long as that evidence is forthcoming, how abandonment is brought about does not matter. Thus, if two people on probation desist from breaking and entering, as long as the change of purpose is evident, it is irrelevant that one talked the other one out of it.[16]

3. MISTAKE

The defense of mistake is another one in which purpose and inferences of character play an important role. In general, to excuse, a mistake must be about part of the definition of the criminal act.[17] For example, a mistaken belief about the day of the week is irrelevant to a charge of unlicensed sales of liquor, but it is relevant to a charge of selling liquor on Sunday or election day. If a mistake is not relevant to the definition of a criminal offense, it does not prevent inference of an undesirable character trait, for the person still intends to do a wrongful act and thus evidences a disregard for the harm involved.

As long as a mistake blocks inference of an undesirable character trait, it makes no difference how unreasonable the mistaken belief may be. However, should the crime be one for which there is a lesser offense of doing the act negligently, then an unreasonable mistake should not prevent conviction for the lesser offense. A mistake is unreasonable if it may be avoided by the exercise of reasonable care, so an unreasonable mistake

---

[14] *Model Penal Code*, sec. 5.01 (4).

[15] Fletcher, *Rethinking Criminal Law*, p. 191.

[16] Ibid., p. 194.

[17] Ibid., pp. 696-97; Gross, *Criminal Justice*, pp. 259-62.

constitutes negligence.

Finally, an actor's purpose may define the crime of which he is guilty. Suppose a defendant breaks and enters a business mistakenly believing it to be a dwelling. As his purpose is to burglarize a house, he is guilty of an attempt at that rather than burglary of a business. His act manifests a desire and disposition to burglarize a dwelling rather than a business.

The excuse of mistake of law indicates a special feature of several affirmative defenses. These defenses require more than evidence to block the inference of an undesirable character trait; they require evidence that the conduct manifested a desirable character trait. Except for a small class of cases, the defense of mistake of law requires that one acted upon an authoritative opinion of the law.[18] The advice of one's lawyer does not count; the authority required is that of an official, of someone who is in authority, not merely of someone who is an authority upon the law. For example, consider the case of a minister who checked with the attorney general's office before placing a sign to aid in soliciting couples for marriage.[19] When charged with violating a regulation about the placement of such signs, his unsuccessful defense was that he relied upon an authoritative opinion of the law. In this case, as in many others, both the predominant view and the Humean character view imply that the unfortunate minister should have been excused. On the predominant view, he lacked a fair opportunity to discover the law. On the Humean view, his conduct exhibited a desirable character trait, namely, of being disposed to discover the law and conform to it.

These two rationales give differing results in other cases. If the excuse of mistake rests on a person lacking a fair opportunity to conform to the law, then a person's attempt to discover the law should be irrelevant. Thus, were it not possible to discover the law on a matter, a person should be excused even if he made no attempt to discover the law. On the Humean character view, however, such a person would not have manifested the desirable character trait of trying to conform to the law; one could instead infer an attitude of indifference to the legality of his conduct. Consequently, no excuse but blame and punishment would be appropriate.

This general pattern applies to all defenses which are justifications. As exceptions to general laws prohibiting certain conduct, a person's conduct must not merely be such that it is justified, but he must have acted for the reason specified by the justification. Only if a defendant proves that he acted for that reason can one infer a desirable character trait. Otherwise,

---

[18]See *Model Penal Code*, sec. 2.04 (3); Gross, *Criminal Justice*, pp. 271-72.

[19]Hopkins v. State, 193 Md. 489, 69 A. 2d 456 (1950).

room is left to infer that he was at least negligent with respect to the harm. Suppose that *D* shoots his mortal enemy *V* as *V* approaches him. Further suppose that unbeknownst to *D*, *V* was carrying a pistol in his pocket and was about to shoot *D* with it had *D* not killed him first. *D*'s purpose was to kill *V*, regardless of self-defense. Consequently, one may still infer the undesirable character trait of being disposed to kill one's enemies.

Unlike mistakes about the elements of the definition of crimes which may be unreasonable, the law usually requires that mistakes relevant to justifications be reasonable. On the character view, the reason may be to make sure the person was actually acting for the reason the justification provides. Suppose *V* approaches *D* with a hot dog in plain view in his hand and *D* shoots him. At trial, *D* claims that he thought the hot dog was a piece of lead pipe and that *V* intended to beat him with it, so he killed *V* in self-defense. The unreasonableness of the mistake makes it possible that *D* had the undesirable character trait of killing enemies or at least of a careless disregard for their lives. In some areas, the law may simply declare that no mistake can be plausible enough to evidence a desirable character trait. For example, the *Model Penal Code* does not allow a defense of mistake of age for rape of a person under the age of ten years.[20] It is simply not plausible that a person who committed such an act had the permissible disposition to have intercourse only with mature consenting persons.

4. MENTAL ABNORMALITY

The Humean character view of criminal responsibility most differs from the current law with respect to its treatment of mental abnormality excuses. Given the current problems with mental abnormality defenses in the criminal law, this divergence does not automatically signify a defect in the theory. Three central points may be made about the general approach of the Humean character view. First, whether the accused could have helped doing what he did, whether he had the capacity to conform to the law, is itself irrelevant to an excuse. Second, it is irrelevant because the conduct of a mentally abnormal person may be good evidence of an undesirable character trait justifying a social response. Consider, for example, a psychopath who is fascinated by the sounds people make as they take their last breaths while being strangled to death.[21] If he goes around strangling people so he can hear this sound, then he obviously has an undesirable character trait and a social response is appropriate. Hence, he has no

---

[20]Sec. 213.6 (1).

[21]Richard B. Brandt, *Ethical Theory* (Englewood Cliffs, N.J.: Prentice-Hall, 1959), p. 522.

excuse. Third, although psychological disorders enduring to the time of trail do not excuse, temporary ones disappearing before trial almost always do so. Temporary insanity prevents the conduct from indicating a character trait--an undesirable disposition the actor still has.

Many people would reply that convicting and punishing the mentally abnormal would be unjust. However, the Humean character view does not necessarily require that the mentally abnormal be punished. Indeed, if punishment would not be effective in correcting or eliminating the undesirable character traits, then punishment would not be an appropriate social response. For many persons who commit wrong acts, punishment is an appropriate response because it corrects their character trait or prevents the development or expression of similar character traits of others. For some people, among them many of the mentally abnormal, another form of social response may be more effective and appropriate. The general point is that social response to an undesirable character trait need not be of only one kind. It need not be fixed by the method of determining an undesirable character trait, for example, by violation of the criminal law.

The most interesting aspect of the Humean character view is that it offers a third approach in the current debate about punishment and treatment. The issue has generally been framed as between (1) a thoroughgoing attempt to treat dangerous persons without any consideration of excuses at the conviction stage and (2) a punishment system incorporating the predominant view's requirement that those who are punished have had the capacity and a fair opportunity to conform to the law.[22] The Humean character view is concerned to respond to undesirable character traits, but it does not eliminate excuses. As indicated above, defenses of lack of mens rea, accident, mistake, abandonment of attempts, and justifications would still have a place in the criminal law, along with others not discussed, such as duress. Nonetheless, some forms of mental abnormality and perhaps other conditions which do not prevent the inference of an undesirable character trait would no longer excuse. The choice of social response would then be determined by its effectiveness in correcting or preventing the undesirable trait as well as other considerations, such as the cure not being worse than the disease.

Nonetheless, it might be claimed that the Humean view, like the treatment view, would support punishment or treatment without the requirement of an overt act. That is, were it possible to diagnose undesirable character traits before people commit criminal acts, then they

[22]See generally, Barbara Wooton, *Crime and the Criminal Law* (London: Stevens & Sons, 1963); Hart, *Punishment and Responsibility*, chap. 8.

are blameworthy and a social response appropriate. This criticism ignores the previous distinction between blame or blameworthiness, expressing blame, and punishment or other organized social responses. Blameworthiness is only a necessary, not a sufficient, condition for punishment. To grant political or legal authorities the power to punish for mere undesirable character traits, which may or may not ever be manifested in overt socially harmful behaviour, unreasonably risks freedom for security. Less drastic measures which do not restrict liberty, as are often provided by school and social counseling, may help people remove such traits before social harm eventuates.

The concern of the criminal law with social harm also explains why, even on a Humean view, the law is not ordinarily concerned with motives. Criminal harm may spring from good or bad motives. A desire for wealth, even greed, is acceptable provided it is pursued in nonharmful ways, e.g., business. The criminal law is concerned with more specific dispositions which produce social harms. Hence, motives are not usually relevant, at least to conviction. At least as the law currently is, a generous disposition to alleviate pain does not justify killing people in pain--euthanasia--although it may be relevant to sentencing.

This paper has not attempted a complete justification of the Humean character view of criminal responsibility but only to argue for its plausibility and general compatibility with the current criminal law. However, it indicates that the Humean character view is worthy of more serious consideration than it has received. It is not only compatible with the emphasis upon mens rea and the distinctions between acting purposely, knowingly, recklessly, and negligently, but these elements are important for warranting the inference of an undesirable character trait and distinguishing between the undesirability of the character traits inferred. It seems more compatible with the law of attempts than approaches to criminal law based on producing harm or the dangerousness of acts. It provides a rationale for conviction and punishment for impossible attempts as well as the broad outlines of a basis for the excuse of mistake. It further explains the burdens upon defendants and the requirement of reasonableness in defenses of mistake of law and justifications. It provides a third approach between recognizing the excuse of mental abnormality and abandoning all excuses in a thoroughgoing treatment system without implying punishment or treatment if undesirable character traits may be detected without a person having committed a criminal act. A view with all these strengths is certainly worth being taken more seriously than it has been.

PUNISHMENT FOR ATTEMPTS

The law of attempts has fascinated writers in criminal jurisprudence, because it often brings into sharp and crucial focus both conceptions of criminal conduct and normative principles for dealing with it. This paper focuses on a small but important aspect of criminal attempts--the amount of punishment appropriate for them. Should attempts be punished equally with completed crimes? Recent theoretical arguments strongly support punishing attempts equally with completed crimes, yet many criminal codes, including the Canadian Criminal Code, generally prescribe a lesser punishment for attempts than completed crimes.[1] Following the theory that punishment is based on the dangerousness of the offender, the Model Penal Code prescribes equal punishment for attempts and completed crimes except for those crimes carrying the highest penalty.[2] Should criminal codes, in particular the Canadian Criminal Code, be revised to conform to the thrust of recent scholarship? Or are the codes based on a commonsense insight which recent scholarship has failed to grasp?

Crimes are commonly analyzed into four elements: intent (or other culpable mental element), act, harm, and a causal connection between the act and harm. Historically, criminal theory has shifted its emphasis on conditions for criminal liability from "external" results (harm) to "internal" mental states (intent).[3] For example, attempts do not involve resultant harm, and the early common law did not recognize attempts as crimes.

---

[1]*Criminal Code*, R.S.C. 1970, c. C-34, Sec. 421. Most but not all of the exceptions in which attempts are punished equally with completed crimes are crimes the success of which depends on the conduct of another person. For examples, attempts to corrupt municipal officers [Sec. 112 (2)], to bribe judicial officers (Sec. 108), to procure for prostitution [Sec. 195 (1)], and to obtain goods by false pretenses (Sec. 320) all require the act of another person for completion; in these attempts the actor has done all that he would do in a successful crime. Among the exceptions are attempting to injure animals by placing poison where they may readily consume it (Secs. 400, 401) and high treason by killing or attempting to kill Her Majesty [Sec. 46 (1)(a)]. See also Wayne R. LaFave and Austin W. Scott, Jr., *Handbook on Criminal Law* (St. Paul, Minn.: West Publishing Co., 1972), p. 452.

[2]American Law Institute, *Model Penal Code: Proposed Official Draft* (Philadelphia: American Law Institute, 1962), Sec. 5.05.

[3]George P. Fletcher, *Rethinking Criminal Law* (Boston: Little, Brown and Co., 1978), pp. 234, 472.

W. L. Robison (ed.), The Legal Essays of Michael Bayles, 129–138.
© 2002 *Kluwer Law International. Printed in the Netherlands.*

If one focuses on intent, no apparent reason exists to punish attempts differently from completed crimes. This general focus is exhibited in the Model Penal Code. Its rationale for punishing attempts equally with completed crimes is that the actors equally evidence being dangerous persons in need of a corrective sanction.[4] Consistently followed, this rationale leads to eliminating the requirement of an act for criminal liability. If the purpose is to remove or reform dangerous persons, then when evidence of dangerousness is obtained independent of an act, sufficient reason exists for corrective measures.[5] If one rejects the removal or reform of dangerous persons as a justification for punishment,[6] then one must also reject this rationale for the equal punishment of attempts and completed crimes.

two other recent theories of attempt--those of Lawrence Becker[7] and Hyman Gross[8]--focus on the elements of act and harm, yet by their theories, all, or at least some, attempts should be punished equally with completed crimes.

Becker's primary purpose is to develop a new theory of crimes to explain and justify why certain conduct, such as theft, is in the public criminal law and other perhaps equally damaging conduct, such as default on a contract, is not. The harm of crimes, he argues, is a threat to the stability of the social order. Criminal conduct exhibits socially unstable character traits which, if acted upon by many persons, provide others a reason to also abandon socially stable behavior in their own defense.[9] Criminal conduct is thus socially volatile, and that is the social harm which justifies treating criminal conduct by public rather than private law techniques. Becker in effect views crimes as a public good problem in which each person has a good reason to act in a socially stable manner (refrain from force and fraud) as long as he or she has assurance others

---

[4]LaFave and Scott, *Criminal Law*, p. 453.

[5]While this emphasis has not yet led to dropping the act requirement, it probably has led to a weakening of it. For example, instead of the last step or an unequivocal act being required for attempt liability, any substantial step in carrying out the crimes suffices. See Fletcher, *Rethinking Criminal Law*, pp. 166-70.

[6]Space does not permit arguing against this justification of punishment. For one recent criticism, see Hyman Gross, *A Theory of Criminal Justice* (New York: Oxford University Press, 1979), pp. 385-9.

[7]Lawrence C. Becker, "Criminal Attempt and the Theory of the Law of Crimes," *Philosophy & Public Affairs* 3 (1974): 262-94.

[8]Gross, *Criminal Justice*, pp. 423-36.

[9]Becker, "Criminal Attempt," pp. 273-4.

will do so too. The criminal law provides that assurance by punishing conduct which creates social instability or volatility.

Becker uses this theory of criminal harm to justify equal punishment for attempts and completed crimes.[10] Attempts produce the same instability (harm) as completed crimes, for they give other people good reason to depart from socially stable patterns of conduct. As the intent or culpability and the harms are the same in attempts as in completed crimes, punishment should be equal.

A number of difficulties confront Becker's theory. First, social instability or volatility is not sufficient to distinguish criminal from contract or tort law. Were people able to break contracts with impunity, the stability of economic institutions would be threatened. As Hobbes recognized,[11] even in individual contracts, without assurance of performance by the other party, no one has a reason to comply. The underlying public good argument in Becker's analysis pertains to having a legal system backed by the power of the state, not to the division of law into separate branches.

Second, even if Becker's analysis explains why crimes are distinct from defaults on contracts, it is not appropriate for justifying the amount of punishment for crimes. One may distinguish the questions "Why should crimes be treated differently from contractual defaults?" and "How much should a crime be punished?" The harm done to particular victims (rather than society at large) may be relevant to the latter issue. Becker is aware of this objection and replies to it. He claims that if one separates these issues, then one must punish premeditated murder and motor vehicle homicide the same, because the harm to the victim is the same in each. Mens rea will thus be neglected.[12] However, Becker's reply is effective only against the claim that harm to the victim is the sole consideration in determining the amount of punishment. It does not count at all against the claim that harm to the individual victim is one consideration among several in determining the amount of punishment. Because Becker excludes individual harm as a basis for justifying punishment for attempts,[13] a criticism need only

---

[10]Ibid., p.. 275-6.

[11]Thomas Hobbes, *Leviathan*, ed. Michael Oakeshott (Oxford, Basil Blackwell, n.d.), Chap. 14, p. 89.

[12]Becker, "Criminal Attempt," p. 277.

[13]Ibid., p. 271. He says that to justify lesser punishment for attempts, "one must show that attempts produce less specifically *criminal* harm than do completed crimes." As he recognizes only social harm as criminal harm (p. 270), individual harm is excluded. This poses another difficulty for Becker, for assault or battery with a deadly weapon can create as much social harm as murder and attempted murder. At least the difference in social

maintain that it is one relevant consideration.

Third, Becker's view treats all attempts the same, yet a rather vast range of conduct can constitute an attempt of the same crime. Consider the following conduct which may be attempts at murder: *A* shoots and wounds *B*, *A* shoots and narrowly misses *B*, *A* is about to shoot at *B* when the police apprehend him, *A* is aiming at *B* but desists when he hears the police coming, *A* is lying in wait for *B*, *A* is lying in wait for *B* but his gun does not have sufficient range to hit B (or is unloaded). It is not clear that all of these attempts deserve the same punishment, let alone that they all deserve punishment equal to that for the completed crime. Becker takes such cases merely to illustrate the problem of determining whether an attempt (as opposed to mere preparation) has occurred at all; once one decides an attempt has occurred, it deserves the same punishment as a completed crime.[14] Even on his own theory, Becker needs to show that each of these attempts produces the same amount of social instability. It is implausible that impossible attempts provide the same reason for resort to socially unstable conduct as do attempts with a high probability of success. The same type of difference holds between secret and public attempts.

Hyman Gross avoids the last two difficulties with Becker's view. He distinguishes different types of attempts and argues for punishing only one kind the same as completed crimes. Moreover, he does not ignore the harm or threat of harm to individual victims.

Gross distinguishes between abortive and completed attempts. All attempts are incomplete versions of the crime, since the harm of the full offense does not occur.[15] In abortive attempts, the criminal conduct has not proceeded far enough for the harm to occur, although a threat of it may exist.[16] Some crimes, such as homicide, battery, and arson, require that a certain result occur. A distinctive feature of these sorts of crimes is that the result--death, injury, destruction--can result from nonhuman as well as human causes.[17] In abortive attempts at these crimes, conduct has not proceeded far enough to produce a result, for example, a potential murderer is aiming a gun but has not yet fired. In other crimes, such as rape and burglary, the harm is constituted by the doing of the act.[18] In abortive attempts at these crimes, the actor fails completely to perform the

instability produced by these different crimes is much less clear than the conviction that they deserve different amounts of punishment.

[14]Ibid., pp. 288, 290-1.

[15]Gross, *Criminal Justice*, p. 425.

[16]Ibid., p. 426.

[17]Fletcher, *Rethinking Criminal Law*, pp. 385-6.

[18]Gross, *Criminal Justice*, p. 426.

act, for example, a rapist accosts and grabs a victim, but penetration does not occur. Completed attempts pertain to crimes involving a resultant harm. In completed attempts, the actor does all that he might reasonably do to bring about the resultant harm, but by chance it does not occur, for example, a potential murderer fires and misses, or an arsonist's small fire is put out by a gust of wind before it damages property.

Gross argues for punishing completed attempts the same as completed crimes. Punishment should be proportional to culpability,[19] which is determined by intentionality, harm, dangerousness, and legitimacy.[20] As the resultant harm fails to occur only by chance, the actor's conduct in a completed attempt is as dangerous as in a completed crime and his culpability is the same. Gross does not claim the actor in a completed attempt is as dangerous a person as the actor in a completed crime; rather, he claims the acts of the two are equally harmful or dangerous and, therefore, equally culpable. (This argument applies even to impossible attempts if there was reason for the actor and others to believe the harm could occur; for example, the impossibility was due to a hidden defect in the bullet.) Finally, to clarify the basis for equal punishment, Gross proposes redefining crimes by their degree of dangerousness--as harmful, imminently dangerous, or creating a present danger.[21] In harmful conduct, the occurrence of harm is imminent and avoided only by chance, whereas in imminently dangerous conduct it would be irrational to ignore the danger.[22] As a resultant harm need not in fact occur for conduct to be harmful, both completed attempts and completed crimes involve harmful conduct.

To determine the defect in Gross's analysis, one must distinguish between first- and second-order interests. The interest violated by completed resultant-harm crimes is a first-order interest in the thing destroyed. Death, injury, and damage to property directly violate first-order interests in continued life, bodily integrity, and possession of property. Attempts violate, not those first-order interests, but second-order interests in their security.[23] Security is the assurance that another interest

---

[19]Ibid., pp. 433, 438.

[20]Ibid., pp. 77-82.

[21]Ibid., pp. 434-6.

[22]Ibid., pp. 428-9.

[23]Ibid., pp. 124-5. This analysis also applies to crimes which are not based on resultant harm. Rape violates sexual integrity or autonomy, while attempted rape violates the security of sexual integrity or autonomy. This analysis does not apply directly to crimes defined by a further intent, such as burglary. However, an attempt always violates a

will not be adversely affected. Although people value security for the sake of the underlying first-order interest, the interest in security is not the same as the first-order interest. Two people might equally value their interest in continued life, bodily integrity, or property, yet value their security differently. Some people are more risk averse than others. As the value of first-order interests does not determine that of security, it is a distinct interest. More directly to the point, few people value security the same as the first-order interest to be secured. An increased risk of loss of life (short of a probability of 1) is not considered the same as the loss of life. Consequently, the harm done by at attempt, even a completed attempt, is not as great as that done by a completed crime.

Even on Gross's own theory, this last point is sufficient to defeat his argument for equal punishment. The linchpin of his argument is the claim of equal culpability is harm, which is determined by the importance of the interest violated.[24] Since attempts violate only the less valued second-order interest in security and completed crimes the underlying first-order interest, the harm of attempts is less than the harm of completed crimes, so the culpability is less, and the punishment should be less.

One might try to defend Gross's position by claiming that only the first-order interest is relevant to determining the harm dimension of culpability. For example, both attempted and completed homicide concern the first-order interest in life, so the harm dimension of culpability is the same. Only degrees of dangerousness can distinguish the culpability of attempts and completed crimes, and it is the same for completed attempts and crimes. Both are harmful conduct.

Even granting this redefinition of the harm dimension of culpability, the degree of dangerousness of conduct will not justify the same punishment for completed attempts and crimes. Completed crimes do not all involve conduct of the same degree of dangerousness. Consider two purposeful murders. The first murderer kills his victim by cutting the brake hose on the victim's automobile, and the victim dies from injuries in an accident due to brake failure. The second murderer, at a distance of ten feet, aims and fires an automatic rifle at the victim who is killed instantly. Both actors have committed murder, but the degree of dangerousness in cutting an automobile brake hose is considerably less than that in shooting at a person with an automatic rifle at point blank range. Degree of dangerousness is not relevant when the harm in fact results. As the conduct in completed crimes can have different degrees of dangerousness, one cannot use that as a basis for assimilating completed attempts to

second-order interest in the security from harm to the interest violated by the completed crime.

[24]Ibid., p. 118.

completed crimes. A completed attempt at murder by cutting an automobile brake hose is not as dangerous conduct as that in killing a person by shooting him or her with an automatic weapon at point blank range.

Gross could respond that if there is a difference in the degree of dangerousness, then cutting an automobile brake hose should not be punished as severely as shooting at point blank range, even if death in fact results from the former and not the latter (the victim has a bullet proof vest on).[25] He thus consistently ignores the harm actually caused and looks only to the harm threatened and the seriousness of the threat. The issue, then, is whether good reason exists for the actual harm to be taken as relevant to determining the amount of punishment.

One might think that a reason for ignoring actual harm is chance, another factor Gross mentions to support equal punishment for completed attempts and crimes. For the difference between failure and successful completion of the crime is due only to chance. The culpability of the actors is the same, even if Gross's analysis of culpability does not show this. However, this argument will not save Gross's views, because some abortive attempts manifest the same intent as completed ones and fail (are aborted) due only to chance. The conduct is not finished because police or other factors intervene by chance. Consequently, the element of chance cannot justify the distinction between amounts of punishment for completed and abortive attempts.

George Fletcher defends the relevance of actual results and lesser punishment for attempts than completed resultant-harm crimes.[26] He notes that people feel more guilt and remorse for even inadvertently causing harm than for close calls. Moreover, he suggests, people would be outraged were they punished the same when they failed to cause harm as when they did. Consequently, they cannot defend treating others in a way they would not consider acceptable if it was applied to themselves. However, unless one is satisfied with a naive universalizability requirement, Fletcher's argument is insufficient; for he fails to justify the differences in attitudes toward amounts of punishment when the harm does and does not occur.

To do so, one needs to explain why the result (death, injury, destruction) is conceptually and morally relevant. The conceptual relevance is easily noted. If asked what did the accused do, "he caused death" and "he burned a building" are different responses from "he tried to kill someone," "he endangered someone's life," or "he tried to start a fire." When the result occurs, a first-order interest is violated, but when it does

[25]Gross, *Criminal Justice*, p. 434.

[26]Fletcher, *Rethinking Criminal Law*, pp. 482-3.

not only the second-order interest in security is violated. Language notes this difference by including the occurrence of the result in descriptions of acts. In short, it is perfectly appropriate and normal to use the occurrence of a result (consequence) to distinguish between different acts. Even though the description of an attempt may also apply when one is successful, some descriptions apply only to completed crimes.[27] This is sufficient to conceptually distinguish them.

The moral point is more difficult, for those guilty of completed attempts and crimes have the same intent, and it appears mere good (bad) luck that some succeed and others fail. The ultimate question, then, is whether one who fails only by luck or chance should benefit by receiving a lesser punishment. If one looks first at the victim, it is not so odd for luck or chance to be permitted to make a difference. If the actor fails by chance, then good luck or fortune befalls the victim. Only the victim's security interest, not the underlying interest, is violated. People are perfectly happy to let the victim benefit from this good luck.

Why should not the actor also benefit from this luck? It might be said that the actor does not deserve it. But neither does the victim, even an innocent victim. Luck and chance, if they really are luck and chance rather than the fruit of previous hard work, are simply not a matter of desert. Consequently, one has no basis for denying the criminal good luck on the ground that it was undeserved. To do so is to usurp God's role in the fantasy world of perfectly apportioned happiness and desert. The law is a human concern, and human beings lack the knowledge and power to assure that happiness and moral worth are perfectly apportioned. Moreover, as noted above, some abortive attempts are abortive due only to chance or luck, yet Gross does not propose punishing abortive attempts and completed crimes equally. If actors are not to benefit from their good luck, then at least those attempts aborted due only to chance should also be punished equally with completed crimes.

One must offer a reason to deprive an attempter of the good luck in failing. As punishment involves a deprivation requiring justification, the burden of proof is upon those who wish to impose it, and thus upon those who wish to punish attempts or completed attempts equally with completed crimes. Any such argument, it seems, will have to be based upon a general theory of punishment. To completely justify punishing attempts less than

---

[27]Gross individuates acts by responsibility and culpability. Two descriptions are of different acts if the responsibility or culpability of the actor may differ between the descriptions. *Criminal Justice*, pp. 135, 217. Consequently, either he cannot distinguish completed attempts and crimes or the culpability differs (assuming responsibility does not).

completed crimes would thus require showing that no plausible theory of punishment can meet the burden of proof. That would involve a detailed analysis of theories of punishment. However, as the burden of proof rests upon those who do wish to punish attempts equally with completed crimes (and two recent theories to do so have been refuted), it should suffice to sketch why such a proof is unlikely to be forthcoming.

On a retributive view, punishment is to be proportional to the crime. The difficulty with it lies in determining what the crime is or how one determines it seriousness. If the harm done is even part of what the punishment should be proportional to, then attempts should be punished less than completed crimes, for they harm only the security interest and not the first-order interest. If harm done plays no role in determining the seriousness of the crime, then one is left only with intent and the act. However, it is difficult to see what dimension of the act is relevant, unless it be the conceptual differences discussed above which depend upon whether or not the harm actually occurred. Consequently, on a retributive view, to deny the relevance of the occurrence of harm and to justify equal punishment for attempts and completed crimes, one has to base the seriousness of the crime simply upon the intent. In consistency, the act requirement should be dropped and the mere intention to commit a crime should be punished the same as its successful completion. Only contingent difficulties of proof of intent would stand as a bar to such punishment.

Alternatively, one might contend that effective deterrence requires equal punishment for attempts and completed crimes. With completed attempts, no questions can be raised about a lesser punishment providing an incentive for the actor to chance his mind. However, it is not clear that persons contemplating crimes are deterred by the prospect of punishment for failure as much as by that for success. After all, in contemplating a crime, people usually plan on success. Granted, were attempts not punished at all, general deterrence might be weakened for, one might say, there's no punishment in trying. Nonetheless, it does not follow that general deterrence requires completed attempts to be punished equally with completed crimes.

Nor is there any better reason to suppose specific deterrence requires equal punishment. The certainty and swiftness of punishment are the crucial elements in negative reinforcement, not the amount. Moreover, one may always wonder whether many attempters do not fail in part because they lack the full resolve of those who succeed.[28] Thus, no clear reason exists to think that general or specific deterrence requires equal

---

[28]Such a general difference in resolve is well documented between those who only attempt suicide and those who succeed.

punishment.

Nor is there any reason to think a reform or rehabilitative view of punishment requires equal punishment for attempts and completed crimes. Indeed, a reformist view does not support equal punishment for persons who commit the same completed crime. The punishment should be designed to best rehabilitate the offender, and different persons committing the same crime might require different penalties or programs to be rehabilitated. Of course, some attempters might need the same penalty as some persons guilty of the completed crime, but some of the latter might need less than some attempters. In short, because reform or rehabilitation is directed to the individual and not the crime, it does not have any implications about general punishments for particular crimes, let alone equal punishment for attempts and completed crimes.

Thus, the case has not been made for depriving those guilty of completed attempts of their good luck in failing. Retribution does not require it unless only intent counts. Neither general nor specific deterrence obviously requires equal punishment. Reformative views do not even require equal punishment of those who are guilty of the same type of completed crime. As punishment involves a deprivation requiring justification, the burden of proof is on those who wish to impose it. In the world of practical affairs, although good reasons exist to aid victims of bad luck and thus promote human well-being, the benefits of good luck may be allowed to rest where they fall. A few would-be murderers and arsonists may benefit, but only in proportion to the benefit of their victims. To let everyone benefit from his or her non-deserved good luck is not unjust and will not clearly make the world a worse place in which to live.[29]

---

[29]This paper is a revised version of one presented at the Canadian Philosophical Association meeting in Montreal, June, 1980. I wish to thank Marsha Hanen for her valuable comments.

THE PURPOSES OF CONTRACT LAW

In recent years, interest in the theory of contract law has increased. Many articles and several recent books have developed philosophical or jurisprudential perspectives on contract law.[1] This introduction aims to place the major views in perspective by considering what theories might try to do and briefly outlining the major approaches to the central questions of contract law. The theories cannot be developed in detail.

THE FUNCTIONS OF CONTRACT THEORY

Gerald Fridman begins his paper in this symposium by suggesting that lawyers and philosophers may have different purposes in examining contract law. Philosophers, he suggests, are often concerned to examine the language of lawyers about contracts or the ethical and other reasons for recognizing and enforcing contracts, while lawyers are concerned to determine whether a legally binding arrangement has been made. Fridman is correct to note that theories of contract law can be developed for different purposes, and he is perhaps correct about the usual emphases of philosophers and lawyers. However, it is better to note the different functions a theory of contract law can have without identifying these functions with one or another group of theorists.

At least three distinct functions can be served by a theory of contract (or other part of) law: prediction, explanation, or justification. Most theories seek to serve all these functions but differ in the relative emphasis they place on them. Fridman implicitly ascribes the function of prediction to lawyers--to determine whether a legally enforceable arrangement has been made. Doing this primarily involves predicting what courts would do were they confronted with the arrangement. Lawyers, however, usually want to do more than predict what courts will do; they want to be able to draft arrangements and make presentations that will persuade courts to enforce them. Consequently, a predictive function is often best fulfilled by stating the theory in the terminology courts use. Due to the doctrine of precedent, judges usually at least state their decisions in terminology of previous cases. Unless one is a total cynic about judicial

[1] Among the books are the following: P. ATIYAH, PROMISES, MORALS, AND LAW (1981); C. FRIED, CONTRACT AS PROMISE (1981); I. MACNEIL, THE NEW SOCIAL CONTRACT (1980).

W. L. Robison (ed.), The Legal Essays of Michael Bayles, 139–152.
© 2002 *Kluwer Law International. Printed in the Netherlands.*

behavior, one can reasonably expect to influence their decisions by arguments framed in that terminology. Consequently, if the primary function of a theory is predictive (and persuasive), it is likely to be stated in standard legal terminology, drawing heavily on the reasons and language of appellate court opinions.

A second function of contract theory is to explain. Explaining is not the same as predicting. The view that explanations and predictions are symmetrical has largely been abandoned in philosophy of science. It is even more obvious that they are not the same in law. While the doctrine of freedom of contract might have been a good basis for explaining court decisions in the early twentieth century, it would have been a poor basis for predicting future developments of contract law.

Explanations can occur on at least two different levels. At the first level, a theory might seek to increase understanding of how various court decisions fit together and how the law develops. Explanations of this sort may be closely tied to the type of prediction discussed above. By classifying cases under various legal doctrines, one can see how they fit together and predict how new cases will be decided. However, insofar as explanations are based on past cases, they might not be reliable guides to future decisions. Judges change their minds, new judges with different views are appointed, and the law develops. Nonetheless, the doctrine of precedent works to preserve the same general rationale and pattern of decisions, so one can often perceive developing trends and extrapolate them into the future.

Explanation can also be sought at a second level--that of understanding the role of contracts and contract law in society. While explanations of the first level are likely to stick closely to the principles enunciated by courts, explanations at this second level are much less likely to do so. Instead, they are apt to draw on economic, sociological, and historical perspectives. The terminology is likely to be that of the social sciences. The explanations are likely to be by causes rather than by reasons as on the first level. If one can identify underlying causes and trends, then predictions can be made. However, because the explanations are by causes rather than reasons, explanations of this second level are less likely than those of the first level to provide practicing lawyers persuasive arguments to use in court.

A third function of contract theory is justification. The aim is to justify contract decisions, doctrines, and principles. Because explanations of human conduct often indicate its significance for individuals and society, justification can be closely tied to explanation. Nonetheless, to explain is not to justify, so justification will often involve indicating that elements of contract law are not the best and should be revised or reformed. Some theorists assume that the bulk of contract law must be justified; that any theory that implied the bulk of contract law is unjustified must be mistaken. This approach corresponds to a common approach to ethical theory in which the aim is to formulate general principles that will account for and systematize strongly held moral beliefs, such as that torture, lying, and breaking promises are wrong. Here is not the place to discuss the appropriateness of this method, but one should realize that with it justification will only result in incremental revision. Radical reform cannot be developed.

Although the functions of prediction, explanation, and justification are often related to one another and most theories seek to fulfill all three, they are not identical and can lead in opposite directions. An explanation of a doctrine may indicate that it is simply not justified. Moreover, explanation and prediction do not necessarily go together. Consequently, one must determine which function is predominant in a theory one examines or constructs. Often, strong disagreement between theories or their proponents stems from unrecognized differences in emphasis on functions.

The Questions and Traditional Answers

In contract action, the plaintiff needs to show that there was a contract imposing a duty to the plaintiff on the defendant, that the defendant breached that duty, and that a particular legal response (usually the payment of damages) is appropriate. Traditional contract law had (and to some extent still has) several doctrines surrounding each of these elements that often made it hard for plaintiffs to prove their cases. It is useful to briefly note them. Proving the existence of a contract was (and is) often difficult. First, there had to be an offer specifying all the major terms and acceptance of that precise offer. If a business sent an offer on its printed form to purchase 1000 widgets from another firm, which accepted the offer on its printed form, a contract might not have existed. The acceptance form would probably not have the identical conditions as the original offer form. Second, the existence of a contract required consideration--something provided in exchange for the promise. Standardly this might be paying money or a promise to do something in return. Later the law came to also recognize detrimental reliance, for example, taking a lost dog to its owner in response to an advertisement offering to pay a reward for the dog's return.

Once a plaintiff establishes that a contract exists, the plaintiff still have to prove that under the contract the defendant owed a duty to him or her. Historically, courts were strongly inclined to restrict duties to those expressly stated in the contract. The parol evidence rule rarely permitted verbal evidence of promises not included in a written document. Moreover, the doctrine of privity restricted duties to the other parties to the contract. If a person bought an item for another person to use, the seller had no duty to the second person because that person was not a party to the contract. Over time the courts have relaxed these stringent rules, often implying promises in contracts and making exceptions to the parol evidence and privity rules.

Generally, showing that the defendant breached the duty has not been a major focus of court cases. It is often clear that the defendant did or did not do something, for example, complete construction of a barn. The issue is most likely to be disputed when the defendant's duty requires conduct meeting some standard, for example, supplying merchandise that is fit for normal use or building a house that meets construction standards.

Finally, the plaintiff must show that a certain legal response is appropriate. The general principle is that contract damages should place a plaintiff in the position he or she would have been in had the defendant performed as specified in the contract. The plaintiff is supposed to receive his or her "expectation interest"--what the plaintiff expected to make from the deal. Three important rules have limited these damages. First, the plaintiff is required to mitigate damages by trying to secure substitute performance. Second, damages are also limited to those the defendant should have foreseen as likely to result from his or her breach. Third, penal damages are not awarded; the purpose of damages is simply to compensate the plaintiff.

Courts do not generally award specific performance. By trial time the performance would often not be of benefit to the plaintiff; indeed, the rule requiring plaintiffs to mitigate damages increases the likelihood of this being so. In a few cases, courts will order specific performance, usually when something unique is involved, such as the transfer of land or of a unique art object.

The traditional rules of contract law yielded harsh results in many situations. The difficulties of the parol evidence and privity rules were mentioned above. Perhaps the most difficult aspect, and one not yet fully resolved, stems from the concept of contractual duties. If no contract exists, then no duty exists and contract law is necessarily silent. For example, if because of mutual mistake no contract exists, then a plaintiff has no contractual recourse no matter how much he or she may have expended. The courts did and do in fact usually provide remedies, but conceptually they are not considered to be in contract. On the other hand, if a contractual duty does exists, then the defendant is liable for full contractual damages. Today, however, courts often manage to provide lesser damages (the plaintiff's reliance interest) if full damages would be inappropriate.

RECENT THEORIES

Although recent theories of contract law differ in the extent to which they retain or coincide with traditional contract law, on the whole they find the extant contract law acceptable. The following discussion emphasizes their conception of the purpose of contract behavior and law and briefly indicates some of their implications for answers to the three central questions: When does a contract exist and impose a duty? What constitutes breach of a contract? What legal remedy is appropriate?

Agreement and Promise

One type of recent contract theory takes agreement or promise as the central element. This type of theory has a long history and many variations which cannot be considered here. The paper by Gerald Fridman in this symposium sketches an agreement theory. The primary purpose of contract law, he contends, is to enforce the agreement of the parties. For there to be a contract, substantial agreement must exist and the parties must have freely intended to be legally bound. In interpreting contracts, courts are primarily trying to carry out the intent of the parties. A breach occurs when one party foils the intentions of the other party. The breaching party can then be held to pay damages for consequences of the breach that were foreseeable at the time the agreement was made. In short, throughout, the purpose of contract law is to carry out the intentions of the contractors, including the payment of damages in case of failure to perform.

A similar yet distinct view advanced by Charles Fried holds that the purpose of contract law is to enforce promises. In making a contract, one invokes the practice or convention of promising, which provides a way of getting others to trust one to perform in the future. Once one has done so, it is wrong not to fulfill one's promise for the reasons Kant gave, namely, it violates trust and exhibits disrespect for the other person.[2] On this view, if things go awry and no contract is made, then the promise principle does not provide a basis for relief. Instead, other principles apply, such as the principle of benefit which requires compensating others for non-gift benefits received from them.[3] In general, expectation damages are appropriate for breach of contract, because they provide the benefits the plaintiff was promised.

Páll Árdal in his paper in this symposium presents an argument

---

[2]C. FRIED, *supra* note 1, at 17.
[3]*Id.* at 25.

that, if correct, undermines Fried's account. Árdal contends that no prima facie obligation to keep promises exists (thus under-cutting the moral basis of Fried's promise principle). Promises are symbolic acts involving a commitment to the realization of what is promised. As such, nothing inherent in them supports their being kept. Whether promises should be kept depends on their content and the interests of the promisor and promisee. Moreover, implicit promises, a favorite way for judges to achieve fair decisions, are not really promises at all. Árdal illustrates the implications of his view by considering an actual case.

The differences between Fridman's agreement and Fried's promise theories are subtle. As Fridman notes, on his view all contracts involve promises, but not all promises imply contracts. Fried would agree. The central difference between them appears to concern what makes contracts binding. On Fridman's view, it is the agreement (intention) of the parties to be legally bound. On Fried's view, promises are morally binding and courts enforce some but not all of them to maintain trust in society and the freedom of individuals to determine the major aspects of their lives.

The theories of Fridman and Fried are both close to traditional contract law doctrines. That is, the terminology and statements are close to those found in judicial opinions. Moreover, they both emphasize the freedom of people to make arrangements as they desire. Indeed, Fried greatly emphasizes the importance of contract law in enabling individuals to maximize their freedom by making specific arrangements for the future. Both views also confront the difficulties of traditional contract law when no contract is found to exist. Fried refers such problems to other parts of the law, such as restitution.

In this respect, both views appear unable to explain much of the law surrounding contracts. The inability to explain these matters within the framework of contract theory might not bother Fried, for he does not appear to seek to explain as much as to justify contract law. He claims to show that the promise principle is the moral basis of contract law.[4] Although he also hopes to explain contract law, he wants to explain it on a moral basis. Although Fridman appears to take prediction as primary, he is more concerned with explanation than Fried is. Indeed, he might plausibly contend that one advantage of his view over the promise view is that it can explain more of contract law.

Economic Analysis

In contrast to the agreement and promise theories, the economic theory of

---

[4] *Id.* at 1.

contract law primarily emphasizes the explanatory function of theory. Moreover, the aim is to explain contract law at the second level. It is not strongly argued that the language of judicial opinions explicitly conforms to the theory, although it is often urged that judicial language is not incompatible with it. Like the agreement and promise theories, however, the economic theory takes the freedom to contract to be important. The freedom is not important for the sake of the autonomy or freedom of individuals, but because free exchange between individuals tends to maximize value. Value is determined by the free preferences of individuals, so if two persons voluntarily arrange an exchange, say, money for goods, then both individuals' preferences will be satisfied; both will get something more valuable to them; and value will be maximized.

Thus, according to the economic theory the primary purpose of contract law (indeed, all law) is to maximize value. The test for rules of contractual liability is whether they "will create incentives for value-maximizing conduct in the future."[5] Thus, the requirement of consideration for a contract is explained on the ground that without it no exchange occurs (so value cannot be increased) or the courts have no way of determining whether the transaction would maximize value.[6] The defenses of fraud and duress can also be explained as rebutting the presumption that the exchange would maximize value.[7] Finally, most of the traditional rules of damages can be explained as maximizing value.[8] The plaintiff should receive expectation damages so that the defendant breaches only when he or she can make enough from an alternative arrangement to compensate the plaintiff. No penal damages are imposed because that would discourage a person from breaching a contract when more value could be realized by breach and compensation. Similarly, a plaintiff should have a duty to mitigate damages, for otherwise resources will be wasted, that is, not used to maximize value.

One would expect an economic theory to explain much of contract law, for it is predominantly the law of the market. It has become popular to challenge the economic theory as a justification of contract and other law. Obviously, even if it does provide a good second level explanation of contract law, this need not amount to a justification of contract law. In particular, value maximization need not be one's only or even main concern. One might also be concerned with equality of distribution. The expression "value maximization" obscures an important point, namely, that

---

[5]R. POSNER, ECONOMIC ANALYSIS OF LAW 68 (1977).

[6]*Id.* at 69-70.

[7]*Id.* at 79-80.

[8]*Id.* at 88-93.

the primary value in question is wealth. Other values are included only insofar as they are part of the preferences of the parties to the exchange. And a preference for equality by a poor party to a projected exchange is not likely to be reflected in the resulting bargain, say, in a lower price. Consequently, while economic theory might fulfill the function of second level explanation reasonably well, it is not likely to fulfill the function of justification well.

A promise theory and an economic theory might differ with respect to penal damages. If the purpose of contract law is to enforce promises, then it might be plausible to invoke penal damages to encourage people to fulfill their promises. Fried does not discuss penal damages, but he does support expectation damages when they exceed reliance costs as taking persons and their assumptions of obligations seriously.[9] Penal damages might also be imposed, it seems, to encourage trust and make people take their assumptions of obligations seriously. However, while an economic theory supports expectation damages, it would never support penal damages, because they would prevent value maximization.

Relational Analysis

According to relational theory, economic analysis best applies to a form of contract that is becoming less important in modern society. Contracts occur along a spectrum of relations between people, varying from quick, one time transactions between strangers at one end (the purchase of gasoline at a distant independent station) to indefinitely continuing relationships at the other (employment or marriage). Although all contracts involve some more complex set of relationships between the parties and contracts fall on a continuum, frequently relational theorists speak of two contrasting types--discrete transactions and relational contracts. Different goals are involved in these two types of contracts and they involve different norms. The elements of exchange and choice keep contract distinct from tort law, which also deals with the relationships between people.[10]

Ian Macneil has set out the different norms which he claims are involved in these two types of contracts.[11] Discrete transactions are governed by a norm calling for planning and bringing the future into the present on the basis of consent. One might say that the discrete norm promotes abstractness; that is, it ignores the identities of the parties and tries to eliminate temporal differences. In contrast, the relational norms

---

[9]C. FRIED, *supra* note 1, at 20-1.

[10]I. MACNEIL, *supra* note 1, at 50.

[11]*Id.* at 59-70.

promote concreteness by emphasizing role integrity (which partly defines the parties), preservation of the relation (rather than viewing it as a one time matter), harmonization or elimination of conflicts in the relation, and consideration of "supra-contract" norms (noncontract norms that apply to the relationship).

Elsewhere Macneil analyzes the values involved in the norms for these types of contracts.[12] He contends that relational analysis is value neutral in the sense that different societies will instantiate the norms in their own social contexts. Thus, relational analysis does not necessarily imply a commitment to liberalism. Instead, the norms are ones that must generally be involved if exchange relations are to occur. Not each norm must be fully realized in each contract, but in general practice these norms must be followed.

It thus becomes clear that relational analysis, like economic analysis, emphasizes second level explanation. The norms are not capable of justifying contract law, because they are descriptive. Although Macneil claims that the norms not only describe the way people behave "but the way they *ought* to behave," at best they describe how people *think* they ought to behave.[13] The norms are hypothetical; if one wants to preserve relations, then one ought to behave in such and such a manner. The norms describe "the behavior that does occur in relations, must occur if relations are to continue, and hence ought to occur so long as their continuance is valued."[14] If one wants to end a relationship (employment, marriage), then one need not be concerned to conform to the norms.

The relational theory is more of a framework for legal analysis than a theory for a specific legal system. As B. J. Reiter notes in his paper in this symposium, it is like an engine waiting to be powered. One must add the particular social relations of a society before one can draw any particular conclusions. As such, relational theory can explain exchange relations in any society. This is another reason why it is incapable of providing justifications.

In his paper in this symposium, Phillip Mullock tries to provide an alternative perspective on the same phenomena the relational theory addresses. He wants to look at relations from the point of view of participants in them, which he calls a hermeneutical approach. Mullock develops the concepts of conventional action and conventions to explain exchange relations. Conventional action is more inclusive than promising, so by implication Mullock also rejects promise theories of contract law.

---

[12]Macneil, *Values in Contract: Internal and External*, *78* NW. U.L. REV. (1983).

[13]I. MACNEIL, *supra* note 1, at 38.

[14]*Id.* at 64; *see also id.* at 59.

Obligations can arise from conventional actions without promises, although the obligations are not as strong or inclusive as those arising from promises. Although Mullock does not develop the point in great details, he notes that his theory provides a basis for contractual damages that do not go to the full extent of expectation damages.

Reasonable Expectations

Another recent theory of contract law contends that "the fundamental purpose of contract law is the protection and promotion of expectations reasonably created by contract."[15] Because two parties are involved, only those expectations of which the other party was or should have been aware are to be protected.[16] On such a theory, the existence of a contract itself may become a secondary consideration, for the primary one will be to protect and promote reasonable expectations arising out of relations. (Thus, the theory is closely connected to the relational theory.) The existence of a traditional contract is only one factor to consider in deciding to impose liability, and then only because it affects reasonable reliance and expectations. A person should be held liable when that person should realize that another might reasonably rely to his or her detriment or entertain reasonable expectations on the basis of the first person's conduct.[17] Thus, tort and contract law tend to merge. Traditional contracts only establish or acknowledge relations from which reasonable reliance and expectations arise.

In his paper in this symposium, Reiter explores the significance of a requirement of good faith for contract theory. He argues that an adequate theory will be two-tiered, that is, have some very general principles at one level and more specific principles at a lower level. Contracts derive their binding force or moral justification from community views. Moreover, contract law cannot be sharply separated from other areas of law. Reiter then explores the importance of these and other points for Fried's view of contract as promise.

The crux of a reasonable expectations theory is how one determines what expectations and reliance are reasonable. Cases often involve differing expectations of the parties, and courts must decide which set to enforce. Thus, one needs a method to determine which expectations are

---

[15]Reiter & Swan, *Contracts and the Protection of Reasonable Expectations*, in STUDIES IN CONTRACT LAW 6 (B. Reiter & J. Swan eds. 1980).

[16]*Id.* at 7.

[17]Reiter, *Contracts, Torts, Relations and Reliance* in STUDIES IN CONTRACT LAW 242 (B. Reiter & J. Swan eds. 1980).

reasonable or justified.[18] The usual approach, which Reiter adopts, is to look to express commitments in contracts, clear implications from the wording of the contract, or the general practice in such activities. Although contractors can mutually recognize almost any obligations by their contractual promises, in the final analysis even the expectations and reliance arising from the depend on accepted norms requiring the fulfillmentof promises. Consequently, the ultimate standards for reasonable expectations and reliance are accepted community norms.

The question that arises whether such a theory can have a justificatory function. Particular legal decisions and doctrines can be justified by reference to the agreement of the parties to the contract and accepted social norms (including holding people to the arrangements they accept). However, can one justify the accepted social norms? Obviously, any such justification is apt to be complex. One is apt to have a form of positivism, namely, the function of law is to provide fair and just enforcement of certain social norms, whatever they might be, in order to promote a smoothly functioning society (or whatever). This type of justification differs significantly from Fried's argument for the promise principle, for Fried claims that the promise principle is justified for any society.

Another potential difficulty for the reasonable expectations theory is that expectations and reliance appear to point to different contract damages. In a classic paper, Lon Fuller and William Perdue argued that reliance can be the basis for justifying damages yet expectation be the basis for determining the amount of damages.[19] Essentially, in contracting with one party a person relies on that person and forgoes opportunities to contract with others. In the final paper in this symposium, Richard Bronaugh examines the possible import of lost opportunities for contract damages. In particular, he criticizes the Fuller and Perdue argument. One cannot, Bronaugh argues, rely on a promise by the other party in contract formation, for no promise exists until the offer has been accepted. Thus, one cannot rely on a promise in accepting the offer.

CONCLUSION

What, if anything, hinges on these different theories? As the discussion of the functions of theory sought to indicate, they will agree about the solution to many contract cases. If P orders 1000 widgets from D but D ships only 500, then P is entitled to expectation damages. This result

---

[18] P. ATIYAH, *supra* note 1, at 67-8.

[19] Fuller & Perdue, *The Reliance Interest in Contract*, 46 YALE L.J. 52 (1936).

ensues whether one argues on the basis of agreement, promise, economic value maximization, relational theory, or reasonable expectations. Similarly, they all imply that if D enters a contract under duress, D need not perform. The core and clear cases of contract law will likely remain untouched no matter which of these theories one adopts.

This does not mean that the theories imply the same solutions in all cases. Significant differences arise in borderline cases. For example, they might not provide the same solution to a case of mutual mistake as in Sherwood v. Walker.[20] In that case, Walker sold Sherwood a presumably barren cow, but the cow turned out to be fertile and worth much more than the contract price. Walker thereupon refused to deliver the cow to Sherwood. Fried considers mutual mistake to vitiate the contract.[21] An economic analysis, however, would be concerned to allocate the risks that the cow is fertile so as to maximize value; the seller should probably assume the risk of a barren cow being fertile because the seller is in a better position to know.[22] A reasonable expectations approach would probably come to the same conclusion for essentially the same reasons.[23]

In other cases, the economic and reasonable expectations theories might differ. For example, the economic theory would imply warranties only if the seller could most cheaply detect and provide for the eventuality. However, community expectations might not be the most efficient; that is, the community might well expect a party to assume liability even if that party is not in the best position to do so efficiently. To the extent a reasonable expectations theory evaluates reasonableness by community standards and they are not the most efficient, it will differ from the economic theory. At this point it is tempting for a reasonable expectations theorist to argue that community expectations are not reasonable. If one makes that argument then it is not accepted community norms that ultimately count, but some notion of reasonableness that is independent of community norms. This will greatly change the type of justification such a theory can provide for contract law. It then becomes less culturally relative and more of the sort Fried attempts to provide.

At this point, one must return to the functions of a contract theory. The crucial question is what one wants a theory for. Until one becomes clear what one wants a theory to do, arguments for and against one or the other are often confused and misplaced. For example, if one wants a

---

[20]66 Mich. 568, 33 N.W. 919 (1887).

[21]C. FRIED, *supra* note 1, at 59.

[22]R. POSNER, *supra* note 5, at 73-4.

[23]Swan, *The Allocation of Risks in the Analysis of Mistake and Frustration,* in STUDIES IN CONTRACT LAW 201-04 (B. Reiter & J. Swan eds. 1980).

theory to provide a moral justification of contract law, then criticisms that Fried's promise theory does not comprehend as much of contract behavior as does Macneil's relational theory are simply misplaced. Similarly, if one wants a theory to explain the role of contract behavior in society, arguments that Macneil's relational theory does not provide an adequate justification are irrelevant. Many theorists hope to provide a theory that fulfills all three functions, but there is no priori reason to believe this is possible. Indeed, unless one assumes that the law is always as good as possible, it is a priori implausible that a theory that provides an adequate explanation will also provide a satisfactory justification.

Does this mean that several theories can be correct? Yes, it does, but "correct" is relative to purposes--a correct prediction, a correct explanation, or a correct justification. Nor can one clearly argue that one function has precedence over the others. Unless it is justified, the law is an ass. But any justification that ignores how the law functions in society at both the general level and as perceived by participants in the legal system (judges and lawyers) will be irrelevant to society and merely an ass of another color. Thus, an adequate justificatory theory must rest upon an adequate explanatory one. But if one wants to promote the well-being of citizens, one will need a justificatory theory to know that one is doing good, not harm. In this sense, and this sense only, the justificatory function of legal theory is primary.

LABOUR, LAW, AND SOCIETY

Labour law directly affects most people's daily lives, yet, except for Marxists and Marxians, scholars of jurisprudence and the philosophy of law have largely ignored it. This neglect might be due partly to labour law's variability from country to country and partly to its detailed and esoteric nature. However, labour law involves major issues of society and life. One can define labour law narrowly as the law pertaining to employer-employee relations, or one can define it broadly as all extant and possible law concerning work in society. The essays in this collection take a jurisprudential or philosophical approach to North American labour law in the broad sense. Obviously, in this small collection many important topics are not addressed. This introduction tries to place the papers in a general framework that includes some of the important topics not addressed.

I. RIGHTS AND WORK

To evaluate extant labour law, one needs a conception of the role of work and labour in society and a framework for evaluating it. This basically means that one needs a theory of society and labour as well as a political-legal philosophy--a very tall order indeed. The first three articles in this collection discuss some of the issues involved in developing such a basis for evaluation.

Work is a major factor in the lives of most normal adults. One can distinguish between work and employment, for many people who work, such as housewives, are not employed. 'Labour' can be used to refer to either work or employment. Although in their papers Richard De George and Adina Schwartz expound at some length on the importance of work and its social organization, it is useful to note briefly three aspects of the importance of work to most people's lives. First, work is economically important in most people's lives. Employment, whether by others or oneself, is the primary source of income for the vast majority of people. However, the work of people who are not employed is also economically important in their lives. The work of housewives or househusbands (undoubtedly together the largest group of persons who work but are not employed) is economically important to the family. Indeed, some women do not seek employment outside the home, because the costs of replacing their services in the home exceeds their potential earnings. In nonmerchanized agriculture and some small family businesses, the work of children is also a significant economic benefit to the family.

W. L. Robison (ed.), The Legal Essays of Michael Bayles, 153–164.
© 2002 *Kluwer Law International. Printed in the Netherlands.*

Second, work is important simply due to the amount and kind of activity it involves. Any activity that occupies 35 or more hours a week must loom important in people's lives. The nature of any activity occupying so much of a person's waking life must also be important. Work can be physically difficult or easy, mentally difficult or easy, stressful or relaxing, boring or interesting, and so on. It can develop one's capacities and require using one's abilities to the fullest, or it can allow them to atrophy. Most work does both, developing some abilities and causing or allowing others to atrophy. Although people prefer different types of work, most people probably prefer work that requires them to use many of their abilities.[1]

Third, the type of work one does is important because of its effects on one's relations with others. At a simple level, most people develop friendships with some of their co-workers. Even the interpersonal relationships of people who work alone, such as housewives, are strongly influenced by their work; for example, neighboring housewives often form informal groups that meet for coffee. In a more complex way, people often identify themselves with their work. When strangers meet on airplanes or trains, one of the early questions asked of each other is what work they do. People identify themselves as politicians, car salespersons, business persons, teachers, engineers, and so forth, and such identification affects the way others interact with them. For example, to tell a stranger on a train that one is a philosopher is often to invite a puzzled look and an abrupt halt to conversation.

Although the nature and organization of work has never been stagnant, during this century they have been subject to change at an ever increasing rate. During the early part of the century, factory work changed to assembly-line work. Farm labourers have all but disappeared from the land, at first replaced by independent farmers with mechanized equipment, and now by large agribusinesses. Small businesses took second place to large corporations and are now regaining importance, but often as franchises in large chains. The percentage of professionals in the labour force has increased greatly, and now even many of the previously independent practitioners--lawyers and doctors--are employees of large firms. Railroaders have given way to truckers. In mid-century industrial society, blue collar workers were the largest segment of workers. In the present North American post-industrial service economy, white collar workers form the largest segment. Yet, society and labour law may not have adequately altered to reflect these changes.

The remaining years of this century are likely to bring even greater

---

[1]See J. RAWLS, A THEORY OF JUSTICE 426-28 (1971)

changes, changes that raise significant issues for society and labour law. Perhaps the major source of changes is technological development bringing about an electronic information society. Developments in electronics are quickly changing the nature of work. It is certainly conceivable that by the end of the century, mail and books as we currently know them will disappear. Letters and letter-carriers will be relics of the past, replaced by immediate electronic communication between home computers over telephone lines. Books may also be stored in large central computer banks with people able to call them up by computers and print out a copy if they want one. (This introduction is being written on a computer, largely eliminating the need for a secretary and decreasing the amount of paper used.) In factories, electronic robots are beginning to displace workers.

These technological changes will significantly affect the nature of much work. The hope has been that the changes will eliminate the drudgery of work so that people will have jobs making greater use of their abilities. Yet, a recent study reported in the news suggests that the effect may be the reverse. In the computer industry, about 25 percent of the jobs are interesting, upper middle income ones, while 75 percent are uninteresting, low paying jobs, such as assembling computers. A large scale change of this sort would tend to eliminate the large middle class and split society into two groups of upper middle and low income. Such changes could have major effects on society.

Another major effect of these technological developments may be the elimination of many jobs. Although the effect of the new technology on employment is a matter of considerable dispute, the intermediate range outlook for employment in Canada is not bright. Some forecasts in the fall of 1983 predict average unemployment of 10 percent for the next five years. In some ways Canada is special because of its previously high proportion of workers in resource extraction, yet, at the same time data from Great Britain, whose labour force is not heavily engaged in resource extraction, show unemployment at 13 percent. If work, usually employment, plays such an important role in the lives of most people, these unemployment rates will have a major effect on the lives of many people.

One response to the foregoing scenarios would be to recognize a right to work. Both Richard De George and David Beatty in their papers argue for such a right, but they provide quite different arguments for it. De George bases his argument on human rights, starting with the right to work recognized in the United Nations Declaration of Human Rights.[2] This right can be interpreted by, and derived from, other human rights. De

---

[2]G.A. Res. 217 A (III), U.N. Doc. A/23 (1948).

George argues that the human rights to life, personal development, and respect support the human right to work interpreted as a positive right, that is, as one imposing an obligation on society to provide work, not merely prohibiting interference with people working if they can find employment. De George also notes changing social conditions that make the right to work more important to recognize now than in the nineteenth century. He discusses how North American (especially United States) ideology of free enterprise and collective bargaining have operated to prevent the recognition of a right to work. A right to work has not developed from collective bargaining, because it has not been in the interest of unions and union leaders to press for it.

De George does not discuss in detail how a right to work might be implemented. One method often discussed, one which De George does not strongly favor, is for the government to be the employer of last resort. An alternative or at least supplement is to provide workers tenure. Even if it might not be feasible to require companies to continue the employment of workers during a deep recession, it might be feasible to require them to retain or retrain workers who become obsolete or would otherwise be jettisoned into the sea of technological change.

Against this suggestion it might be argued that placing the burden of technological change on enterprises rather than society as a whole through government programs might be unfair. The total social costs and benefits of technological change are the same, whether the government or enterprises pay for the costs. Moreover, it is often not possible to predict what changes will affect an industry. For example, if biotechnologists develop a new strain of corn with nitrogen fixing properties, much of the chemical fertilizer industry would become irrelevant in a very few years. As this scientific breakthrough cannot be predicted and the costs of retaining employees would force many of the companies into bankruptcy, this solution would be unfair.

Yet, one might argue that enterprises should pay their true social costs; that worker displacement is a cost of the introduction of new technologies; so enterprises should have to absorb the costs of worker displacement. Doing so would lead to better judgments about the value of introducing new technologies. Although this argument might be appropriate for some technological changes, such as word processors, the above example of a nitrogen fixing strain of corn illustrates a difficulty with it. The technological change in one industry (farming) might have major impacts on enterprises in other industries (chemical fertilizer). In short, it is not technological change by the chemical fertilizer plants that would produce the worker displacement, so those enterprises should not have to absorb the costs. The costs should be spread among all those who benefit from the change, and eventually that is everyone is society.

David Beatty's argument for a right to work at a decent wage is only part of a broader set of principles for labour relations. He argues from what he takes to be central elements of liberal theory of law for a regime of industrial democracy. The central principle of the liberal theory of law, according to Beatty, is the moral equality of persons. More specifically, each person has a right to equal respect for liberty. In the realm of civil and political rights, this principle implies certain substantive rights, such as freedom of speech, and certain procedural rights, such as one person, one vote. In the area of labour relations, the theory implies substantive rights, in particular, the right to work at a decent wage. It also has procedural implications, in particular, that workers have an equal right to participate in decisions that importantly affect them in their work. Collective bargaining, as practiced in North America, Beatty claims, does not secure the procedural rights in a liberal theory of labour relations and should be greatly modified to a system of industrial democracy. This would involve broader definitions of worker groups and a collegial rather than adversarial model of labour relations wherein workers participate with management in industrial decisions rather than bargain with management over a comparatively narrow range of issues.

In her paper, Adina Schwartz criticizes a common methodological approach which she claims De George and Beatty use. This approach rests on two principles. The principle of metaethical individualism is that one first determines the justifiable rights and claims of individuals and then evaluates social institutions by their ability to recognize and satisfy those rights and claims. The principle of the priority of pure normative theory is that normative principles are universal--independent of time and social conditions. A pure normative theory is developed and then applied to particular social conditions.

Because the social organization of work relates to how people produce and reproduce social life, Schwartz claims, this approach will not work, and an alternative is needed. What is produced, the work process by which it is produced, and the distributional structure in society are all interrelated and affect other aspects of social life such as the family and friendships. Metaethical individualism requires that the claims of individuals be identified and justified without assuming work structures. But the main types of theory, Schwartz claims, presuppose certain social structures. Thus, their argument is circular. Instead, Schwartz contends, we should ask what types of work structures make sense for us in our historical and social context. We can then consider what changes in work and other social structures would be required, use a consistent set of values to evaluate the costs and benefits of changing society, and then decide whether the changes are worthwhile. Within limits, reasonable people might disagree about the appropriate changes, but at least there is a basis for reasonable argument.

Schwartz's methodological critique extends far beyond the area of labour relations and applies to the evaluations of all parts of law and other social institutions. However, it is important to examine evaluative theories closely to make sure that in practice, as opposed to theory, the methodological assumptions she criticizes are indeed made. For example, while Schwartz suggests that De George makes these assumptions, it is not completely clear that he does. He recognizes that a right to work will emerge only in certain types of social conditions. Similarly, although Beatty appears to make the assumptions, the liberal theory of law is one that has developed in Western societies during the last century or two. It certainly is not one that characterized ancient Athens. One might view it as a very general statement of what kinds of institutions "make sense to us."

II. Rights and Collective Bargaining

In North America, there are in effect two different coexisting regimes of labour law--the common law of contract governing people employed by individual contracts and the law governing collective bargaining by unions. Superimposed on both are certain statutory conditions concerning such matters as minimum wages, employment of children, unemployment insurance, and social security. Most of the focus of labour law, at least as taught, is on collective bargaining. However, most employees in the United States and Canada are not covered by collective bargaining agreements.

One can approach collective bargaining by considering problems frequently encountered in individual contracts. First, usually these contracts are not written, so many of the terms are not clearly spelled out. Second, employers can terminate the employment without giving reasons. (In Canada, reasonable notice must be given, and the reasonableness of the notice is based on the length of time the employee has been employed by that employer.[3]) Third, the conditions of employment are determined by bargaining between the individual and the employer. Given a large supply of labour, an individual has relatively little bargaining power. Wages are usually set by market forces. With current and expected rates of unemployment (at least in Canada), individuals do not have much bargaining power and the market tends to keep wages low. In short, except for people with special skills in short supply, individuals have little ability to determine the conditions under which they work, because compared to employers they

---

[3]*See, e.g.*, Employment Standards Act, ONT. REV. STAT. ch. 147. §13 (1970).

have little bargaining power.

Around the time of World War Two, collective bargaining laws were established in North America. Recognizing the unequal bargaining power of most employers vis-à-vis most employees, the aim of the laws was to permit workers to organize and bargain as a group with employers. Organized employees have more bargaining power than individuals and so the two parties then approach bargaining equality. The underlying normative principle is that the agreements of two equal parties are fair. Consequently, the laws were primarily designed to establish fair procedures for two such parties to work out an agreement.

The law of collective bargaining generally aims to ensure that the bargaining process is fair. It determines the size of the employee bargaining units, certifies bargaining agents, requires bargaining in good faith, broadly specifies the scope of issues to be determined by a contract, regulates the methods of exerting pressure on the other party (strikes, lockouts, etc.), and sets up procedures for handling impasses in the bargaining. Many of these tasks are assigned to a labour board.

Although much of the detail of labour law is the same in the United States and Canada, there is a difference in the legal attitude toward collective bargaining. The U.S. position is one of neutrality towards collective, while Canadian law supports it.[4] This raises the question of the value of collective bargaining. Three plausible reasons can be offered to support the value of collective bargaining: its effects on renumeration; its effects on working conditions, particularly respect for, or fair treatment of, employees in the workplace; and the intrinsic value of participating in union and bargaining activities.[5]

None of these reasons presents an overwhelming argument for the value of collective bargaining. The economic benefits of collective bargaining are not so clear.[6] Some gain may be realized, but the acceptance of reduced compensation by many union employees of financially troubled businesses during the 1981-82 recession and the widespread layoffs of unionized employees indicate that unionization and collective bargaining are not absolute protections against wage rollbacks and unemployment. Second, it is not clear how much of the noticeable improvement in workplace fairness during the last quarter century has stemmed from collective bargaining and how much has stemmed from human rights legislation and other protections. Unionization does not appear to have

---

[4]*See* P. WEILER, RECONCILABLE DIFFERENCES: NEW DIRECTIONS IN CANADIAN LABOUR LAW 25 (1980).

[5]*Id.* at 24-33.

[6]*Id.* at 28-29.

done much to protect female employees from sexual harassment, especially from male employees in the same bargaining unit. Third, the value of participation can easily be exaggerated. For example, it is hard to take the following claims literally.

> ...[C]ollective bargaining is the most significant occasion upon which most of these workers ever participate in making social decisions about matters that are salient to their daily lives....[C]ollective bargaining is intrinsically valuable as an experience in self-government. It is the mode in which employees participate in setting the terms and conditions of employment rather than simply accepting what their employer chooses to give them....[7]

The participation of the average rank and file union member is hardly the momentous occasion these claims suggest. Consequently, skepticism about the value of collective bargaining is reasonable.

In view of the structure of collective bargaining law, five sets of issues arise. (1) Who should engage in collective bargaining? This issue involves questions of the definition and size of bargaining units and whether certain types of employees should be denied collective bargaining. (2) What matters or topics should be subject to collective bargaining? Besides wages and hours, many other matters might be the subject of negotiation, such as job tasks, safety conditions, and even the products and services of a company. (3) How should an agreement be interpreted and implemented? Should the usual standards of contract interpretation apply, or are there special principles for collective agreements? Usually, disputes are resolved by arbitrators with possible appeals to courts, but other methods are certainly possible. (4) What should be done or permitted if an agreement cannot be reached? This includes questions of strikes, lockouts, secondary boycotts, picketing, mediation, and arbitration. (5) What legal procedures and mechanisms should be used to oversee all of these matters? This includes courts, labour boards, and various other techniques. This set overlaps with (3) above, but it is broader in scope in covering the issues in (1), (2), and (4) as well.

The last two papers in this collection address some of these issues. In her paper, Susan Sherwin in effect considers an aspect of what should be the subject of collective bargaining. Her question is when should a substantive matter be imposed by the state rather than left to collective bargaining. She notes several reasons for the state to be reluctant to impose substantive conditions on agreements, such as the need to vary conditions

---

[7] *Id.* at 32, 33.

for different workplace arrangements and the difficulty of obtaining compliance with conditions to which the parties did not agree. Taking affirmative action programs for women as an example of a substantive matter that might be imposed by the state, she sketches the arguments for affirmative action. She then argues that affirmative action programs are not likely to result from collective agreements, because, for a variety of reasons, it is rarely in the interest of either party to press hard for them. For example, when women constitute a minority of the bargaining unit, the majority is likely to be willing to sacrifice affirmative action for benefits for the majority, such as higher wages. Drawing on her analysis, Sherwin concludes that besides labour codes setting minimal standards for all employment, the state should substantively intervene only on behalf of minority groups subject to systematic discrimination.

In the course of her analysis, Sherwin remarks on the vulnerability of public employees in bargaining with the government. One may be puzzled to find Sherwin viewing public employees as particularly vulnerable in negotiations, while others claim that they have power not possessed by employee groups in the private sector. In part, this difference of opinion may be due to the different levels of government they consider. Sherwin primarily considers public employees at the provincial level where the government can legislate wages and override the bargaining process (as several Canadian provincial governments did in 1982 in the name of reducing inflation). Local governments lack such powers.

The paper by Morley Gorsky focuses on a particular question in the interpretation of collective agreements, namely, management rights clauses. These are general clauses purporting to retain rights for management to take actions not covered by other parts of the agreement. They come into question when matters such as the assignment of overtime are challenged as arbitrary or discriminatory. Although Gorsky emphasizes the interpretation of a recent decision of the Ontario Court of Appeal, the discussion has a much broader significance, going to the very root of the concept of collective bargaining. The broad issue concerns the impact of collective bargaining legislation on the relation between the parties. As noted above, the intent of the legislation was to make the parties to the employment contract more nearly equal. The fundamental question concerns interpreting the change in status brought about by the legislation. On the extreme management rights view, it leaves the common law intact except for altering the power of the parties; thus, management retains all the rights it had at common law, namely, to run the business as it see fit, unless rights are explicitly bargained away. On an extreme union rights view, collective bargaining legislation changes all that and the parties became moral equals, so management is subject to all the requirements of fair dealing unless the union explicitly bargains away such rights. Gorsky argues that both the U.S. Supreme Court and the Ontario Court of Appeal have opted for a moderate position between these two possible extremes. Some minimal elements of fairness must be followed by management even if the agreement does not explicitly so provide. The discussion shows how broad philosophical views of labour relations are important in questions of interpretation and implementation of the details of agreements.

Underlying Gorsky's discussion is the usual method of enforcement of collective agreements in North America. The agreement provides for arbitration of grievances. Sometimes a single arbitrator is agreed to by both parties. Sometimes panels of three arbitrators are used, one from management, one from the union, and one supposedly neutral. However, arbitrators are restricted to interpreting a contract, and matters of law can be appealed in the courts. In the case Gorsky discusses, the arbitrator was held to have acted beyond her authority.

Sometimes employees do not wait for arbitration but engage in wildcat strikes, which are illegal while an agreement is in force. Courts often issue back to work orders. An interesting side aspect of this has recently developed in Canada. A citizen of Montreal who held a monthly bus pass filed a class action suit against the bus drivers' union for the lost value of the pass due to an illegal strike. The Supreme Court of Canada refused the union's motion to have the employers names as co-defendants.[8] The possibility of such suits may drastically increase the costs to some employees of wildcat strikes.

None of the papers in this collection focuses on what happens when the parties fail to agree. In the first instance, at least in the private sector, the parties are left to their own resources. This means that they try to exert pressure on one another, perhaps by employees sticking strictly to the work rules and slowing production, but more usually by strikes or lockouts. Usually neither party is anxious to have work cease through a strike or lockout, because employees lose wages and employers lose income from reduced sales. However, in some circumstances, at least from the employer's point of view, a strike is not that damaging, for example, when there is a large stockpile of goods and falling demand for them. In other situations, when there is a strong demand for the product, a strike can be very costly to employers. In any event, the result of a strike or lockout is usually increased incentive on both parties to come to an agreement. Governments will often make mediators available to help the parties reach an agreement.

In the public sector, strikes are usually illegal and courts will issue back-to-work orders. However, if public employees are denied the right to

---

[8]*Riders Free to Sue Union in Montreal,* THE GLOBE AND MAIL, Sept. 29, 1983, at 11.

strike, then their main bargaining weapon has been removed and their power decreased. This seems to undermine the foundation of collective bargaining--increasing employee bargaining power so that the parties are equal. Yet, governments are also unlikely to resort to a lockout, so in effect both are weakened. Despite legal prohibitions, public employees do go on strike, and rarely can or do governments take the action of President Reagan during the 1981 air controllers' strike and simply fire all striking employees.

A variety of techniques can and have been used to resolve public sector disputes when the parties cannot agree. The dominant method is interest arbitration: an arbitrator simply settles the terms of the contract. However, because such arbitrators are likely to split the difference, this method does not provide the parties a strong incentive to moderate their positions in hopes of reaching a negotiated settlement. If an agreement is not reached and the arbitrator splits the difference, an extreme position will prove more beneficial than a moderate one. To avoid this problem and encourage settlement by negotiation, sometimes 'final-offer' arbitration is used. Here, each side makes a final proposal, and the arbitrator is limited to choosing one or the other. As one might lose, there is a stronger incentive to settle. A defect of this approach is that both offers might have elements totally unacceptable to the other party, elements that would never have survived a negotiated settlement, and the arbitrator must choose one or the other. Finally, limited strikes by public employees might be permitted. The strikes can be limited as to who may strike. For example, striking nurses might be required to keep some beds open, such as intensive care beds, and to assist in nonelective surgery. Alternatively, strikes can be limited in duration. For example, Ontario physicians have used rotating limited strikes. Physicians in different localities would cease work for one day a week, with the possibility of escalating to ceasing work for two days, three days, and so on and in more localities.

III. Adjudication, Administration, and Collective Bargaining

The final question raised above was what type of procedure should be used to oversee collective bargaining. As has been indicated, a mixture of adjudicative and administrative methods are used. Labour boards are administrative agencies, but some of them, such as the National Labor Relations Board in the United States, operate much like courts. Courts are also involved in various aspects, such as handling appeals on matters of law from arbitrators' decisions and issuing back to work orders for illegal strikes. Alternatively, the British Columbia Labour Relations Board has broad jurisdiction over the whole range of issues and normally works in an administrative fashion.[9]

Collective agreements are a form of what have been called relational contracts.[10] These contracts are not one time transactions between strangers, such as buying a bottle of pop at a refreshment stand while visiting a park. Rather, they regulate ongoing relations between the parties. Both workers and management expect to continue their relationship, though in somewhat modified form, beyond the expiration of the current agreement. Indeed, industrial relations are often compared with family relations, another primary example of a continuing relationship. Yet this analogy may not bode well for an adjudicatory approach to collective bargaining and industrial relations, for the law and courts have been notoriously inept in familial relations. Indeed, the general trend has been to take courts out of family disputes as much as possible by allowing no-fault divorces, domestic agreements, and using family counselors. One might view these changes as applying elements of the more successful labour law to family relations by setting a framework and allowing the parties to reach their own agreements.

More radical approaches to labour law involve abolishing collective bargaining as it has been practiced in North America. One alternative is to turn to government regulations, which might involve a regulated economy. The other alternative is some form of industrial democracy, as advocated by Beatty. To complete the divergence of views in this collection, Sherwin generally supports continued collective bargaining with minor modifications in both the private and public sectors.

Thus, the papers in this collection represent a wide spectrum of views on a number of topics in labour law broadly construed. They also illustrate the relevance of jurisprudential and philosophical views to general and specific issues in labour law. A number of directions for reform are suggested. Both De George and Beatty call for recognition of a right to work, and Beatty also recommends a major restructuring of labour law towards industrial democracy. These are general suggestions for reform requiring many details to be worked out. More specific reforms-government required affirmative action programs in Canada-are suggested by Sherwin. During the next decade, labour issues are likely to loom large on the social scene as unemployment remains high and technological change alters the nature of work. Analyses such as those in this collection, whether or not one agrees with them (and the authors do not agree with one another), are needed to contribute to resolving the challenges that lie ahead.

---

[9]Weiler, *supra* note 4.

[10]*See* I. MACNEIL, THE NEW SOCIAL CONTRACT: AN INQUIRY INTO MODERN CONTRACTUAL RELATIONS (1980).

LEGALLY ENFORCEABLE COMMITMENTS

ABSTRACT. A continuing issue of contract law is what purported contracts should be legally enforced. This article considers what principles rational persons would want courts to use in enforcing commitments in a society in which they expected to live. By reviewing the promise, economic value, and reasonable expectations approaches, the principles of freedom of transfer, enforceable commitments, and collective good are developed. Then, less general principles of consideration, past benefits, reliance, gratuitous commitments, and contract modification are presented. These latter principles specify the more general principle of legally enforceable commitments. The resulting set of principles provide the basic outlines of legally enforceable commitments that would be acceptable to rational persons living in a contemporary, industrialized Western common-law society.

INTRODUCTION

A continuing issue of contract law is what purported promises, agreements, or contracts should be legally enforced. Classic common-law theory usually addresses this issue though the doctrine of consideration: only those promises for which consideration is given are legally enforceable. The intent to enter contractual relations has also often been mentioned as another factor but its importance is questionable. In the absence of consideration, an intent to enter contractual relations would not suffice; and if a court finds consideration, it will also find an implied intent to contract unless there is a very explicit statement to the contrary.

My aim here is to consider what commitments should be legally enforceable. Although the terms 'promisor' and 'promisee' will be used, the term 'commitment' is used to avoid possible limitations imposed by the concepts of promise and agreement. If one person sells a boat to another representing it as fourteen feet long, it seems odd to say that the seller promises that it is fourteen feet long; however, the seller certainly makes a commitment to its being that long. In other situations the "promisor" might not say anything but the "promisee" reasonably relies on a commitment. Without any linguistic communication, however, one might hesitate to say a promise was made.

W. L. Robison (ed.), The Legal Essays of Michael Bayles, 165–190.
© 2002 *Kluwer Law International. Printed in the Netherlands.*

Normative analysis. The purpose herein is to consider what commitments should be legally enforced, not to determine which ones have been or will be enforced.[1] Because there is little agreement on methods for establishing such normative claims, it is important to state the method used even though space does not permit a defense of the method.

The central normative question is: What principles would rational persons accept courts using to decide cases in a society in which they expected to live?[2] As acceptable principles could and should vary with the type of society, the society is assumed to be an industrialized Western one with a common-law system. The crucial concepts to clarify are those of principles and rational persons.

Principles and rules can be distinguished from each other.[3] One the one hand, rules apply in an all-or-nothing way; if they apply to a situation, they determine its evaluation. For example, a law requiring two witnesses to a will not in the handwriting of the testator is a rule. If a will has only one witness, it is invalid. In contrast, when principles apply, they do not necessarily determine an evaluation. For example, it might be a principle that people should be free to dispose of their property by devise as they wish.

It does not necessarily follow that a freely made will should be upheld because a contrary principle, for example, that a person should make adequate provision for children, might also apply. On the other hand, because principles do not apply in an all-or-nothing way and can conflict, principles have 'weight'. Conflicting principles must be weighed or balanced against one another, and some have more weight than others. Because rules apply in an all-or-nothing fashion, they do not have to be weighted or balanced against one another.

Some scholars reject this distinction between principles and rules, contending that principles differ from rules only by being more general.[4] In this view, both rules and principles have weight and can be balanced

---

[1]See Michael Bayles, 'Introduction: The Purposes of Contract Law,' *Valparaiso University Law Review* 17 (1983): 613-615.

[2]See also Richard B. Brandt, 'A Motivational Theory of Excuses in the Criminal Law,' in J. Roland Pennock and John W. Chapman (eds.) *Criminal Justice: Nomos XXVII*, (New York: New York University Press, 1985), p. 169.

[3]Ronald Dworkin, *Taking Rights Seriously* (Cambridge: Harvard University Press, 1977), pp. 22-28; Michael D. Bayles, *Principles of Legislation* (Detroit: Wayne State University Press, 1978), pp. 42-44.

[4]Joseph Raz, 'Legal Principles and the Limits of Law,' *Yale Law Journal* 81 (1972): 823-54.

against one another. This contention does not affect the following arguments because the essential features are the possibility of weighing or balancing and different levels of generality. The following discussion presents some principles for different types of commitments.

A rational person uses logical reasoning and all relevant available information in acquiring desires and values, deciding what to do, and accepting legal principles.[5] Logical reasoning is not restricted to deductive logic but also includes inductive logic or scientific method. A rational person considers arguments for and against principles, accepting the sound arguments and rejecting the unsound ones. All relevant available information is all pertinent information that a person in the situation can obtain. It is information, not knowledge, that a rational person has. People are rational if they use the best information available, even if it later turns out to be incorrect; indeed, it would be irrational to use information that, on the basis of presently available evidence, appeared incorrect even if it were later found to be correct. Information is relevant to the acceptability of a legal principle if it indicates that the principle's use by courts has or lacks some normative characteristic, such as fairness, or that the probable consequences of such use, including effects on third parties, would be good or bad.

Some normative basis must be used in determining what legal principles are justifiable or acceptable, but it need not be a moral of legal one. Much legal analysis and justification is in terms of people's interests. There is little reason to believe that these interests or desires (the difference is not important here) are irrational. Herein certain basic desires are assumed to be rational, namely, those for wealth, security, bodily and mental integrity (including life), prestige or reputation, and freedom. Most of these have been justified elsewhere.[6]

Finally, it is assumed that rational persons could be either party to a case. This assumption is implicit in the very question being asked, for it concerns the acceptability of legal principles for a society in which one expects to live. In contract cases, many principles can be used by plaintiff or defendant. In arguing for a legal principle, one must then consider its acceptability from both parties' points of view.[7] This type of argument is common in courts. An example is the following argument by Judge Turnage for the rule that rejection of a purchased option does not terminate

---

[5]Richard B. Brandt, *A Theory of the Good and the Right* (Oxford: Clarendon Press, 1979), pp. 10-16; Bayles, *Principles of Legislation*, pp. 51-54.

[6]Bayles, *Principles of Legislation*.

[7]See also David A.J. Richards, 'Human Rights and the Moral Foundations of the Substantive Criminal Law,' *Georgia Law Review* 13 (1979): 1414-15, 1436.

the right to accept later unless the other party has materially changed position.

> This rule fully protects the rights of both parties. It extends to the option or the protection he requires in the event a rejection of the option is communicated to him and he thereafter changes his position in reliance thereon to his detriment. At the same time it protects the right of the option holder to have the opportunity to exercise his option for the full period for which he paid, absent the material change in position.[8]

This argument shows that it is a reasonable rule whichever party one might be. One has no reason to think that people are more likely to have written than purchased an option.

Contract law. Contracts are often defined as promises or agreements enforceable at law.[9] Contract law might then be taken to be the law pertaining to the enforcement of promises or agreements. However, this narrow conception of contract law is inadequate for material normally included in contract law, let alone for evaluating the law. Many court cases normally included in contract law do not, for one reason or another, involve enforceable agreements or promises. Indeed, often it is found that no contract has been made. In short, contract law concerns more than enforceable contracts and agreements; it also concerns failed attempts to make them. This narrow conception of contract has made possible talk of the death of contract,[10] because nontraditional principles have come to play such an important role in failed attempts to contract.

An extremely broad conception of contract law is as the law pertaining to private transfer of property or services. So conceived, contract law includes many subject not usually thought to belong to it, such as wills and inheritance, gifts, restitution, fraud, and conversion of property. This extremely broad conception of contract law can be subdivided by the use of two distinctions. The first is simply whether an intended transfer is a present or future one. The second distinction is among 'plus sum', 'zero sum', and 'minus sum' interactions. In plus sum interactions, more value exists after the interaction than before; that is,

---

[8]Ryder v. Westcoat, 535 S.W. 2d 269 (Mo. Ct. App. 1976).

[9]Arthur Linton Corbin, *Corbin on Contracts,* 1 Vol. edn. (St. Paul, Minn.: West Publishing Co., 1952), p. 5; G. H. Treitel, *The Law of Contract*, 5th edn. (London: Stevens & Sons, 1979), p.1.

[10]Grant Gilmore, *The Death of Contract* (Columbus, Ohio: Ohio State University Press, 1974).

value is increased. The general concept of a plus sum interaction has three subcases. One party might lose but the other gain more than the first loses; one party might remain the same and the other gain; and both parties might gain. If Arnold purchases a watch from a store, then presumably both he and the store benefit and the interaction is a plus sum one of the last type. In zero sum interactions, the same amount of value exists after the interaction as before. If two people each mistakenly take the other's similar umbrella from a stand, the interaction is a zero sum one. An interaction would also be a zero sum one if one party gained precisely what the other lost. In minus sum interactions, less value exists after the interaction than before. If two people have an automobile accident, value is decreased. Either one party is the same and the other worse off or both are worse off.

How one classifies some interactions depends on how value is conceived. For example, gifts are usually treated as zero sum interactions, probably because there is only a one way transfer. But the parties to a gift transfer might think of it as a plus sum interaction. The recipient of a book might value it more than a donor who has already read it. The donor might value the recipient having the book and indicate this by paying to mail the book to the donee. Voluntary gifts can then increase economic value and be plus sum interactions. Gift interactions can also be minus sum ones, for example, when a recipient places less value on a gift than the donor or the market. One often receives gifts that one did not want and puts away in a drawer or closet. Perhaps on average gifts are zero or modest plus sum interactions, the plus sum ones barely offsetting the minus ones.

With these two distinctions, transfers of property or services can be classified as follows.

	ZERO SUM	PLUS SUM
PRESENT	gift intervivos gift causa mortis	barter cash sales
FUTURE	conditional deeds succession	executory contracts

All of the transfers in the zero sum column are considered in property law. Gifts causa mortis and deeds with conditional delivery are placed near the border of present and future, because gifts causa mortis are present transfers with a right to revoke, whereas conditional deeds involve future transfers when the condition is met.

Logically, one might expect contract law to concern all the transfers in the plus sum column. However, there are two main problems with that.

First, the concept of a plus sum interaction needed is a special one. Contract law is not limited to interactions which are in fact plus sum ones; it includes cases when something goes wrong and the interaction is not a plus sum one. One must view the interaction from a prospective or *ex ante* perspective; it is expected to be a plus sum interaction. As noted above, one party can lose and the interaction still be a plus sum one if the other party gains more than the first loses. Nonetheless, if the interaction is voluntary, rational parties expect it to be beneficial to them, although they need not expect or even consider whether it will be beneficial to the others. The concept then is of mutually expected beneficial plus sum interactions. Each party hopes to get something that is of more value to it than what is given. Because each party expects to benefit, based on the parties' expectations, *ex ante* the interaction is a plus sum one of the third type--in which both parties gain. Court cases arise when something goes wrong and the transfer does not occur or is for some other reason not mutually beneficial as expected.

Second, many commentators claim that contracts necessarily involve a promise.[11] If promises always relate to the future, then contract law excludes all present transfers such as barter.[12] This creates a problem for cash sales of goods as in purchasing groceries. Of course many sales of good are partially 'executory', for example, one party is to perform at a future date. Moreover, even most present sales involve commitments to the future, for example, warranties. Nonetheless, a cash payment for goods "as is" (no warranties) is included in the Uniform Commercial Code[13] and thus part of what is usually considered contract law. We have placed cash sales of goods in the present category, but near the border because of the future effect of warranties. If one party in a sale is to perform in the future, then sales of goods belong to executory contracts as that term is meant in the table, namely, as all those in which at least one party makes a commitment to something in the future.

Finally, 'interaction' rather than the more usual 'transaction' has been used because of its durational openness. 'Transaction' suggests a discrete even, whereas 'interaction' can apply to a long-term relationship. Much traditional contract law focuses on brief interactions between strangers. Yet, in the contemporary world, many contracts, such as employment, franchise, and installment contracts, pertain to a course of

---

[11]John D. Calamari and Joseph M. Perillo, *The Law of Contracts*, 2d edn. (St. Paul, Minn.: West Publishing Co., 1977), p. 1; Corbin, *Corbin on Contracts*, p. 7.
[12]Corbin, *Corbin on Contracts*, p. 6.
[13]U.C.C. sec. 2-316 (3) (d) (1978).

dealing between parties.[14] Although many of these long-term or relational contracts are treated in special fields, such as labor law, it is desirable to develop contract principles that can cover both them and discrete transactions.

Thus, the main function of contract law is to regulate mutually expected beneficial interactions transferring property or services between private persons[15] and to provide civil remedies when they go wrong. Failed mutually expected plus sum interactions usually become zero sum or minus sum ones. Most minus sum interactions are treated in tort law, but because many failed mutually expected plus sum interactions become minus sum ones, there is an overlap of tort and contract principles, especially for remedies. This does not mean that tort and contract law are the same; they take different perspectives. Tort law takes an *ex post* view of interactions as minus sum ones. Criminal law also regulates plus sum and minus sum interactions, but it can be distinguished by its remedy--punishment.

AIMS

Most theories of contract law adopt a single aim: the enforcement of agreements or promises. maximizing economic value, or fulfilling reasonable expectations. An advantage of this approach is that it provides a unity to the field. However, human beings, and courts composed of them, are not such single-minded machines. People can have more than one purprose for their activities or institutions and reconcile or balance them when they conflict. Consequently, none of these theories alone provides an adequate basis for evaluating the law. Nevertheless, it is useful to briefly examine their claims, and then to bring together the insights they provide.

Agreement and promise. The classical view is that contract law is to enforce the agreement or promises of the parties. On the agreement version, the purpose of contract law is to carry out the wills of parties who intended to be legally bound by an agreement.[16] On the promise version, the purpose of contract law is to enforce the moral obligation to keep

---

[14]See generally Ian R. Macneil, *The New Social Contract* (New Haven and London: Yale University Press, 1980).

[15]See Anthony T. Kronman, "Contract Law and Distributive Justice," *Yale Law Journal* 89 (1980): 472.

[16]G. H. Fridman, 'On the Nature of Contract,' *Valparaiso University Law Review* 17 (1983): 631.

promises when the institution of promising is intentionally invoked.[17] Three claims are central to both versions. (1) The parties intend to bind themselves. (2) The parties freely choose to bind themselves. (3) Legal enforcement increases freedom or autonomy by enabling people to make definite arrangements for the future.[18]

There are problems with this view as the sole purpose of contract law. First, much of contract law concerns situations when, for one reason or another, agreements or valid promises were not made. The purpose of enforcing agreements or promises thus does not reach them. The heroic approach is to call such situations contractual accidents or gaps falling outside of contract law proper.[19] But this is like saying principles of building construction pertain only when they are followed and have no relevance to situations when they are not.

Second, the first two claims are sometimes denied in the law. Parties can be legally bound although they did not intend to bind themselves legally. Indeed, it is not at all unusual for parties to find they have legally binding contracts or promises when they did not so intend. Contrarily, some contracts are not legally enforced even if the parties want and intend them to be, for example, gambling contracts. Whether one is legally bound depends on the rules of law, although often one can avoid legal obligations by explicitly stating that one is not making legal commitments. It follows that parties do not always freely choose to bind themselves. One should distinguish two aspects of freely binding oneself--entering a contract and choosing the terms of a contract. Terms of a contract are often set by law (for example, a marital contract), but one is free to enter it or not. In a few cases, a contract is not even entered freely. Different conceptions of freedom can pertain here, but on almost any of them some contracts are not entered freely, for example, an agreement with a judge not to do some act.[20]

One's overall freedom is increased by being able to make legally binding agreements. One has options to bind oneself in the future. But it is the ability to bind others to one, not the ability to bind oneself, that is the most valuable aspect of contract, although being able to bind oneself and doing so might be necessary to get others to bind themselves. One is freed

---

[17]Charles Fried, *Contract as Promise* (Cambridge: Harvard University Press, 1981), p. 16; see also P.S. Atiyah, *An Introduction to the Law of Contract*, 3rd edn. (Oxford: Clarendon Press, 1981), p. 3.

[18]Fridman, 'Nature of Contract,' p. 636; Fried, *Contract as Promise*, pp. 20-21.

[19]Fried, *Contract as Promise*, p. 69.

[20]Atiyah, *Law of Contract*, p. 23.

from worry and actions to ensure the promised performance. Thus, enforcement of agreements or promises cannot be the sole aim of contract law, because it simply fails to cover a multitude of situations arising in it. Nonetheless it, and especially the freedom it provides, can still be purposes of contract law.

Maximizing economic value. Economic analysts view law, at least private law, as designed to maximize economic value or wealth.[21] The point or test of legal enforcement (imposition of liability) is to create incentives for value maximizing conduct in the future.[22] A more contract specific and sophisticated aim is to "maximize the net beneficial reliance derived from promise-making activity."[23] 'Beneficial reliance' is reliance on commitments that are kept so that one benefits. 'Detrimental reliance' is reliance when a commitment is not kept and one loses. A balance must be struck between the benefits from fulfilled commitments and the losses from unfulfilled ones. In reciprocal or bargained for contracts, these two considerations can be balanced by the parties in their negotiations. For example, if Bradford is negotiating a contract to loan Caswell a sum of money, the interest to be charged will reflect Bradford's estimate of the likelihood of Caswell repaying. The greater the risk of nonrepayment (loss), the higher the interest (benefit) will be. In nonreciprocal contracts, the law must be more active, because these considerations are not balanced by the parties adjusting the terms.

On this economic view, freedom is subordinated to increasing wealth. Freedom of parties is not important for its own sake but because value is determined by the free preferences of persons. Free choice in entering contacts and fixing their terms is essential, because it ensures that both parties expect to benefit from them and value is thus increased. If a person did not (freely) intend to make a commitment, then its enforcement is not justified, because there is not reason to believe the person thought it would be beneficial.[24] The economic view supports a freedom the promise theory does not, namely, the freedom to breach contracts. If a party finds that another deal can provide more benefit even if damages are paid, then

---

[21]Richard A. Posner, *The Economics of Justice* (Cambridge: Harvard University Press, 1983), pp. 88-115.

[22]Richard A. Posner, *Economic Analysis of Law,* 2d edn. (Boston: Little, Brown and Co., 1977), p. 68.

[23]Charles J. Goetz and Robert E. Scott, 'Enforcing Promises: An Examination of the Basis of Contract,' *Yale Law Journal* 89 (1980): 1321.

[24]Anthony T. Kronman and Richard A. Posner, 'Introduction: Economic Theory and Contract Law,' in Anthony T. Kronman and Richard A. Posner (eds.), *The Economics of Contract Law*, (Boston: Little, Brown and Co., 1979), p. 5.

that party is free to break the contract. Indeed, to maximize value, the party should do so. Similarly, if the original judgment about expected benefit from the contract were incorrect and one would lose from completing the deal, one is free to and should breach if the damages would be less than the costs of performance.

The economic view focuses on the fact that contracts are mutually expected to be beneficial, that is, value increasing interactions. One has good reasons to accept the economic purpose. Laws facilitating mutually expected beneficial plus sum interactions are desirable, since one can expect to benefit whichever party one is. Moreover, one has no reason to object to rules that enable others to break contracts provided one receives benefits equivalent to what one would have received had the contract been performed. However, economic theorists tend to discount the costs of breach by the other party, in particular, the costs of suing for compensation. Possible legal expenses and judicial error are costs of another's breach that must be subtracted from the benefits of the contract. Consequently, one would not accept allowing others to breach whenever, after subtracting one's expected benefits, they gain.

Maximizing beneficial reliance comes close to maximizing the trust which promise theorists see as central. On a promise view, the principles of mutual trust and respect are the basis for enforcing promises.[25] Beneficial reliance amounts to action in trust that promises will be fulfilled. Thus, both views fasten on essentially the same element but describe it in different terminology--mutual trust and beneficial reliance. They have different views as to the ultimate purpose or benefit of enforcement. Promise theorists view the benefit as freedom, while economic theorists view it as material gain. The difference is subtle, because an important point of contractual freedom is to be able to improve one's situation materially by arranging the future. However, freedom to contract includes the freedom to make expected detrimental commitments as well as beneficial ones, although a rational self-interested person would not do so.

Reasonable expectations. Another view contends that "the fundamental purpose of contract law is the protection and promotion of expectations reasonably created."[26] In a contractual setting, only those reasonable expectations of which the other party was or should have been

[25]Fried, *Contract as Promise*, p. 17.

[26]Barry Reiter and John Swan, 'Contracts and the Protection of Reasonable Expectations,' in Barry J. Reiter and John Swan (eds.), *Studies in Contract Law*, (Toronto: Butterworths, 1980), p. 6.

aware are to be protected.[27] This view emphasizes one being responsible for another reasonably relying on, or having expectations due to, one's words or actions.[28] If one is or should have been aware that one's actions would create expectations in another, then one is responsible for fulfilling (not frustrating) those expectations.

The central problem for this view is to specify when expectations and reliance are reasonable.[29] One might determine reasonableness of contractual expectations and reliance by social practices. Courts often use commercial customs and practices as a basis for interpreting contracts.[30] However, for many contracts no such commercial basis exists. Instead, one has to turn to what the average person would have expected or to a normative theory about reasonable expectations. Using the expectations of the average person will not provide a sound normative basis for contract law. Even if one thinks it valuable to satisfy people's expectations, this will not help. The average person's expectations are often determined, directly or indirectly, by what the law is. Thus, the argument might be circular: the law should be such and such because that complies with what people expect, but they expect that because the law is such and such. A normative basis should thus be able one to evaluate the expectations of people. The concept of a rational person as used here can fulfill that role. But then the view simply amounts to claiming that contracts should be enforced when rational persons have good reasons for doing so. This does not provide an aim for contract law.

The aim of protecting reasonable expectations and reliance is closely related to the aims of the promise and economic views. Reasonable expectations arise from promises, and their protection and promotion largely involves enforcing the promises. Promoting and protecting reasonable reliance is similar to the economic view's concern to maximize beneficial reliance. The economic theory, however, provides a criterion for determining when and how reliance should be protected, thereby specifying what reliance is reasonable. The reasonable expectations view does not provide guidance here.

Specific aims. With different language and emphasis, each of the views is concerned to promote and protect mutually expected beneficial plus sum interactions involving the transfer of property or services and the interests arising therein. It is possible to pick out specific aims common to

---

[27]Reiter and Swan, 'Contracts,' p.7.

[28]Barry Reiter, 'Contracts, Torts, Relations and Reliance,' in Barry J. Reiter and John Swan (eds.) *Studies in Contract Law*, (Toronto: Butterworths, 1980), p. 242.

[29]P. S. Atiyah, *Promises, Morals, and Law* (Oxford: Clarendon Press, 1981), p. 68.

[30]*Restatement (Second) of Contracts* secs. 219-22 (1979).

these views and to add one that they ignore. Both the promise and economic views emphasize freedom to enter contracts and fix their terms. Although the reasonable expectations view does not emphasize freedom, it does emphasize responsibility for the exercise of freedom, for expectations and reliance voluntarily created. Consequently, the freedom to transfer property and services in mutually expected beneficial interactions is common to each. This aspect is contained in the following principle. *(1) The principle of freedom of transfer: (a) property and services should be voluntarily transferable from one person to another; and (b) involuntary transfers should be not be allowed.* This principle is a very general one, covering gifts and testamentary dispositions as well as contracts.[31]

The expected benefit of entering interactions involving commitments rests on the assurance that they will be fulfilled. The views' emphasis on trust, beneficial reliance, and fulfillment of reasonable expectations all support legal assurance. Promises are more trustworthy if supported by law; beneficial reliance is more likely when the law enforces most commitments; and expectations and reliance are reasonable if the law will protect them. Not all commitments need be or should be legally enforced. Much depends on whether the interaction is expected to be a plus sum, zero sum, or minus sum one. One has good reasons for the promotion and enforcement of commitments in mutually expected beneficial plus sum interactions, because one can expect to benefit from them. This rationale does not apply to zero sum and minus sum interactions. In an expected minus sum interaction, at least one party and often both will lose, so one has no reason to support commitments to them. In zero sum interactions, either both parties will be left as they were or one will gain what the other loses. With an equal chance of being either party, one would be indifferent to them. Again, however, whether an interaction is zero sum depends on what counts as value. If one counts the psychological satisfaction of a donor or the greater value to the donee, then the giving of gifts can be a plus sum interaction. One might thus rationally desire to bind oneself legally to giving a gift in the future. Moreover, as a potential donee in a zero sum interaction, one does not want it turned into a minus sum interaction with oneself the loser.

(2) The principle of enforceable commitments: commitments in transfers of property or services should be supported and enforced (a) in mutually expected beneficial plus sum interactions, and (b) in zero sum interactions if (i) it is necessary to prevent loss due to reasonable reliance by intended beneficiaries or (ii) donors indicate they are enforceable. This principle encapsulates the reasoning of the previous paragraph. It extends

[31]See also Fried, *Contract as Promise,* p. 39.

to wills and gratuitous conditional deeds, for by making such instruments a donor indicates that they are enforceable. It also protects reasonable reliance on gratuitous promises. This principle assumes that, in accordance with the principle of freedom of transfer, the commitments are voluntary.

Of course, as with all principles, there can be sufficient reasons against complying with it. In law, a crucial concern is not bothering with de minimis or trivial matters. This consideration is largely met by the costs imposed on parties in lawsuits for enforcement of commitments. Although none of the views considered makes note of the point, one also has another good reason to limit enforcement of commitments. *(3) The principle of collective good: enforcement of commitments should be limited by social policies for the collective good.* Courts have always so limited commitments, refusing to enforce contracts contrary to public policy. One stands to benefit from justifiable policies of this sort. Although one might want to enter into an arrangement involving a commitment contrary to such a policy, for most people the chances of this being so are small. Even if one would want to make or receive such a commitment in a particular case, it does not follow that a legal principle of enforcing such commitments would benefit one. One would have to consider the detrimental effects on one as a member of society from their enforcement. Consequently, for almost everyone, the expectable benefits from the principle outweigh the expectable benefits of not having it. However, few policies are likely to restrict enforcement, because mutually beneficial interactions do not usually impose harm on others. The primary instances of this occur when collective restraint from conduct is necessary for some good, for example, refraining from anticompetitive business practices.

Grounds for Enforcement

The principle of enforceable commitments is too general to be applied directly in contract cases. It needs to be spelled out in more detailed, although still general, principles. Doing so both clarifies the extant law and exhibits defects of extant legal doctrines.

Consideration. The hoary doctrine of consideration has created despair for several scholars as well as hundreds of students. A primary, though not the only, purpose of the doctrine of consideration is to distinguish those promises or commitments that are legally enforceable from those that are not. According to classical theory, only those commitments for which consideration is received are legally enforceable. Consideration for a promise is an act, a forbearance, a change in a legal relation, or a promise, bargained for and given in exchange.[32] It is either a detriment to the promisee or a benefit to the promisor.[33] One difficulty is that, given a court's view of the justice of the case, almost anything can count or not count as considerations. In *Hamer v. Sidway*,[34] a nephew's refraining from smoking, drinking, swearing, and playing cards or billiards for money constituted consideration for an uncle's promise to pay $5,000, but in *Kirksey v. Kirksey*,[35] a widowed sister-in-law with her children moving sixty miles across rural Alabama in the nineteenth century was not consideration for a promise of a place to live.

Charles Fried claims that the doctrine "is too internally inconsistent" to serve as a basis for contractual obligation.[36] He is referring to a deeper inconsistency than the seeming one between the cases just mentioned. Although consideration is required for binding contract, the adequacy of consideration is supposedly not examined by courts.[37] In practice, under other names courts do sometimes evaluate the adequacy of consideration,[38] but they do so much less than were it official policy to do so. In any case, the theoretical problem remains. The failure to inquire into the adequacy of consideration implies that people's free arrangements should be respected and enforced, but the doctrine of consideration limits the free arrangements that are respected and enforced.[39]

The conflict involved here goes to two purposes underlying the enforcement of commitments in plus sum interactions--freedom and maximizing value. The failure to inquire into the adequacy of consideration recognizes the freedom of persons to make their own arrangements. The requirement of consideration helps ensure that the interactions are mutually expected to be beneficial and thus increase value. Consider the following hypothetical contract. Didway transfers goods "as is" to Evans in exchange for Evan's paying Didway $100. Didway prefers $100 to the goods, and Evans prefers the goods to $100. The transaction is mutually expected to be beneficial, a plus sum interaction. Moreover, Didway receives a benefit of $100, which constitutes a detriment to Evans. Similarly, Didway's

---

[32]*Restatement (First) of Contracts* sec. 75 (1933).

[33]Joseph Chitty, *Chitty on Contacts*, 2 vols., 25th edn. (London: Sweet & Maxwell, 1983), sec. 146.

[34]124 N.Y. 538, 27 N.E. 256 (1891).

[35]8 Ala. 131 (1845).

[36]Fried, *Contract as Promise*, p. 35.

[37]*Restatement (Second) of Contracts* secs. 17, 79 (1979).

[38]Atiyah, *Law of Contract*, p. 105.

[39]See also Atiyah, *Law of Contract*, p. 94.

detriment (giving up the goods) is a benefit to Evans. The doctrine of consideration rests on these elements of mutual benefit and detriment. Yet, courts will not inquire into whether the goods are worth $100. The economic rationale is that only Evans can determine what the goods are worth to him. Even if no one else would play more than $75 for them, it does not follow that Evans has not benefitted, only that he probably could have obtained a better bargain. For a court to refuse to enforce the deal because the goods are not worth $100 is to interfere with Evan's freedom to make his own value judgments and lead his own life.

This exchange does not involve commitments, but one can easily modify it into an executory contract with mutual commitments by simply having Didway and Evans exchange promises to act as above. Here one has mutually exchanged promises, and the promises are taken to be consideration for each other. Around the beginning of the twentieth century, there was much academic debate as to how a promise could be consideration for another promise,[40] and some contemporary scholars still query how promises can provide consideration.[41] Promises cannot be beneficial to promisees or detrimental to promisors unless they are binding, but they are not binding unless consideration is given and a contract is formed.

The answer to this alleged problem lies in two factors. First, as discussed more fully in the next section, a central element of consideration is that it is bargained for the promise, which occurs in this case. Second, not just any promise will do. The promise must be to something that itself would be consideration. For example, if a person is already under an obligation to the other to do the promised act, the promise will not constitute consideration.[42] There is no benefit to the promisee or detriment to the promisor, so the interaction would be a zero sum rather than plus sum one. One might still contend that a promise is not sufficient to constitute consideration, but it is just as valuable as what is given, namely, a promise. Reciprocal bargained for promises constitute consideration for each other if the promised acts would constitute consideration, because each gets as much as he gives. One simply discounts the promised acts of each by the probability of their occurrence.

In the standard case, the benefit is received by the promisor and the

---

[40]See generally Richard N. Bronaugh, 'A Secret Paradox in the Law,' *Law and Philosophy* 2 (1983): 193-232.

[41]Atiyah, *Law of Contract*, p. 94.

[42]*Restatement (Second) on Contracts* sec. 73 (1979); Lingenfelder v. Wainwright Brewery Co., 103 Mo. 578, 15 S.W. 844 (1891).

detriment is that of the promisee. These relations are not essential.[43] If Frick hires Graham to drive her son's car from Ontario to Florida, then Graham clearly performs a detrimental act, but Frick's son receives most of the benefit. Nonetheless, the interaction is still reasonably foreseen as a plus sum one. Frick thinks that she is better off having her son's car driven to Florida than retaining the money paid to Graham. Nor does it make any difference if Graham's brother drives the car, that is, the detriment for Frick's promise is to someone other than the promisee.

(4) The principle of consideration: consideration should be treated as evidence that an interaction is mutually expected to be beneficial and thus as providing a reason to enforce a commitment. Consideration indicates that the promisor expects to obtain something valued, although it need not pass to that party. In *Hamer v. Sidway*,[44] the uncle wanted his nephew to refrain from smoking and so on. When a person is to receive something asked for in exchange for a promise, there is reason to believe that the person expects to gain from the interaction. In *Kirksey v. Kirksey*,[45] there was little reason to believe the brother-in-law wanted the widow to live on his land, that he received anything he valued. However, there may have been others reasons for enforcing the brother-in-law's promise. Consideration is not a necessary condition for enforcing commitments,[46] but it is a good reason for doing so. It shows that the interaction is likely to be a plus sum one, and there are good reasons for enforcing commitments to promote such interactions. The mistake of classical contract theory is to turn good evidence of an interaction being a plus sum one into a necessary condition for enforcing a commitment.

Past benefits. The general English rule is that past consideration or benefit is not sufficient to make a promise legally binding.[47] The argument is that the benefit was not bargained for and the promise was not given for it. Thus, the bargain requirement of consideration is used as a necessary condition for a commitment to be enforceable. However, there are certain situations in which even English law allows past consideration to make a commitment enforceable--where an act was done or promise made at the promisor's request or a debt unenforceable by a statute of limitations is

---

[43]*Restatement (Second) of Contracts* sec. 79 (1979).

[44]124 N.Y. 538, 27 N.E. 256 (1891).

[45]8 Ala. 131 (1845).

[46]See also Melvin Aron Eisenberg, 'The Principles of Consideration,' *Cornell Law Review* 67 (1982): 640.

[47]Atiyah, *Law of Contract*, pp. 97-98; Chitty, *Chitty on Contracts*, sec. 162; F. R. Davies, *Contract*, 3rd edn. (London: Sweet & Maxwell, 1977), p. 27.

acknowledged.[48] American courts are more generous with respect to past benefits.

A case illustrates past benefits. In *Sheldon v. Blackman*,[49] a niece gave up her job and took care of her aunt and uncle for thirty-four years. After thirty years, his wife having died, the uncle made a note for $30,000 payable to the niece on his death. The court upheld the note and provided reasonable compensation for services rendered thereafter. A reasonable person could certainly value thirty years service as worth $30,000 even with the dollar's much greater value then. In this case, there was no past legal obligation rendered unenforceable by law nor a bargaining for the service and note.

The sort of case is recognized by *Restatement (Second) of Contracts* sec. 86 (1979) which allows enforcement of promises made in recognition of previously received benefits to the extent necessary to prevent injustice, provided the amount is not disproportionate to the benefit. However, it does not permit recovery if the benefit was conferred as a gift or otherwise the promisor was not unjustly enriched.[50] The underlying principle of this section is 'unjust enrichment'--benefits given for which compensation is expected. However, it allows for variation from the market value of the benefits, since they can be worth more to one person than another.

This principle is not comparable with the case law or logical. In *In re Hatten's Estate*,[51] a man whose estate was valued at $3,000,000 had given a $25,000 note for meals and other services (such as being driven to various places) rendered over a number of years. Although the value of the services was $6,000, the plaintiff was allowed to recover on the note. The meals appear to have been provided originally as gifts--having a friend to dinner. After Hatten had told the plaintiff that she would be compensated, she might have expected compensation and failure to compensate then [would] constitute unjust enrichment. However, if there is unjust enrichment, the promise is unnecessary since the plaintiff can sue under the law of restitution.[52] In *Webb v. McGowan*,[53] a promise to pay a weekly sum to a worker injured in saving the employer's life was upheld. It is highly unlikely that at the time he acted the worker expected to be compensated for any injuries. Moreover, failing to compensate a good

---

[48]Chitty, *Chitty on Contracts*, secs. 165-6, 171.

[49]188 Wis. 4, 205 N.W. 486 (1925).

[50]*Restatement (Second) of Contracts* sec. 86 (2)(a)(1979).

[51]233 Wis. 199, 288 N.W. 278 (1940).

[52]Eisenberg, 'Principles of Consideration,' p. 664.

[53]27 Ala. App. 82, 168 So. 196 (1936).

Samaritan is not obviously unjust; indeed, if compensation were expected for good Samaritanism, it would no longer be such. Physicians can expect payment for emergency services, so one does not view their services as good Samaritanism. The *Restatement's* theory tries to force these situations into a mold they do not fit.

There are good reasons to accept sec. 86 without the limitations for gifts and lack of unjust enrichment. Two mistaken assumptions underlie the failure to recognize past benefits as a broad basis for enforcing commitments. Perhaps the major one is treating bargaining as a necessary condition for enforcement.[54] A bargain is evidence of a mutually expected plus sum interaction. However, there can be actual plus sum interactions without a bargain and consideration, including some gifts. The second mistaken assumption is treating contracts as discrete interactions. On a relational view of interactions, one can consider the receipt of the original benefit and the later return as one interaction. As a benefit was received, the entire interaction is a plus sum one. Granted, it might not have been mutually expected to be beneficial, for the promisee might have rendered the benefit without expectation of recompense, although many people today do expect reciprocation of gifts. Contract law might have originated in reciprocal gift giving in primitive societies. Reciprocity, or reciprocity along with benevolence, is the primary motivation in the past benefit cases.[55]

As a promisee, one will benefit from enforcement of a promise in return for a past benefit. As a promisor, one can view it as a mutually beneficial interaction. If one does not, one need not make the promise. However, the amount involved should be such that the promisor could reasonably consider it reciprocation for the benefit received. *(5) The principle of past benefits: a commitment made in recognition of a previously received benefit should be enforceable unless a reasonable person in the promisor's position could not view it as reciprocity for the benefit.* To avoid fraud, especially when the promisor is dead, one might reasonably require clear and convincing proof of the promise. If the amount promised exceeds reasonable reciprocity, a court could either not enforce it or reduce the amount to a reasonable sum. The practical results are likely to be the same in either case, because if the court refuses to enforce the promise, a valid claim for compensation for unjust enrichment is likely to remain. Both the principle of past benefits and that of consider-

---

[54]See also Joel Levin and Banks McDowell, 'The Balance Theory of Contracts: Seeking Justice in Voluntary Obligations,' *McGill Law Journal* 29 (1983): 40.

[55]Stanley D. Henderson, 'Promises Grounded in the Past: The idea of Unjust Enrichment and the Law of Contracts,' *Virginia Law Review* 57 (1971): 1158.

ation indicate that situations come under part (a) of the principle of enforceable commitments--that the interaction is a mutually expected beneficial one.

Reliance. Suppose a promisor has not benefitted, but the promisee detrimentally relied on the promise. Except for the psychological benefits a promisor might have received from the promise, the interaction was not mutually expected to be beneficial. In *Ricketts v. Scothorn*,[56] a grandfather gave his granddaughter a note payable on demand for $2,000 plus interest so that she would not have to work, and she quit her job for about a year. The court held she could recover from his estate. Here, one might argue, there was as much consideration as in *Hamer v. Sidway*.[57]

A clear instance of no benefit being received by the promisor is *Feinberg v. Pfeiffer Co*.[58] In 1947, Pfeiffer's board adopted a resolution providing Mrs. Feinberg, an employee since 1910, $200 a month for life on retirement. She retired two years later, and payments were made until 1956, when they were reduced to $100. The court did not find consideration in the extra two years Mrs. Feinberg worked, because she was paid for that. Although the board made the resolution in recognition of Mrs. Feinberg's long employment, that could not constitute past benefit, for she had also been paid for it. Instead, the court specifically relied on *Restatement (First) of Contracts* sec. 90 (1933) which provides that "a promise which the promisor should reasonably expect to induce action or forbearance of a definite and substantial character on the part of the promisee and which does induce such action of forbearance is binding if injustice can be avoided only by enforcement of the promise." In *Restatement (Second) of Contracts (1979)*, the corresponding section (90(1)) has been modified to drop the requirement of definite and substantial character, to cover third parties as well, and to provide that the remedy can be limited.

The *Restatement's* requirement that reliance be reasonably expectable by the promisor has been criticized as redundant, for the very purpose of a promise is to induce behavior. The crucial element, it is claimed, is whether the reliance is reasonable.[59] At one level, whether reliance is reasonable, like reasonable expectations, depends on whether a promise is enforceable. Consequently, reliance is reasonable to the extent the promise will be enforced. At a more specific level, what is reasonably

---

[56] 57 Neb. 51, 77 N.W. 365 (1898).

[57] 124 N.Y. 538, 27 N.E. 256 (1891) (uncle requests nephew to cease smoking).

[58] 322 S.W. 2d 163 (Mo. Ct. App. 1959).

[59] Melvin A. Eisenberg, 'Donative Promises,' *University of Chicago Law Review* 47 (1979): 20-21; Eisenberg, 'Principles of Consideration,' p. 659.

expectable by the promisor and what is reasonable reliance by the promisee are inter-dependent. Conduct in reliance that is not of a sort foreseeable by the promisor is not reasonable, and unreasonable conduct in reliance is not usually foreseeable. It is preferable to use a promisor's foreseeability as the test, because that indicates the extent of commitment undertaken. It designates the scope of the promisee's conduct for which the promisor is responsible. Also, it more clearly covers third parties.

Except for the psychological benefit to the promisor, these situations involve zero sum interactions. However, if such commitments are not enforced, then zero sum interactions become minus sum ones. A relying promisee will have incurred costs. For example, Mrs. Feinberg is likely to have spent savings on the assumption that she would have a continued $200 a month income. Thus, these cases fall under the principle of enforceable commitments (b) (1) of preventing loss due to reasonable reliance by intended beneficiaries. *(6) The principle of reliance: a commitment should be enforceable to the extent necessary to prevent loss due to foreseeable reliance.* This principle is acceptable whether one is promisor or promisee. It enables one to make enforceable promises in zero sum interactions and still withdraw from them at an anticipated cost. As a promisee, one can place more trust and reliance in such promises, because one need not fear loss.

It is worth noting that *Kirksey v. Kirksey*[60] could have been decided on this basis had it been available. A similar case decided on this ground was *Greiner v. Greiner*[61] in which a mother promised to give her son land if he came and lived on it. Indeed, *Kirksey* is better supported, because the widow asked only $200 damages, not a continued place to live, whereas in *Greiner* the son requested and received the land, which was more than necessary to prevent loss.

For the principle of reliance to operate, a promise need not be definite enough to form a contract were there consideration. In *Hoffman v. Red Owl Stores*,[62] Red Owl had been engaged in extended negotiations with Hoffman concerning his purchase of a franchise grocery store. At first Red Owl told Hoffman that the $18,000 he had would be sufficient. Hoffman sold his bakery and bought a small grocery for experience, then Red Owl told him to sell it and purchase a larger one, which he did. On Red Owl's recommendation, Hoffman also bought a lot and moved to another city. Finally, Red Owl escalated its demands to $24,000, then

---

[60] 8 Ala. 131 (1845) (widowed sister-in-law invited to come live on land).
[61] 131 Kan. 760, 293 P. 759 (1930).
[62] 26 Wis. 2d 683, 133 N.W. 2d 267 (1965).

$26,000 and finally broke off negotiations. The court used sec. 90 of *Restatement (First) of Contracts* to require Red Owl to compensate Hoffman.

It has been objected that his case is not the enforcement of a promise at all but a tort action, because there was no promise sufficient to establish a contract and the plaintiff received only the costs of reliance.[63] But these contentions rest on the narrow concept of contract law as enforcing promises and are contrary to the jury and appellate court findings. The jury found that representations (commitments) were made by Red Owl and relied on by Hoffman, and the appellate court explicitly used *Restatement (First) of Contracts* sec. 90. Commitments were made even if they were not sufficient to constitute a franchise contract.

The principle of reliance does not require that the action itself be detrimental. Instead, the loss could result from the failure to enforce the commitment. The point is illustrated by *Central London Property Trust Ltd. v. High Trees House Ltd.*.[64] High Trees leased a block of flats from Central London just prior to World War II and subleased flats, but the building was not full. Consequently, Central London agreed to accept payment of half of the rent. In 1945, the receiver of Central London sued for the full back rent. The court held that the promise was intended to create legal relations and the promisor knew that the promisee was going to act on it. Consequently, it held that back rent could not be collected, but as the promise was made because of the low tenancy rate in the flats, it did not extend beyond the time income from them became reasonably sufficient to play the full rent on the lease.

This case does not directly involve detrimental reliance, because High Trees' reliance was beneficial to it. However, not enforcing the promise and permitting Central London to recover all back rent could have involved a loss for High Trees. If it did have the money, it might have made other uses of it (new investments, dividends, and so on) just as Mrs. Feinberg might have spent some of her savings. As there is no way accurately to determine this matter, it is reasonable to use the amount promised. However, in *High Trees* it is reasonable to take the promisor as foreseeing reliance only while rents were low, whereas in *Feinberg* the promisor should have foreseen reliance during retirement, that is, for the rest of Mrs. Feinberg's life.

Gratuitous commitments. Finally, none of the subordinate principles discussed this far covers zero sum interactions in which donors indicate that promises should be legally enforceable--part (b) (2) of the

---

[63]Fried, *Contract as Promise*, p. 24.

[64]1947 K.B. 130 (1946).

principle of enforceable commitments. Historically, such promises could be made enforceable by making them under seal, but in many American (but not English and Canadian) jurisdictions the use of the seal has been severely restricted or abandoned.[65] As a result, in *Dougherty v. Salt*[66] an aunt's promissory note playable to her eight year old nephew was hold not enforceable. Rational persons might want to commit themselves legally to a future gratuitous transfer of property or services, and from an economic viewpoint even a completely gratuitous promise can increase value[67] and thus be a plus sum interaction.

There are a number of arguments against enforcement of gratuitous promises,[68] but none of them are completely decisive. First, it is claimed that the injury from breach is slight, for if a promises were relied on it would be covered by the principle of reliance. Although the injury might be slight, a child promisee in a situation like *Dougherty*[69] might be counting on the gift to attend college. The frustrated expectations can be as great as with any promise. Second, the promisor is not enriched at the promisee's expense. Again this is true. These first two points only show that, ignoring the psychological benefits to the promisor, the situation is not covered by the principles of past benefits and reliance. Third, it is claimed that no social interests are implicated in such promises. However, they can increase economic value, and there can be social interests in trust irrespective of reliance. Fourth, there are serious problems of proof, for people might simply fabricate claims. But this only requires limitations on the promises that will be enforced, not denying legal enforcement to all of them.

Two more serious objections arise even for formalized or written promises where the evidentiary problems are not great, namely, the difficulties created by improvidence and ingratitude.[70] For example, suppose an aunt promises to pay her nephew $5,000 in two years, but when the times comes, due to unforeseeable losses, she will be unable to

---

[65]Lon L. Fuller and Melvin Aron Eisenberg, *Basic Contract Law,* 4th edn. (St. Paul, Minn.: West Publishing Co., 1981), p. 16; U.C.C. sec 2-203 comment 1 (1978); Chitty, *Chitty on Contracts*, sec 25; G.H. Fridman, *The Law of Contract in Canada* (Toronto: Carswell Company Ltd., 1976), pp. 188-90.

[66]227 N.Y. 200, 125 N.E. 94 (1919).

[67]Kronman and Posner, 'Introduction,' p. 8.

[68]Eisenberg, 'Donative Promises,' pp. 3-5.

[69]227 N.Y. 200, 125 N.E. 94 (1919).

[70]Eisenberg, 'Donative Promises,' pp. 13-16; Eisenberg, 'Principles of Consideration,' p. 661.

provide for herself or her family if she does. Alternatively, suppose the nephew has, without her consent, taken her automobile for a cross country trip and wrecked it. Although European countries recognize improvidence and ingratitude as defenses, the contention is that common-law courts are not equipped to analyze difficult family situations. But this surely exaggerates the point. Proof of financial hardship is addressed by courts all the time in child support and bankruptcy cases. Ingratitude is a more difficult point, but it should not cover such factors as a nephew's political or social views. It might be restricted to damage to property (an offset) of personal injury. At the weakest, one could even allow the promise to be revoked in writing for any reason prior to the time for performance; this would still permit enforcement of unrevoked promises.

(7) The principle of gratuitous commitments: a written and notarized commitment, stating that it is to be legally binding, should be enforceable, without consideration, past benefit, or reliance, to the extent appropriate in view of any changed circumstances. The principle is clearly acceptable from a promisee's viewpoint, and since one need not make a promise but can legally bind oneself if one wants, it is acceptable from a promisor's viewpoint. The restriction on enforcement 'in view of changed circumstances' permits courts to consider improvidence and ingratitude on the basis of individual cases. This principle basically corresponds to the Model Written Obligations Act.[71] American law accords with this principle when the promise is of a charitable donation, although a mighty effort has been made to find consideration.[72] Moreover, Totten trusts and gifts by written instruments delivered to third parties are similar to such enforceable commitments.

A distinct form of gratuitous commitment often arises when parties seek to modify a contract by agreement. The traditional common-law rule was that consideration is necessary for a promise made in modification--a gratuitous commitment is not enforceable.[73] In *Alaska Packers' Ass'n v. Domenico*,[74] Alaska Packers hired workers as sailors and fishermen to go to Alaska for the salmon season. Once in Alaska, the workers quit and refused to work until the superintendent promised them higher pay. On their return, the workers were paid the original wages and signed a release.

---

[71]9C U.L.A. 378 (1943).

[72]Allegheny College v. National Chautaugua Co. Bk., 246 N.Y. 369, 159 N.E. 173 (1927).

[73]See Stylk v. Myrick, 170 Eng. Rep. 851 and 170 Eng. Rep. 1168 (1809) (seamen in Russia demand higher pay when two desert the ship); a consideration interpretation has been strongly criticized, Gilmore, *Death of Contract*, pp. 22-28.

[74]117 Fed. 99 (9th Cir. 1902).

They then sued for the extra pay promised in Alaska. The court held for Alaska Packers on the ground, among others, that there was no consideration for the extra play. The workers only promised to do what they were already legally obligated to do, so they incurred no detriment and the packers no benefit. The doctrine of consideration is not needed to settle *Alaska Packers'*. The sailors had Alaska Packers' superintendent over a barrel. If no promise was made, the fishing season was likely to be a total failure. In effect, the agreement was economically coerced.[75]

There are cases where the request for modification by one party seems more reasonable. In *Gilbert Steel Std. v. University Construction Ltd.*,[76] Gilbert Steel requested a price increase in steel being furnished for two apartment buildings under construction by University. An oral agreement was reached to modify the written contract, but a written agreement was never made. While University Construction accepted deliveries with invoices indicating the new prices, it did not pay in full. Gilbert Steel then sued for the remainder due. The court found for the defendants, holding that there was no consideration for the variation, and rejecting detrimental reliance as a legal basis for claims and on factual grounds.

Should modifications be enforceable? Contractors supplying goods assume risks of price increases unless they specifically contract otherwise. An alternative available to University Construction was to refuse to agree to the price increase and, if Gilbert defaulted, to purchase the steel elsewhere and sue for the difference in price. As the apartment buildings were only partially constructed at the time, this alternative might have involved a delay in construction. However, it is doubtful that the delay would have been significant; there is no showing that the needed steel was not available from other sources. By agreeing to the change, University seems to fall under the principle of reliance so its promise should be enforced. The court, of course, did not accept the principle of reliance. Moreover, it claimed that Gilbert could not show detrimental reliance. The reason is that had University refused to pay the higher price, Gilbert would have been liable for the increased costs of steel University purchased elsewhere. Thus, such modifications do involve gratuitous commitments.

(8) The principle of modifications: good faith modifications of contracts regardless of consideration, past benefit, or reliance should be enforceable. One has a good reason to accept this principle. Many modifications are routinely made by business-persons without significant cost to either party, for example, modifying time and place of delivery.

---

[75]See *Restatement (Second) of Contracts* sec. 175 (1979).

[76]67 D.L.R. 3d 606 (Ont. 1976).

Also, if one takes a relational view of contracts, many modifications occur in the context of ongoing business dealings between parties. If one agrees to a modification in favor of the other party in this contract, a modification might be made in one's favor in a subsequent one. In short, neither party need be worse off, and both might benefit in the long run. Thus, the principle of modifications falls under (b) (2), and sometimes perhaps (a), of the principle of enforceable commitments. One can always protect oneself from unacceptable modifications by refusing to agree. If there is excessive economic pressure, the modification would not be in good faith. The requirement of good faith is complex.[77] Here it need only be noted that it rules out more than extortion and coercion.

It has been suggested that the chief goals of the law should be to enforce voluntary modifications and not to enforce involuntary ones.[78] But that is too narrow a basis for refusing to enforce modifications, unless one takes an exceptionally broad view of coercion and includes any exploitation of unfair advantage within it. Although the Uniform Commercial Code does not require consideration for modifications in contracts for the sale of goods, it does impose a duty of good faith requiring a "legitimate commercial reason" for the modification.[79] *The Restatement (Second) of Contracts*[80] enforces modifications if fair and equitable in view of unanticipated circumstances or required by justice in view of reliance on the promise, but this is too restricted a principle.[81] There is no reason to require that reasons for modification stem from unanticipated circumstances. Detrimental reliance need not arise in contract modifications, and in any case, it is covered by the principle of reliance.

---

[77]See Robert S. Summers, "'Good Faith' in General Contract Law and the Sales Provisions of the Uniform Commercial Code," *Virginia Law Review* 54 (1968): 195-267; Barry J. Reiter, 'Good Faith in Contract,' *Valparaiso University Law Review* 17 (1983): 705-34.

[78]Robert A. Hillman, 'Contract Modification Under the Restatement (Second) of Contracts,' *Cornell Law Review* 67 (1982): 681.

[79]U.C.C. sec 2-209 (1) and comment 2 (1978).

[80]Sec. 89 (1979).

[81]Hillman, 'Contact Modification,' pp. 692-702.

PRINCIPLES FOR LEGAL PROCEDURE

NORMATIVE ANALYSIS

This paper presents basic justifiable principles of legal procedure, especially civil procedure. As the purpose here is to justify procedural principles, it is important not to assume constitutional requirements for procedure. The issue is which principles are justifiable, not which are constitutionally required. Of course, justifiable principles might then be used in interpreting constitutional provisions. Since constitutional provisions are not assumed and there is little agreement on methods for establishing such normative claims, it is important to state the method used even though space does not permit a defense of it. The central normative question is: What principles would rational persons accept courts using to decide cases in a society in which they expected to live?[1] As acceptable principles could and should vary with the type of society, the society is assumed to be an industrialized Western one with a common-law system. The crucial concepts to clarify are those of rational persons and principles.

A rational person uses logical reasoning and all relevant available information in acquiring desires and values, deciding what to do, and accepting legal principles.[2] Logical reasoning is not restricted to deductive logic but also includes inductive logic or scientific method. A rational person considers arguments for and against principles, accepting the sound arguments and rejecting the unsound ones. All relevant available information is all pertinent information that a person in the situation can obtain. It is information, not knowledge, that a rational person has. People are rational if they use the best information available, even if it later turns out to be incorrect; indeed, it would be irrational to use information that, on the basis of presently available evidence, appeared incorrect, even if it were later found to be correct. Information is relevant to the acceptability of a legal principle if it indicates that the principle's use by courts has or lacks some normative characteristic, such as fairness, or that the probable

[1]See also R. B. Brandt, 'A Motivational Theory of Excuses in the Criminal Law', in *Criminal Justice: Nomos XXVII*, ed. J. Roland Pennock and John W. Chapman (New York: New York University Press, 1985), p. 169.

[2]Richard B. Brandt, *A Theory of the Good and the Right* (Oxford: Clarendon Press, 1979), pp. 10-16; Michael D. Bayles, *Principles of Legislation* (Detroit: Wayne State University Press, 1978), pp. 51-54.

W. L. Robison (ed.), The Legal Essays of Michael Bayles, 191–210.
© 2002 *Kluwer Law International. Printed in the Netherlands.*

consequences of such use, including effects on third parties, would be good or bad.

Some normative basis must be used in determining what legal principles are justifiable or acceptable, but it need not be a moral or legal one. Much legal analysis and justification is in terms of people's interests. There is little reason to believe that these interests or desires (the difference is not important here) are irrational. Herein certain basic desires are assumed to be rational, namely, those of wealth, security, bodily and mental integrity (including life), prestige or reputation, and freedom. Most of these have been justified elsewhere.[3]

Finally, it is assumed that rational persons could be either party to a case. This assumption is implicit in the very question being asked, for it concerns the acceptability of legal principles for a society in which one expects to live. In procedure, many principles can be used by plaintiff or defendant. In arguing for a legal principle, one must then consider its acceptability from both parties' points of view.[4] This type of argument is rather common in courts. An example is the following argument by Judge Turnage for the rule that rejection of a purchased option does not terminate the right to accept later unless the other party has materially changed position.

> This rule fully protects the rights of both parties. It extends to the option or the protection he requires in the event a rejection of the option is communicated to him and he thereafter changes his position in reliance thereon to his detriment. At the same time it protects the right of the option holder to have the opportunity to exercise his option for the full period for which he paid, absent the material change in position.[5]

This argument shows that it is a reasonable rule whichever party one might be. One has no reason to think that people are more likely to have written than purchased an option.

Principles and rules can be distinguished.[6] On the one hand, rules apply in an all-or-nothing way; if they apply to a situation, they determine its evaluation. For example, a law requiring two witnesses to a will not in the handwriting of the testator is a rule. If a will has only one witness, it is

---

[3]Bayles, *Principles of Legislation.*

[4]See also David A. J. Richards, 'Human Rights and the Moral Foundations of the Substantive Criminal Law', *Georgia Law Review* 13 (1979): 1414-15, 1436.

[5]Ryder v. Wescoat, 535 S.W. 2d 269 (Mo. Ct. App. 1976).

[6]Ronald Dworkin, *Taking Rights Seriously* (Cambridge: Harvard University Press, 1977), pp. 22-28; Bayles, *Principles of Legislation,* pp. 42-44.

invalid. In contrast, when principles apply, they do not necessarily determine an evaluation. For example, it may be a principle that people should be free to dispose of their property by devise as they wish. It does not necessarily follow that a freely made will should be upheld, because a contrary principle might also apply, for example that a person should make adequate provision for children. On the other hand, because principles do not apply in an all-or-nothing way and can conflict principles have 'weight'. Conflicting principles must be weighed or balanced against one another, and some have more weight than others. Because rules apply in an all-or-nothing fashion, they do not have to be weighed or balanced against one another.

Some scholars reject this distinction between principles and rules, contending that principles differ from rules only by being more general.[7] On this view, both rules and principles have weight and can be balanced against one another. This contention does not affect the following arguments, because the essential features are the possibility of weighing or balancing and the different levels of generality.

ADJUDICATION

In considering principles for legal procedure, it is important to have a clear notion of adjudication as distinguished from legislation, negotiation, and so on. Courts differ from legislatures by the necessity to render decisions applicable to the particular parties in actual cases and controversies and by their limited investigative powers. Legislatures can consider and act on issues not currently disputed and can refuse to consider or act on highly contentious issues. Courts lack such freedom. The U.S. Constitution limits federal courts to cases and controversies.[8] This restriction does not prohibit 'declaratory judgments' when disputes arise concerning a matter of law likely to be involved in an actual controversy, but it does prohibit advisory opinions in which some person or group simply wants an answer to a legal question. Not all common-law courts are so restricted. Some can take issues referred to them by government bodies, such as the legislature, but this method is rarely used.

Courts must render decisions applicable to the parties in the case.

---

[7]Joseph Raz, 'Legal Principles and the Limits of Law', *Yale Law Journal* 81 (1972): 823-54.

[8]Art III, sec. 2; see also Samuel Mermin, *Law and the Legal System -- An Introduction* (Boston: Little, Brown and Co., 1973), pp. 174-76, 179-80, 184-85; Charles Alan Wright, *The Law of Federal Courts,* 4th edn. (St. Paul, Minn.: West Publishing Co., 1983), pp. 53-59.

Of course, the decision can be that no claim has been stated for which relief can be granted, but that is to render a decision. Courts cannot simply decline to decide because the issue is too complex. Appellate courts can often refuse to take cases, but then lower court decisions stand. The U.S. Supreme Court can decide that a matter is a political question for Congress rather than the Court,[9] but that is quite rare. Moreover, when courts give a final decision, it is legally binding on the parties. Of course, collecting a judgment for damages is sometimes harder than getting a favorable judicial decision.

Courts have limited investigative powers. At best, they can investigate matters relating to the specific case before them. They do not have the power to conduct a general investigation into, for example, business practices in an industry. In the common-law system, the burden of amassing and presenting evidence rests with the parties. Since the advent of the 'Brandeis brief' lawyers can and do provide available relevant social information, but courts cannot undertake general social investigations of the sort made by legislative committees and commissions of inquiry. In civil-law countries, courts are more actively involved in amassing and presenting evidence, especially in criminal law cases, but they still do not have the powers of legislatures; they are limited to the case at hand. The assumption made here about the investigative powers of courts generally leaves open the difference between common and civil-law courts.

Further distinctions need to be made between adjudication and other methods of resolving controversies. A prominent conception of adjudication defines it by the form of participation of the parties--"presenting proofs and reasoned arguments."[10] However, this definition tends to beg questions about the best type of procedure, biasing it in favor of an adversary system. A more neutral conception must be a more formal one.

Most features distinguishing adjudication from other forms of dispute resolution are implicit in the conception of courts deciding controversies between particular parties.[11] (1) There is a particular dispute.

---

[9]See Baker v. Carr, 369 U.S. 186 (1962).

[10]Lon L. Fuller, 'The Forms and Limits of Adjudication', *Harvard Law Review* 92 (1978): 364.

[11]See Martin P. Golding, *Philosophy of Law* (Englewood Cliffs, N.J.: Prentice-Hall, 1975), pp. 108-12; Martin P. Golding, 'On the Adversary System and Justice', in *Philosophical Law*, ed. Richard Bronaugh (Wesport, Conn.: Greenwood Press, 1978), pp. 101-02.

(2) Particular parties are involved; the dispute is not between large, amorphous groups such as environmentalists and industry. (3) A third party is involved. (4) A hearing is held in which information concerning the dispute is presented. (5) The third party "settles" the controversy by rendering a decision. (6) This decision is based on principles and rules--those of the substantive law--with reference to the information presented at the hearing.

These features clearly distinguish adjudication from mediation and negotiation. In the latter, no third party is involved; the dispute is settled directly by agreement between the parties or their representatives. In mediation, although a third party is involved, the third party does not render a decision; instead, as in negotiation, the parties agree to a settlement.

The above features do not clearly distinguish adjudication from arbitration. One might suggest that arbitration differs from adjudication by its reliance on private rules created by private agreement of the parties (contracts) rather than public rules.[12] However, courts regularly enforce contracts most terms of which result from agreement of the parties; and arbitrators use public rules in interpreting agreements. Alternatively, one might suggest that the difference is that adjudicators are publicly appointed but arbitrators are chosen by the parties. Although this is usually the case, some arbitrators are appointed by the government, and one can at least conceive of a private court system in which the parties choose the court and judge. The difference between the private and public status of decision-makers is primarily a matter of authority or jurisdiction, not the essence of adjudication. Consequently, no clear and sharp distinction exists between adjudication and arbitration; at most, there is a continuum with privately chosen third parties deciding on the basis or private rules at one end and publicly appointed third parties deciding on the basis of public rules at the other end.

DISPUTE RESOLUTION AND TRUTH

Two general purposes are inherent in the above concept of adjudication--resolving disputes and finding the "truth." That courts render decisions in cases and controversies implies that one purpose is the resolution of disputes. If judicial decisions were not intended to resolve disputes but, say, only to indicate support for one side or the other, there would be little reason to litigate. One must be clear about the sense in which a dispute is resolved. Even after final judgment, losing parties can still think that they

[12]Golding, 'On the Adversary System', p. 101.

were right, and enmity can still exist between the parties. Courts do not necessarily resolve disputes at the psychological level, only at the practical level, and even there they are not always successful. If Abramowitz claims Baxter owes her $5439 and the court finds for her, then she is entitled to use state power to collect. Usually, but not always, Baxter will pay. The difficulty ex-spouses have in collecting spousal and child support indicates that court decisions do not always result in a practical settlement.

The purpose of ascertaining truth is less obviously inherent in the concept of adjudication. Adjudicators are to decide disputes by the application of rules and principles. Even assuming that the substantive rules and principles are correct, a dispute will not be properly decided in accordance with them unless the "truth" or correct facts are determined. The truth needs to be found not for its own sake but to apply the rules and principles to the dispute correctly. The particular aims of the substantive rules and principles--justice, economic efficiency, public policy--make no difference. If the situation is not accurately understood and described, then the aims cannot be rationally served by the decision either as a resolution of the particular case or as a guide in others.[13] To the extent courts formulate rules for practical guidance, they need to be based on accurate information about the situations to which they are to apply, otherwise they might prescribe impractical and even harmful conduct.

Of course, judicial decision making is not a simple application of rules and principles to facts. First, finding facts is not a straight-forward descriptive process. Facts must be classified for the application of rules and do not come neatly labeled.[14] Second, many so-called factual questions are matters of evaluation.[15] Determining whether someone was negligent, reasonable, or insane requires judgment and evaluation. Third, even when the facts are clear, it is not always clear what the rules and principles imply. Is a child on a railroad tie extending over a public river on railroad property or not?[16] Nonetheless, there are core factual matters that one needs to get correct--that the child was on the tie, that the tie was fastened to railroad property, and so on.

---

[13]Robert S. Summers, 'Comment: "On the Adversary System and Justice"', in *Philosophical Law*, ed. Richard Bronaugh (Westport, Conn.: Greenwood Press, 1978), p. 123.

[14]H. L. A. Hart, *Essays in Jurisprudence and Philosophy* (Oxford: Clarendon Press, 1983), p. 63.

[15]P. S. Atiyah, *Law and Modern Society* (Oxford: Oxford University Press, 1983), pp. 34-36.

[16]*Hynes v. New York Cent. R.R. Co.* 231 N.Y. 229, 131 N.E. 898 (1921).

The purposes of dispute resolution and ascertainment of the truth do not provide usable criteria for evaluating legal procedure; they are too general. Dispute resolution is a purpose of the whole of law, substantive as well as procedural. Unlike pure science, the law does not aim at the truth, the whole truth, and nothing but the truth. That would be too expensive and often irrelevant to the purpose of dispute resolution. Yet, disputes could be resolved without any concern for the truth. Arbitrary fiats or flips of a coin could be used practically to resolve many disputes. Consequently, more specific aims are needed to evaluate legal procedures.

ECONOMIC COSTS

Although this section focuses on economic analysis or procedure, it is merely a specific instance of 'single value instrumentalism'. That is, the underlying concept is to design legal procedures as a means to maximize a single value or end. The economic approach seeks to maximize wealth or economic efficiency. Like any other instrument, legal procedure is viewed as an expense incurred in achieving an end, so the aim is to minimize the expense. The costs of incorrect decisions are called error costs, and those of making the decisions direct costs. The short statement of the aim is to minimize the sum of error and direct costs.[17] If 'EC' stands for error costs and 'DC' for direct costs, it can be written as follows:

Minimize Sum (EC + DC)

One does not aim to minimize either costs alone but the sum of the two. If one tried to minimize only direct costs, error costs might become exorbitant. Similarly, at some point the increase in direct costs to achieve accuracy is greater than the savings in reduced error costs.

A homey analogy might help one understand the view. In grocery shopping, one aims to achieve the most value for the least expense. An error cost occurs when one purchases an item at one store, say, a can of beans, when it could have been purchased for less at another. The direct costs are those of obtaining information about prices at various grocery stores and of transportation to and from them. One could drive from store to store with one's shopping list and price the various items, and then

---

[17]Richard A. Posner, 'An Economic Approach to Legal Procedure and Judicial Administration', *Journal of Legal Studies* 2 (1973): 399-400; Richard A. Posner, *Economic Analysis of Law*, 2d edn. (Boston: Little, Brown and Co., 1977), p. 429; Gordon Tullock, *Trails on Trial* (New York: Columbia University Press, 1980), pp. 5-6.

return to the stores buying the items at the lowest price. However, the investment of time and automobile expenses would probably make the total cost greater than simply purchasing all the items at one store. Many shoppers take an intermediate approach. They determine which store generally has the lowest prices for frequently bought staples. They also subscribe to the local newspaper and read the food advertisements for specials. When they go shopping, they do most of their shopping at the low priced store but stop at others nearby to purchase specials. Although some items purchased could have been obtained for less elsewhere, the combined cost of groceries, transportation, and newspaper is less than on any alternative. The economic approach recommends the same general method for evaluating legal procedure.

Legal error costs arise when an incorrect decision made. The defendant is in fact either guilty or innocent. (Criminal terminology is used for ease of expression; for civil cases one can substitute 'liable' and 'not liable' for 'guilty' and 'innocent'.) There are thus four possible outcomes. The court can convict a guilty person (CG), convict an innocent person (CI), not convict a guilty person (~CG), or not convict an innocent person (~CI). Two of these decisions--CI and ~CG--are incorrect, and two--CG and ~CI--are correct. If the aim of the substantive law is economic efficiency, then each incorrect decision results in an inefficient use of resources and is an inappropriate expense. For example, if a tortfeasor is mistakenly found not liable, then economic deterrence will not be achieved; insufficient resources will be spent on safety and the cost of accidents will increase. Moreover, because courts might make such incorrect decisions, some potential defendants will fail to invest in safety equipment, and some potential plaintiffs with good cases will not bother to sue.[18] A very tough estimate is that U.S. courts make incorrect decisions in about one-eighth of cases.[19] In criminal cases, conviction of innocent persons is probably much lower, but still significant--from 1 to 5 percent of cases.[20] The errors of false convictions are likely balanced by many more errors of false acquittals.

Direct costs are those of running the legal system. These include the public costs for judges' salaries, juries, courthouses, and so on, and the private costs of the parties in hiring lawyers, obtaining expert testimony, and so forth. In general, as private costs increase fewer cases

---

[18]Tullock, *Trials on Trai*l, pp. 6-7.

[19]Tullock, *Trials on Trial*, p. 31.

[20]'When Nightmare of False Arrest Comes True', *U.S. News & World Report,* 17 Dec. 1984, p. 45.

are taken to court and public costs decrease, although many other factors influence decisions to go to trial, such as the amount at stake and the estimated chances of winning. The direct costs of settling out of court or plea bargaining are significantly less than trials. Consequently, an increase in settlements decreases direct costs. Most economic analysts assume that increased settlements increase error costs.[21] This assumption appears well founded, because a settlement of a civil case is usually incorrect. Suppose the total damages in a tort case are $10 000. A settlement will almost be between zero and the maximum a losing defendant can expect to pay. However, either the defendant should pay $10 000 or nothing, so the settlement involves the defendant paying less or more than he or she ought. (This argument does not apply under comparative negligence if the plaintiff's negligence is in dispute, for then the defendant's proper liability might be near the settlement.)

In *Mathews v. Eldridge*,[22] the U.S. Supreme Court appears to have adopted a variation of the economic cost approach to determine due process requirements for administrative decisions. Although the Court is concerned to minimize costs, it has not restricted them to the single value of economic costs. The Court has specified that in evaluating procedures one should balance the private interest, the chances of error, and the government's interest. If errors too often favor the government, then the cost to the private interest will outweigh the government's gain. If the errors too frequently favor private parties, then the government's costs will outweigh the private gain. So balancing amounts to cost minimizing. To decide between two administrative procedures, one calculates the costs of each and then uses the one with the lowest total costs.

Two objections are commonly made against the economic approach. First, many people claim that one cannot place a dollar value on the concerns of plaintiffs. The loss of life or limb, it is said, cannot be adequately valued in monetary terms. However, this objection goes as much to substantive law as to procedural law. It applies more to the calculation of monetary damages for tort losses than it does to procedural law. Criminal cases might be a better basis for the objection. Nonetheless, an economic analyst can reply that crime costs money. It can be given a monetary value by considering its actual costs (for example, amount stolen) and the costs of deterring it. Even those plaintiffs in defamation actions who want vindication more than damages indicate how much vindication is worth to them by how much they are willing to spend to obtain it.

---

[21]Posner, 'An Economic Approach', p. 442.
[22]424 U.S. 319, 335 (1976).

The second objection is that the economic approach or any other single value analysis omits important values. One can reasonably be concerned about the fairness as well as total costs of legal procedures. A process might be less expensive than another but unacceptable because distinctly less fair. Other suggested values that might be omitted from an economic analysis are dignity and participation. However, an economic analyst can reply that, as in the case of vindication in defamation cases, one need only place a dollar value on concerns for equality or dignity and the theory can accommodate them. Here, however, the response is not adequate. In the previous objection, the concern was with outcomes. The economic approach is concerned only with the costs of outcomes--producing them and their being incorrect. Concerns for fairness and dignity are not necessarily aspects of outcomes (error costs) or costs of the procedure (direct costs). Fairness is not necessarily the same as the minimization of error.[23] This issue is considered further in the section on process benefits.

The economic approach does at least indicate one important factor to be taken into account in evaluating legal procedure. One has no reason to increase economic costs without good reasons. In short, all else being equal, anyone concerned with wealth has a good reason to prefer lower to higher economic costs, whether they be direct or error costs. *(1) The principle of economic costs: One should minimize the economic costs of legal procedures.*

MORAL COSTS

Another approach to legal procedure emphasizes that values other than economic costs are involved in evaluating outcomes. The moral cost approach of Ronald Dworkin[24] is an instance of 'multi-value instrumentalism', that is, an approach that evaluates procedures by seeking to maximize several values of outcomes. Dworkin contends that utilitarian (including economic) approaches to procedure ignore rights. He focuses on criminal cases in which he claims there is a right not to be punished if innocent. A utilitarian single value instrumentalism looks at what Dworkin calls the "bare harm" inflicted by mistaken decisions; it considers how much suffering actually results from mistaken decisions. Dworkin contends that convicted innocent persons might not suffer any more bare harm than results from failing to convict guilty persons. Consequently,

---

[23]Tullock, *Trials on Trial*, p. 124.

[24]Ronald Dworkin, 'Principle, Policy, Procedure', in *Crime, Proof and Punishment,* ed. C. F. H. Tapper (London: Butterworths, 1981), pp. 193-225.

there need be no greater reason to avoid convicting the innocent than to avoid not convicting the guilty. This gives inadequate weight to a right not to be convicted if innocent.

Economic analysts do argue that there is a greater cost in convicting innocent persons than in failing to convict guilty ones.[25] This then supports the higher burden of proof required for criminal than civil liability. One reason for lower error costs for failing to convict the guilty than for convicting the innocent is that failure to convict one guilty person will probably not have much of an effect on the law's deterrence, and an increased crime rate is the chief error cost. Nonetheless, the fewer guilty persons convicted, the greater the punishment has to be to maintain an effective deterrent. Thus, as the burden of proof requirement is raised, the amount of punishment also needs to be raised to maintain an equal deterrence. It is not clear that innocent persons benefit from a lower chance of a greater punishment.[26]

The moral cost approach implies that there are at least two types of error costs. Consider the two possible mistaken decisions, convicting the innocent (CI) and not convicting the guilty (~CG). The first is worse than the second, regardless of the bare or economic harm involved in the two, because it infringes the right not to be convicted if innocent. Such violations of rights are moral harms or costs. Moral harm can also occur in civil cases. If one party has a right that might be infringed by an incorrect decision and the other party does not, then procedures should be biased against infringing that right and causing moral harm. Often in civil cases a mistake in either direction involves equal moral harm. For example, whether a deserving tort plaintiff is denied recovery or an "innocent" tort defendant is made to pay damages, moral harm is involved. But in some civil cases, moral harm is perhaps greater on one side than another, for example, suffering an uncompensated defamation rather than paying damages for a truthful libel.[27]

The moral costs approach adds another determinant to the economic approach's analysis of error costs. Besides the economic or bare harm costs of error, there are also moral costs. Thus, the aim of legal procedure can be stated as minimizing the sum of the economic and moral error costs and the direct costs. If 'EC' here stands for the economic or bare harm error costs and 'MC' for the moral error costs, then the moral harm view merely adds another term to the economic approach's formula:

---

[25]Posner, 'An Economic Approach', pp. 410-15.

[26]Tullock, *Trials on Trial,* p. 82.

[27]Dworkin, 'Principle, Policy, Procedure', p. 210.

Minimize Sum (EC + MC + DC)

Moreover, according to Dworkin, moral costs is an objective and constant factor across cases of the same type.[28] That is, moral harm is the same whenever the same right is infringed, so moral costs are a constant factor for each type of case.

Moral costs can make a significant difference in the procedures that are justified, because they attach to some errors but not to others. Consider the following diagram of possible decision outcomes.

Decision

outcomes	CG	CI	~CG	~CI
costs		EC + MC	EC	

Since there are greater costs in CI than in CG, one should bias the procedural system to avoid CI errors. That is, CG errors are preferable to CI errors. This effect can be obtained by shifting the burden of proof to make conviction more difficult. In the example of defamation above, the burden would be shifted the other way, making it easier to establish liability; that is, placing the burden of proof of the truth of the statements on the defendant.

One has good reason to add moral costs to economic costs if one has good reason to prefer one type of error over another. To do so, one need not accept Dworkin's notion of rights being involved. One might arrive at the same position as Dworkin regarding the aim of avoiding punishment of innocent persons without invoking rights. So long as CI is less desirable outcome than ~CG, there is a reason to prefer ~CG errors to CI errors. The same result occurs whenever a principle of substantive law is based on something other than economic efficiency. Moral costs are simply the costs of failure to achieve aims other than economic efficiency, such as not enforcing unconscionable contract terms or providing compensation in tort. *(2) The principle of moral costs: One should minimize the moral costs of legal procedures.*

The moral cost approach does not differ from the economic approach as significantly as might appear. First, some economic analysts

---

[28] Ibid., pp. 203, 209-10.

have recognized that the substantive law might have aims other than economic efficiency.[29] If the failure to achieve a substantive aim can be evaluated in monetary terms, the same cost minimizing approach can be used. Second, one cannot plausibly maintain that no monetary value can be placed on moral costs, because the moral cost approach requires balancing monetary error and direct costs with moral costs. Even if a price cannot be directly placed on moral costs, an indirect pricing occurs. One need only consider how much one is willing to pay in economic costs to avoid moral costs. That amount is the price of the moral costs. For example, the cost of increased crime and punishment resulting from placing the burden of proof on the prosecution is the price of the moral harm in punishing the innocent. Third, the moral costs approach is still an instrumentalist one. Legal procedure is simply a means to achieving proper outcomes.

The similarity of the approaches can be seen by considering *Santosky v. Kramer*.[30] This case involved the burden of persuasion a state must carry in proceedings to permanently terminate parental rights. The U.S. Supreme Court used the method of analysis it developed in *Mathews v. Eldridge*[31] used above to illustrate the economic cost approach and which Dworkin thinks might be a utilitarian approach.[32] However, in *Santosky* the Court considered the fundamental liberty interest of parents as specially weighing against errors of wrongly terminating rights. Thus, it required clear and convincing proof rather than a mere preponderance of the evidence. This appears to be a moral costs approach, the Court saying that the moral harm in wrongfully depriving persons of parental rights makes these errors worse than those of failing to terminate rights.

However, one can challenge the application of the moral cost approach in *Santosky* as well as Dworkin's apparent application of it to a case in which a woman had been falsely accused of child abuse by an anonymous informer.[33] Both the Santosky majority and Dworkin emphasize the rights of the parents (to custody of children or not to be falsely accused). Both seem to ignore the rights of children not to be abused. The *Santosky* majority clearly does so; Dworkin is ambiguous about the matter. In both cases, it is important to look past the procedural form to the substance, past the nominal parties of state or society to the children whose interests are involved. Once that is done, there are equally

---

[29]Posner, 'An Economic Approach', p. 401.

[30]455 U.S. 745 (1982).

[31]424 U.S. 319 (1976).

[32]Dworkin, 'Principle, Policy, Procedure', pp. 221-22.

[33]Ibid, pp. 196, 216-18; *D v. National Society for the Prevention of Cruelty to Children*, 1978 A.C. 171.

strong substantive principles on both sides. There is no reason to prefer one type of error to another.

The instrumentalism of the economic and moral cost approaches has a significant implication for legal procedure. One can evaluate procedures as leading to correct and incorrect outcomes (consider error costs) only if outcomes are either correct or incorrect. The economic approach is assured of outcomes being correct or incorrect, if the aim of substantive law is economic efficiency. An outcome either is or is not economically efficient. Similarly, one of Dworkin's major theses is that legal cases always have a right answer.[34] But if they are wrong and there are no correct answers, there are no error costs. If there are no error costs, both the economic and moral cost approaches prescribe minimizing direct costs. Consequently, one should not have a hearing with the presentation of information but merely flip a coin or otherwise inexpensively render a decision to settle the dispute.

One must distinguish some or a few cases not having a correct answer from there never being correct answers for certain types of cases. The dire implications above result only if cases of a certain type never, or almost never, have correct answers. If only a few cases of some type fail to have correct answers, then one might design legal procedures on instrumental grounds for the usual cases with correct answers. Nonetheless, the amount of direct costs one should rationally bear to avoid error costs should be reduced by some amount to account for cases without correct answers.

Another implication of instrumentalist approaches and our first two principles deserve notice. Substance and procedure are closely related. The more significant the substantive issues, whether economically or morally, the greater the error costs. A mistaken judgment in a case involving $500 does not impose the error costs a similar mistake in a case involving $500 000 does. Similarly, moral costs vary with the substantive principle involved or the amount of moral harm (different amounts of punishment). Contrary to Dworkin, the moral harm of imprisoning an innocent person for five years is greater than that of imprisoning an innocent person for five months. The moral harm is greater the greater the violation of a right. Consequently, fewer direct costs are justified in cases involving less significant substantive matters. This reasoning supports less expensive and less elaborate procedures for smaller matters--small claims courts, traffic violations, and so on.

Because they are instrumentalist approaches concerned with the

---

[34]Ronald Dworkin, 'No Right Answer?', in *Law, Morality, and Society,* ed. P. M. S. Hacker and J. Raz (Oxford: Clarendon Press, 1977).

costs of avoiding errors, the economic moral costs approaches focus on truth finding. If there is no truth to be found, there is no reason for legal procedure. They are concerned with dispute resolution only in that decisions give correct answer to disputes. One can view the next approach as adding a concern with resolving disputes, at the psychological as well as practical level.

PROCESS BENEFITS

Another approach to legal procedure is to consider values or benefits of procedures independent of their effect on the accuracy of outcomes.[35] There might be values such as dignity, fairness, and participation served by legal procedures even though they do not increase the accuracy of decisions. One might describe this approach as an 'inherent process value' approach. However, the concept of inherent value can be misleading. It might suggest that the values are independent of the effect of a process. This is not the case, or at least, need not be the case. The moral and economic error costs are the result of incorrect decisions. The inherent values served are simply independent of decision outcomes. Put another way, the causal chain from procedure to economic and moral error costs goes through the decision rendered, while the causal chain from procedures to process values or benefits does not go through the decision. Process values are logically in the position of direct costs, which are also independent of the decision. They are satisfactions derived from the process itself.[36]

The process values served by legal procedure can be viewed as benefits corresponding to direct costs. Both the economic and moral costs approaches view legal procedures as expenses to be borne only if they contribute to reducing error costs. However, one might prefer one procedure to another even if both have the same direct costs and are equally effective in producing a desired outcome, have the same error costs. An analogy illustrates the point. Suppose one wants to lose ten pounds. Further suppose one can do so equally well by a daily exercise program of either calisthenics or tennis. One might prefer tennis to calisthenics, even if tennis costs more. One might consider tennis to have other benefits than mere weight loss. Similarly, one might prefer one type

---

[35]See Robert S. Summers, 'Evaluating and Improving Legal Processes--A Plea for "Process Values"', *Cornell Law Review* 60 (1974): 1--52; Jerry L. Mashaw, 'Administrative Due Process: The Quest for a Dignitary Theory', *Boston University Law Review* 61 (1981): 885-931.

[36]See Marvin E. Frankel, *Partisan Justice* (New York: Hill and Wang, 1980), p. 6.

of legal procedure to another, even though they are equally accurate.

An instrumentalist might contend that these alleged benefits can be included in direct costs. For example, if calisthenics are less desirable than tennis, one can consider how much more one would be willing to pay for tennis than calisthenics. One can then add that amount to the direct costs of calisthenics so that they have a higher costs. However, this approach has a conceptual problem. The greater direct costs of calisthenics are calculated by comparison with another program. To obtain the full costs of a procedure or calisthenics by this approach, one would have to conceptualize a perfect procedure or weight loss program and determine costs of others in comparison to it, but it is not clear that one can conceptualize a perfect legal procedure or weight loss program.

Alternatively, an instrumentalist might contend that one can noncomparatively calculate the costs of procedures. One can ask what outcome benefits one would have to receive to engage in a procedure or calisthenics. (How much would one have to be paid to do calisthenics?) But this shows the defect; the instrumentalist is try to convert the benefits of one activity into the costs of another. One might not have to receive any outcome benefits to play tennis. Some people find it worthwhile in itself. There are costs--time, rackets, and so on--but there are benefits or satisfactions in the playing that outweigh these costs. There are both benefits and cost in tennis, and perhaps in calisthenics. The same can be true of legal procedure. The instrumentalists might be correct to claim that in legal procedure, unlike tennis, the costs are always greater than the benefits, but that can only be a conclusion of weighing or balancing the costs and benefits. It is more perspicuous to consider them as separate items than to use a conclusory sum. Simply speaking of direct costs can lead one to overlook the benefits and thus exaggerate total costs.

The argument so far shows that one might perceive benefits or values in legal procedures independent of outcomes. Moreover, these benefits should be kept distinct from direct costs. Consequently, the formula for evaluating legal procedures needs to have another term added to indicate process benefit. If 'PB' stands for process benefits, the formula can be represented as follows:

Minimize Sum (EC + MC + DC - PB)

Process benefits are subtracted rather than added, because the other terms are costs.

This approach avoids one possible problem of instrumentalism, namely, the implication that if there is no correct outcome, then the least expensive procedure should be used. Process benefits might offset significant direct costs, so a fairly complex and expensive procedure might still be justified. Of course, if 'least expensive' is confusingly taken to mean 'the net of direct costs and process benefits', then one should use the least expensive procedure (S - 1 being less expensive than S). The process benefits approach retains the instrumentalist implication that substance can affect procedure, because error costs are still relevant whenever they exist.

The argument has not yet established that there are any process values or the basis on which they can be determined, only that if there are such values, evaluation of legal procedure should explicitly take them into account. A basis for process values exists in the inherent purpose of dispute resolution. Instrumentalist approaches focus on truth finding, ignoring dispute resolution except as it results from correct decisions. Process benefits contribute to both psychological and practical dispute resolution. Features of legal procedure can contribute to dispute resolution without contributing to accuracy. Without claiming completeness, a number of process benefits and principles can be identified on these grounds.[37]

(3) The principle of peacefulness: Procedures should be peaceful. This principle is one of the foundations of a legal system. Without legal procedures for resolving disputes, they are likely to result in violence and blood feuds. For the same reasons people rationally desire the criminal law, they also want peaceful procedures. This principle is especially important in limiting self-help.

(4) The principle of voluntariness: People should be able voluntarily to have their disputes legally resolved. This principle must be carefully restricted. It states that one should be able, if one chooses, to have disputes legally settled. It does not imply that if one party does not want a legal resolution, that party can veto such a procedure. Instead, the principle applies primarily to plaintiffs in civil cases. Defendants, whether civil or criminal, should not be able to block legal proceedings by failing to consent to them. This principle contributes to dispute resolution by enabling aggrieved parties to obtain an authoritative settlement. It thus also contributes to peace. An alternative would be to have state agents bring all cases. This would involve great public expense or else many disputes that could be legally resolved would not be. Not all disputes are open to legal resolution. For a variety of reasons, such as the trivial nature of the matter, courts should not undertake to resolve some disputes. Many of these limitations are part of the substantive law, for example, not usually allowing tort recover for pure economic loss and not enforcing unrelied on and unwritten gratuitous promises.

---

[37]See also Summers, 'Evaluating and Improving Legal Processes', pp. 20-27.

(5) The principle of participating: Parties should be able to participate meaningfully in the legal resolution of disputes. This principle is evidenced in the common notion of having one's day in court. If one cannot participate, then one is denied one's day in court. The principle contributes to dispute resolution, because parties that have been able to participate are more likely to accept a decision; although they might not agree with the decision, they are more likely to comply with it. Trials *in absentia* and *ex parte* hearings violate this principle and are used sparingly. One value underlying the principle is participating in decisions that significantly affect one's life. One reasonably desires to at least be heard, to have one's say, before decisions affecting one are made. Being permitted to participate also evidences others' respect, that one is to be considered seriously.

(6) The principle of fairness: Procedures should be fair--treat the parties equally.[38] Fairness here essentially means equality of treatment in the procedures. Given an equal chance of being plaintiff or defendant, one would not want the procedures biased toward one side or another, except as that can be justified by considerations acceptable from both perspectives. For example, in the previous section it was noted that the burden of proof can justifiably be weighted due to substantive aims. Parties are less likely to accept decisions as resolving their dispute, either psychologically or practically, if they think the procedures used to arrive at them were unfair. Several subprinciples help spell out fairness.[39] (1) The dispute settler should be neutral. People should not be judges in their own cases; a judge or jury should not be biased.[40] (2) At the hearing, the information of both sides should be presented. (3) Each party should at least be aware of the information presented by the other and have an opportunity to respond to it. The principle of fairness only specifies that the parties have an equal opportunity to participate; the principle of participation provides a reason for significant participation.

(7) The principle of intelligibility: Procedures should be intelligible to the parties. Generally, rationality increases intelligibility.[41] Consequently, the more rational the procedures for ascertaining the truth and arriving at decisions, the more rational parties will assent to the outcomes. That is, if people can understand the process and the reasons for a decision, they

---

[38]See also Dworkin, 'Principle, Policy, Procedure', pp. 206, 209-10; Tullock, *Trials on Trial,* p. 124.

[39]Cf. Golding, *Philosophy of Law,* pp. 122-23.

[40]28 U.S.C. sec. 455 (1982): *SCA Services v. Morgan,* 557 F.2d 110 (7th Cir. 1977).

[41]Summers, 'Evaluating and Improving Legal Processes', p. 26.

are more likely to accept it as settling their dispute. It follows that decisions should be articulated in terms of rational rules and principles and information developed at a hearing or trial.

(8) The principle of timeliness: Procedures should provide timely decisions. Timeliness is a mean between the extremes of haste and dilatoriness. Persons do not rationally want decisions made without adequate time to gather information and reflect on its significance. In part, this concern pertains to outcomes; hasty decisions are more likely to be incorrect. However, the concern the other way, to avoid dilatoriness, is not. People do not want to wait longer than necessary for resolutions of their disputes. Delay in dispute resolution is likely to encourage people to take matters into their own hands. The saying that "Justice delayed is justice denied" is not correct substantively, for a delayed decision can be substantively correct. Nonetheless, delay prevents people planning and living their lives. An instrumentalist approach to delay is likely to ignore this aspect, concentrating only on its effects on settlements and economic costs.[42]

(9) The principle of repose: A final resolution of a dispute should be made. Disputes are not resolved if they can be reopened. If appeals are always possible, if the same issues can be raised in another case, then the dispute is not settled. If people invoke legal procedures to settle disputes, then there must be a point at which they are finally settled, otherwise there is no point in invoking legal procedures.

The inherent purposes of legal procedure are truth finding and dispute resolution. Obviously, people want to achieve these purposes at as little cost as possible. The purpose of truth finding primarily involves the avoidance of economic and moral error costs. The purpose of dispute resolution involves process benefits making a practical resolution more likely. These elements must be considered in a framework of trying to keep the direct costs of legal procedure as low as reasonably possible. The general normative aim, then, is to minimize the sum of economic and moral error costs and direct costs less process benefits.

Finally, one important aspect of legal cases should be noted, namely, they are minus sum interactions. This point is implicit in the assumption that error and direct costs are greater than process benefits. Although individual plaintiffs can gain from legal cases by obtaining damages and other remedies, overall, legal cases are a net loss. Consequently, from a social perspective or that of potentially being either plaintiff or defendant, lawsuits are to be avoided. The justification of a legal system and procedures must be one of lesser evils, that legal

---

[42]Posner, 'An Economic Approach', pp. 420-21.

resolution of disputes is preferable to blood feuds, rampant crime and violence, and so on.

RECONCEPTUALIZING NECESSITY AND DURESS

I. INTRODUCTION

The criminal law has long recognized the defense of necessity and duress. Generally, persons have a defense of necessity if, due to natural events, they have no alternative but to behave in a manner that satisfied the definition of an offense. Persons have a defense of duress if, due to human threats, they behave in a manner that fulfills the definition of an offense. Even these characterizations do not encompass the defenses as formulated in some jurisdictions.[1]

The previous characterizations are intentionally stated in general and vague terms. Over twenty-five years ago, Jerome Hall wrote that "the explication of these rules [of necessity and duress] in English and American law...is disappointing."[2] Despite significant proposals and commentary in the intervening quarter century, Hall's comment is still true. Although progress has been made in recent commentaries, different grounds for the defenses are still often confused. This frequently results in limitations based on different grounds being applied to the same defense. Significant differences between jurisdictions exist. Confusion and disagreement pervade most aspects of the defenses. Does the source of the defendant's predicament, natural or human, make any difference? Should the defenses operate to justify, excuse, or mitigate? What limitations, if any, should be placed on the defenses? Should they be permitted only when the threat is to oneself or relative, or only when the threat is imminent? Should the defenses be permitted for homicide or for those situations in which persons are responsible for getting themselves into the predicament?

---

[1]Both defenses are similar to self-defense, which is the necessary use of reasonable force to protect oneself. One crucial difference between necessity and duress and self-defense is that in self-defense, a person uses force against the source of the threat, whereas in necessity and duress, harms are usually inflicted on non-threatening and innocent persons. In necessity, no one threatens the actor, so there is no threatening person on whom harm might be inflicted. *A* usually coerces *B* to harm *C*.

[2]J. HALL, GENERAL PRINCIPLES OF CRIMINAL LAW 416 (2d ed. 1960).

W. L. Robison (ed.), The Legal Essays of Michael Bayles, 211–242.
© 2002 *Kluwer Law International. Printed in the Netherlands.*

This Article reconceptualizes the traditional necessity and duress defenses as two distinct, rational, consistent, and justifiable defenses--absence of a reasonable alternative and inability to choose rationally. The approach is normative. The following section briefly examines three distinct theoretical grounds for necessity, duress, or both. These grounds are involuntary behavior, inability to choose rationally, and absence of a reasonable alternative choice, or lesser evil. Although the grounds are generally accepted, problems arise from the failure to clarify and distinguish them in defining and justifying necessity and duress defenses.

The third section analyzes the justification of absence of a reasonable alternative, which closely resembles the traditional necessity defense. Such a defense should not be restricted to imminent threats from nonhuman sources. Nor should it be limited to avoiding harms or to the interests of actors or those under their protection. The defense can provide a justification for some homicides, as well as lesser offenses, and need not be restricted to innocent persons.

The fourth section analyzes the inability to choose rationally defense, which resembles the duress defense. However, most of the traditional limitations on the duress defense, including limitations regarding interests, offenses, source and imminence of threat, and responsibility for becoming involved in the situation, are not justifiable. In view of proof difficulties, the defense should be construed as mitigating rather than excusing.

The fifth section considers whether recognition of the proposed defense would diminish the law's capacity to prevent crime. The focus is on the actors' mistaken beliefs about the absence of a reasonable alternative. Only reasonable mistakes should be permitted.

II. GROUNDS

Theorists have suggested three grounds for the defenses of necessity and duress. The involuntary behavior ground provides that criminal offenses require a voluntary act; necessity and duress are legitimate defenses to the extent they show that no voluntary act occurred. The inability to choose rationally ground provides that persons who lack an ability to choose rationally are not responsible; necessity and duress are then legitimate defenses to the extent they show an inability to choose rationally. The absence of a reasonable alternative ground provides that persons who act so as to produce the greatest possible value in the situation should not be criminally liable; necessity and duress are legitimate defenses to the extent they show there was no reasonable alternative. To punish persons who chose the greatest value or least harm possible is contrary to the purpose of criminal law to prevent harm.

A. Involuntary Behavior

The origins of the involuntary behavior ground can be traced to Aristotle. He believed that praise and blame are appropriate only for voluntary actions.[3] Conduct due to compulsion or ignorance is involuntary.[4] Aristotle recognized that the behavior of a person who acts under a threat of a tyrant or who jettisons cargo from a ship in a storm may include both voluntary and involuntary elements, but is more like a voluntary action. He identified actions as compulsory when "the cause is in the external circumstances and the agent contributes nothing."[5]

In many instances, the involuntary behavior ground will not provide a defense. The infrequency of the ground as a defense is evidenced by Hall's need to use hypothetical cases from the literature rather than actual cases to illustrate the ground.[6] A ship cast on shore by a storm is not an illegal entry. If *A* takes *B's* hand with a knife clasped in it and forces *B* to stab someone, *B's* behavior is involuntary. The principle underlying involuntary behavior is that a person could not have acted otherwise even if he had so chosen. Even if *B* chose not to stab another person, *B's* behavior would be the same.

Most modern penal codes require a voluntary act for an offense.[7] An alternative approach is not to require voluntary conduct within the definition of a criminal offense, but, rather, to provide a separate defense of physical compulsion or involuntary behavior.[8] The effect is largely the

---

[3]ARISTOTLE, *Nichomachean Ethics*, in 9 THE WORKS OF ARISTOTLE III. 11109b (W.D. Ross trans. ed. 1915).

[4]"[T]hat is compulsory of which the moving principle is outside, being a principle in which nothing is contributed by the person who is acting..., e.g., if he were to be carried somewhere by a wind, or by men who had him in their power." *Id.* at III.1 1110a. Involuntariness due to ignorance is not relevant to this Article.

[5]*Id.* at III.1 1110b.

[6]J. HALL, *supra* note 501, at 423.

[7]*See Model Penal Code* §2.01(1)-(2) (Proposed Official Draft 1962) (all future citations to the *Model Penal Code* are taken from 1962 Proposed Official Draft).

[8]1 LAW REFORM COMMISSION OF CANADA, REPORT ON RECODIFYING CRIMINAL LAW 25 (Report 30, 1986) [hereinafter cited as L.R.C.C., REPORT]: LAW REFORM COMMISSION OF CANADA, CRIMINAL LAW, THE GENERAL PART: LIABILITY AND DEFENCES 21, 69-70 (Working Paper 29, 1982) [hereinafter cited as L.R.C.C., CRIMINAL LAW]; *see* 1 P. ROBINSON, CRIMINAL LAW DEFENSES §25(b)(2) (1984).

same.[9]

The question then becomes why involuntariness is thought to be relevant to necessity and dures. First, on all three grounds, behavior can be described as involuntary. Behavior is strictly involuntary on the involuntary ground; that is, no minimal choice is involved and the behavior occurs solely due to physical forces, which Hall calls physical causation.[10] Behavior is involuntary on the inability to choose rationally ground because it does not result from a rational, deliberate choice of the actor. Behavior is involuntary on the absence of a reasonable alternative ground because it is what the actor had to do in the circumstances.[11] Although Aristotle clearly articulated the voluntariness both of throwing goods overboard in a storm and acting due to threats, people speak of such decisions as necessary, as in "it was necessary to save the ship." The term compulsion can also be used in a broad sense, as in "to save the ship, they were compelled to cast the cargo overboard."

Second, psychological egoism[12] views acting to save one's life as behavior due to a law of nature. Thomas Hobbes believed in psychological egoism. He thought that one should be totally excused for acts compelled by the "terror of present death...because no law can oblige a man to abandon his own preservation."[13] Hobbes further suggested that such a law could not deter because one would rationally prefer a chance of future death to certain present death.[14]

Thus, a third but distinct reason why involuntariness is thought relevant to necessity and duress is that the law cannot deter people from

---

[9]Differences may arise concerning the burden of proof. Under both approaches, the burden of production is on the defendant because of the presumption of voluntariness. If voluntariness is part of the definition of the offense, the prosecution has the burden of persuasion beyond a reasonable doubt. To defeat the prosecution's burden, the defendant need only show that it is, for example, 20% probable that he acted involuntarily. If, however, physical compulsion is an affirmative defense, the burden of persuasion will probably be on the defendant by a preponderance of the evidence. In that case, the defendant needs to show that it is at least 51% probable that he behaved involuntarily. Consequently, including voluntariness in the definition of offenses makes the defense easier and convictions fewer. Given that it is wrong to convict persons for involuntary behavior and given the increased likelihood of incorrect convictions on the separate defense approach, it is better to include voluntariness in the definition of offenses.

[10]J. HALL, *supra* note 2, at 421.

[11]*See* 3 J. FEINBERG, THE MORAL LIMITS OF THE CRIMINAL LAW: HARM TO SELF 151 (1986).

[12]Psychological egoism is the view that people always act to further their own interests. J. RACHELS, THE ELEMENTS OF MORAL PHILOSOPHY 53 (1986).

[13]T. HOBBES, LEVIATHAN 197 (M. Oakeshott ed. 1962).

[14]*Id.*

acts performed under threat of imminent death. This view received support from authors of significantly opposed ethical theories such as Kant[15] and Bentham.[16] However, the ineffectiveness of deterrence does not imply that conduct is involuntary. One could be capable of acting otherwise if one chose, yet agree with Hobbes that to so choose would be irrational.

B. Inability to Choose Rationally

Penal codes, as well as some authors, suggest that the inability to choose rationally is a basis for necessity of duress. The Law Reform Commission of Canada asserts that laws should not ask more of people than persons of "ordinary courage, strength and fortitude" can bear.[17] Recently, the Supreme Court of Canada found a necessity defense based on "normative involuntariness" when a person's behavior was "compelled by normal human instincts."[18]

The inability to choose rationally is usually more explicit in the context of duress. The *Model Penal Code* bases duress on the standard of a person of reasonable firmness being unable to resist threats.[19] Several authors also equate duress with an inability to choose.[20] These authorities,

---

[15]I. KANT, THE METAPHYSICAL ELEMENTS OF JUSTICE 41 (J. Ladd trans. 1965).

[16]J. BENTHAM, THE PRINCIPLES OF MORALS AND LEGISLATION 175 (Hafner ed. 1948). Bentham referred to both physical danger and "threatened mischief" by others. *Id.*

[17]L.R.C.C., CRIMINAL LAW, *supra* note 8, at 94.

[18]Perka v. The Queen, 13 D.L.R.4th 1, 15 (1984).

[19]518. Model Penal Code 2.09(1).

[20]Lord Widgery has stated that duress is a defense "if the will of the accused has been overborne by threats of death or serious personal injury so that the commission of the alleged offense was no longer the voluntary act of the accused." Regina v. Hudson, 56 Crim. App. 1 (1971). *But cf.* People v. Carradine, 52 111. 2d 231, 287 N.E.2d 670 (1972) (fear for life not valid reason for refusal to testify at trial, contempt sentence upheld). The will being overborne suggests an inability to choose rationally. Although Widgery also states that the act is involuntary, he can charitably be interpreted not to mean involuntary in the sense adumbrated above.

Jerome Hall more directly presents duress as involving an inability to choose when he states that coercion is based on "a well-founded fear." J. HALL, *supra* note 2, at 439. Paul Robinson is quite explicit about the inability to choose rationally, claiming that duress is available if the actor is unable to control his conduct. 2 P. ROBINSON, *supra* note 8, at §177(c)(1); Robinson, *Criminal Law Defenses: A Systematic Analysis,* 82 COLUM. L. REV. 225 (1982). Finally, Hyman Gross clearly notes that such a defense can involve an "inability to choose." H. GROSS, A THEORY OF CRIMINAL JUSTICE 279 (1979). However, Gross prefers to claim that the defense involves lack of an opportunity rather than an ability to choose, because sometimes a person can have the capacity to choose but otherwise lack an opportunity to do so, such as lacking time to choose.

however, do not accurately construe the underlying principle. Criminal liability should not be imposed if a person lacked the ability to choose rationally to conform to the law. In a criminal justice system respecting freedom, people should not be criminally liable without a fair opportunity and capacity to choose to perform a criminal act.[21] This condition is not met if, due to fear or lack of time, a person lacks the ability to make a rational choice. An act is the result of one's training, habit, or perhaps instinct. In one sense, the actor chooses in both of these circumstances to perform one act or another. It is not reflex behavior. But the act does not reflect a choice anymore than does ducking one's head to avoid being hit by a ball or other flying object. Qualifying the inability to choose with the requirement of "rationally" indicates that, while some minimal choice exists, it is not sufficient to enable one to avoid criminal liability.[22]

The inability to choose rationally is a characteristic of a particular person in a specific situation. Some individuals might not be overwhelmed by fear in circumstances that would overwhelm others. Thus, in principle, this ground requires investigation into a given person's capabilities in the circumstances. This ground justifies a defense closer to duress than to necessity. However, most defenders of a duress defense introduce an objective element. The Model Penal Code and Paul Robinson both advocate examining how a person of reasonable firmness would have acted.[23] However, this limitation cannot be based on inability to choose rationally, as a given individual might not be able to choose rationally even

---

[21]*See* H.L.A. HART, PUNISHMENT AND RESPONSIBILITY 152-53, 181, 201 (1968).

[22]This ground also underlies the control test for insanity--the inability to conform to the law. MODEL PENAL CODE §4.01(1); 1 P. ROBINSON, *supra* note 8, §25(b)(2). One lacks an ability to control one's conduct if one lacks an ability to choose, because people control their conduct through the choices they make. The difference between insanity and duress or necessity is that in insanity the inability to control is due to mental disease or defect, whereas in duress or necessity it is due to danger or lack to time. Although the control test of the insanity defense has been under attack, the critics do not deny that theoretically inability to control should excuse. A primary concern has been whether or not psychiatrists can properly diagnose insanity in particular cases. ABA Standing Committee on Association Standards for Criminal Justice, PROPOSED CRIMINAL JUSTICE MENTAL HEALTH STANDARDS 330 (1984); ABA Standing Committee on Association Standards for Criminal Justice, *Recommendations on the Insanity Defense*, 7 MENTAL DISABILITY L. REP. 138 (1983); American Psychiatric Association, *Report on the Insanity Defense*, 7 MENTAL DISABILITY L. REP. 145 (1983). In duress and necessity, the circumstances provide objective evidence lacking for the insanity defense.

[23]MODEL PENAL CODE 2.09(1); 2 P. ROBINSON, *supra* note 8, §177(d); *see also* G. FLETCHER, RETHINKING CRIMINAL LAW 833 (1978). For a defense of necessity, the Supreme Court of Canada asks whether "the danger was one that society would reasonably expect the average person to withstand." *Perka*, 13 D.L.R.4th at 23.

though most people would. Contrarily, a person might be able to choose rationally when most people would not. The inability to choose rationally supports a defense in the former, but not in the latter, case.[24]

C. Absence of Reasonable Alternative

The third ground for a defense of necessity or duress is the lack of a reasonable alternative choice, or lesser evils. Although more closely related to necessity than duress, this ground often underlies the duress defense. For example, we may ask whether the defendant could have avoided the threatened harm without committing the offense. The *Model Penal Code* recognizes the ground in a general choice of evils defense; an act is justifiable if one believes the act is necessary to avoid a harm or evil that is greater than the evil the law sought to prevent.[25] Robinson recognizes this ground as the basis for all justifications and accepts a lesser evils defense.[26] Similarly, Fletcher treats lesser evils as the general basis for justifications.[27] The Law Reform Commission of Canada explicitly recognizes lesser evils as a ground for a necessity defense.[28] The Supreme Court of Canada also claims that the basis of the necessity defense is the fact that "the person had no other viable or reasonable choice available."[29] Finally, Hyman Gross recognizes an interest-based defense when no reasonable alternative exists.[30]

The lack of a reasonable alternative ground is fairly straightforward. If an actor chooses to conform to the law, either great harm will befall the actor or others or some lawful purpose will not be significantly advanced. If the actor performs a prohibited act, either no harm or a lesser harm will result or a lawful purpose will be significantly advanced. In short, the net value of violating the law is significantly greater than that of conformity. Although conformity to the law can include a variety of acts, no plausible lawful alternative will achieve the net value of breaking the law. The "lesser evils" title is not quite appropriate for this ground because, at least in some formulations, conformity to the law might

---

[24]Similarly, the insanity defense is not restricted to those who have average susceptibility to mental disease or defect. Persons genetically susceptible to schizophrenia are entitled to the insanity defense.

[25]MODEL PENAL CODE §3.02(1).

[26]1 & 2 P. ROBINSON, *supra* note 8, §§24(b), 124(a).

[27]G. FLETCHER, *supra* note 23, at 774-98.

[28]L.R.C.C., CRIMINAL LAW, *supra* note 8, at 93, 96.

[29]*Perka*, 13 D.L.R. 4th at 15.

[30]H. GROSS, *supra* note 20, at 170-72, 280.

involve only a failure to further some good, and not involve evil at all. A better term would be choice of values.

The crux of the ground is that although the conduct by definition constitutes an offense and the person has the ability to choose otherwise, the alternatives are not reasonable given the values affected. To return to Aristotle's example, throwing cargo overboard in a storm to save the ship and crew should be a defense to a charge of criminal mischief. Absent any alternative means to save the ship, permitting the ship, cargo, and crew to go down would not be a reasonable alternative to jettisoning the cargo. Although the act meets the definition of an offense, no reasonable alternative exists given the values involved.

D. Confusing the Grounds

Although the absence of a reasonable alternative differs from the inability to choose, the two are often confused. For example, after giving both grounds, the Law Reform Commission of Canada defined the defense of necessity as acting to avoid an immediate harm that is greater than that resulting from the offense and that could not have been avoided by actions causing lesser harm.[31] This definition does not assume an inability to choose rationally; rather, it assumes a highly rational choice.

In a recent case on the necessity defense, the Supreme Court of Canada also confused the two grounds.[32] The case was similar to Aristotle's classic example of jettisoning cargo to save a ship. A ship with a cargo of marijuana near Canada's Pacific coast was headed for Alaska. The ship developed problems, landed on Canadian shores, and unloaded its cargo to facilitate repairs. The defendants raised the necessity defense to charges of importing narcotics and possession for the purpose of trafficking. In discussing the necessity defense, Chief Justice Dickson frequently made reference to "normal human instincts" and whether a person could be expected to withstand the pressure,[33] which suggests the inability to choose rationally. However, he also stated that the defense rests on the absence of a reasonable legal alternative.[34] On this latter ground, the defendant could have jettisoned the cargo at sea and avoided the illegal importation.

Even able commentators have difficulty distinguishing the absence of a reasonable alternative from the inability choose. Gross comments that

---

[31]L.R.C.C., REPORT, *supra* note 8, at 33; L.R.C.C., CRIMINAL LAW, *supra* note 8, at 94, 96.
[32]*Perka*, 13 D.L.R.4th 1.
[33]*Id.* at 14-15.
[34]*Id.* at 15, 17, 22.

one might be fully in control and yet lack an opportunity to choose rationally.[35] He illustrates the point with the example of two mountain climbers who have fallen and are being held by a rope. The rope is frayed and will not hold both climbers for long, so the upper climber cuts the rope letting the other climber fall to his death. Gross believes that the climber's lack of alternative is an excuse.[36] According to Gross, this lack of alternative differs from the interest-regarding ground in which the climber selects the only reasonable alternative. Gross' example of this ground again involves the two climbers, but in this instance the rope is not frayed. To save both climbers, the upper climber must swing onto a rock ledge and gain a hold; but since the rope's attachment is precarious, it is likely to pull free. In this case, Gross argues that the climber does have an alternative.[37]

Gross states that the lack of an alternative will excuse, but he fails adequately to distinguish between no alternative, no reasonable alternative, and no time to rationally consider the alternatives. In the first situation, there are two alternatives: (1) cut the second climber loose; or (2) try to pull both climbers up hoping that the frayed rope does not snap. If Gross did not contemplate the second alternative, he left the first climber dangling into eternity. The first climber must have had some way to get back after cutting the second one loose, and that same method might have been possible for both climbers despite the frayed rope. In Gross' second case, there are three alternatives: (1) cut the second climber loose; (2) swing onto the ledge; or (3) try to pull up both climbers. Perhaps the best interpretation is that, given the circumstances in the first case, the climber did not consider the second alternative; whereas, in the second case, the climber considered the alternatives and made the only reasonable choice. The difference in circumstances, however, is irrelevant. The critical concern is the thought processes of the individual, which could differ between two different persons under any set of circumstances.

III. THE ABSENCE OF A REASONABLE ALTERNATIVE DEFENSE

This section examines the parameters of a defense grounded solely on the absence of a reasonable alternative choice. This defense should provide a justification when conduct that constitutes an offense has significantly more net value, including less net harm, than any available alternative.

The protected interests should not be restricted to those of the actor

---

[35]H. GROSS, *supra* note 20, at 279.

[36]*Id.*

[37]*Id.* at 280.

or those under the actor's protection. The danger of the lesser value need not be imminent nor immediate, although usually the actor must wait until it is clear that no reasonable alternative exists. The defense should apply whether the absence of a reasonable alternative is due to natural forces or human threats. Moreover, absence of a reasonable alternative may be a defense to homicide, at least if more lives are saved than are taken. Logically, the defense should not apply to taking one life to save another, although such conduct is often permissible and punishment is an inadequate deterrence. The defense should also apply regardless of whether the actor was reckless or careless in getting into the situation that leaves him with no reasonable alternative, although the actor may be liable for any offenses committed that lead to such a situation. An actor's personal interests should sometimes be discounted in determining whether alternatives are reasonable.

A. Interests Included

The absence of a reasonable alternative defense involves a comparison of the values or interests affected by alternative choices and acts. The net value of committing the offense[38] must be significantly greater than that of the lawful act. The values to be used are those of society, not those of the actor.[39] In calculating the net value of available alternatives, one must consider all possible resultant harms and benefits and their probabilities. The *Model Penal Code* choice of evils defense is formulated in terms of the harm or evil "sought to be prevented by the law defining the offense charged."[40] This formulation is unclear sincc it could mean the type of harm generally prevented by the offense or the harm at stake in the particular instance. The latter could be more or less than the usual harm resulting from such offenses. The appropriate issue is the net value that is likely to result from the particular act.[41]

The *Model Penal Code* formulation is also limited to avoiding harms, but the logic of no reasonable alternative permits furthering interests. Perhaps no harm would result from a lawful act, but an opportunity to achieve a great good might be forgone. Thus, the definition

---

[38]The term offense is used even though the defense is premised on the idea that the act is not wrongful and thus not an offense.

[39]*See* 3 J. FEINBERG, *supra* note 11, at 209-11.

[40]MODEL PENAL CODE §3.02(1)(a).

[41]2 P. ROBINSON, *supra* note 8, §124(g)(1); *see* L.R.C.C., CRIMINAL LAW, *supra* note 8, at 96-97 ("harm resulting from that offence").

of the defense should include the opportunity to further lawful interests.[42]

This reasoning is potentially objectionable because this inclusion may be too broad. For example, the inclusion would encompass a hungry person stealing food[43] or a homeless person occupying an abandoned building[44] because the resulting good outweighs the harm caused. Seeking food and seeking shelter are lawful, justifiable interests. Although an interest in taking property from another is arguably unlawful, a similar claim might be made about the interest involved in any offense. For example, setting a backfire in another's field to prevent the spread of a fire to a town may be justifiable although setting fire to another's field is not a lawful or justifiable interest. Thus, it may be best to restrict the value analysis to avoidance of harms.

Nonetheless, such a restriction confronts difficulties. Rescue cases involve both benefits and harms. For example, if Anderson is stricken by a heart attack and Bennett, with an expired operator's license, drives Anderson to the hospital, has Bennett furthered Anderson's interest in life or prevented harm?[45] Such conduct should not be excluded from the absence of a reasonable alternative defense. Yet, the same analysis is applicable to stealing food or occupying an abandoned house.

The best approach is to rely on the analysis of the alternatives. In today's society, individuals can usually obtain food and shelter from government programs or charities, and begging is a last resort. Such alternatives may not be available for Anderson. Moreover, when furthering interests is involved, there must be sufficient difference in value so that compliance with the law is unreasonable. The trier of fact can decide the issue of reasonableness in light of community values, a standard function of juries and judges.

Some versions of duress or a combination of duress and necessity limit the interests that can be protected to those of the actor and persons under the actor's protection.[46] The logic of choosing the greater of two values does not require such a limitation. Moreover, unless we take a broad view of persons for whom the actor is responsible, the defense would not include those engaged in a joint enterprise of the actions of a concerned neighbor, such as Bennett driving the stricken Anderson to the

---

[42]*See* 2 P. ROBINSON, *supra* note 8, §124(a).

[43]*See* State v. Moe, 174 Wash. 303, 24 P.2d 638 (1933).

[44]*See* Southwark L.B.C. v. Williams, [1971] 2 All E.R. 175 (C.A.).

[45]*See* Bayles, Book Review, 4 LAW & PHIL. 424 (1985).

[46]L.R.C.C., CRIMINAL LAW, *supra* note 8, at 87 (duress); *see also* G. FLETCHER, *supra* note 23, at 833 (German code defense combining duress and necessity). *But see* L.R.C.C., REPORT, *supra* note 8, at 32 (dropping requirement that persons be under actor's protection.)

hospital. Perhaps the only reason for such a restriction is to reduce the chances of mistake, but that should be considered under principles of mistake. No special restriction is needed.

B. Imminence of Danger

Defenses of necessity and duress often require imminent danger, but imminence is not necessary for absence of a reasonable alternative. According to Fletcher, an imminence requirement is necessary to restrict the actor's choice of the time, place, or victim of the act.[47] Robinson, however, contends that the imminence requirement is unnecessary because the requirement that the act be necessary to avoid harm sufficiently limits the defense.[48] Fletcher, however, does admit some choice. For example, a person trapped by a snow storm may have to break into one of several unoccupied cabins. The alternative of not breaking in is not reasonable under the circumstances. However, there is a choice among the several cabins and victims, the cabin owners.

The question is why there should be a limit on the actor's choice of the time, place, or victim of his act. Ordinarily, choice of time is not within the actor's discretion since he must wait until the last minute to be certain that no reasonable alternative exists.[49] The choice of place and victim, however, is often left to the actor, at least within a circumscribed number, as in the choice of cabins. Yet, the logic of the defense sometimes provides further limits than those due to timing. For example, Rabbinic law permitted a group of women to hand over one woman to hostile forces for defilement.[50] The circumstances required that a choice be made, and the law permitted handing over a prostitute or concubine. A victim had to be chosen, albeit from a limited number--the women in the group. The choice of a prostitute or concubine probably seemed a reasonable choice of the lesser evil. Constraints on choice are sometimes imposed by the competing values of alternatives.[51]

C. Source of Threat

The logic of no reasonable alternative does not provide a basis for distinguishing between situations caused by threats--duress, and those

---

[47]G. FLETCHER, *supra* note 23, at 795.

[48]2 P. ROBINSON, *supra* note 8, §124(f)(1).

[49]W. LAFAVE & A. SCOTT, HANDBOOK ON CRIMINAL LAW 379, 388 (1972).

[50]A. DONAGAN, THE THEORY OF MORALITY 182 (1977).

[51]*See also* 2 P. ROBINSON, *supra* note 8, §124(g)(5)(E).

caused by natural forces--necessity.[52] If the offense has significantly greater net value than the alternatives, it makes no difference why it does. The only considerations are the alternative choices and their value consequences. Consequently, both the *Model Penal Code* and Robinson reject the source of the constraint as irrelevant.[53]

Although the Law Reform Commission of Canada recognizes that both necessity and duress are based on a concept of necessity, it distinguished them by the source of the danger.[54] The Commission rationalizes the distinction of two bases--common law tradition and moral difference. Although common law tradition may have practical advantages in some contexts, it can be rejected here, since the purpose of this Article is rational normative analysis. The moral difference rationale distinguishes duress and necessity as follows: In the case of duress, the actor avoids the harm but does not promote a value supported by law; whereas, in the case of necessity, the actor may avoid the harm and promote a value supported by law. Granted, an actor subject to threat by another person is not likely to be asked by that person to perform an act promoting a value supported by law. Nevertheless, the distinction between dangers caused by human or natural forces does not correspond to the distinction between avoiding harms and promoting values. Consequently, any moral difference that exists between the latter does not support distinguishing the former.

Other arguments might be made for distinguishing duress and necessity on the basis of the source of the danger. One might argue that if the constraint arises from a natural source, it is easier to avoid the harm than if the constraint arises from a human source. For example, a human threatener is likely to pursue the threatenee if the latter tries to escape the danger. However, this argument merely shows that human-imposed constraints are likely to be more difficult to avoid, and, therefore, that reasonable alternatives are less likely to be available.

Another argument for using the source of danger to distinguish necessity and duress is that humans may elect not to act on their threats, whereas natural forces operate by the inexorable laws of nature. But this argument also addresses the question of the availability of reasonable alternatives. Consequently, this argument also relates to whether reasonable alternatives, such as escape, are available and should be left to

---

[52]*See* 3 J. FEINBERG, *supra* note 11, at 146-50.

[53]MODEL PENAL CODE §3.02(1); 1 P. ROBINSON, *supra* note 8, §27(b).

[54]L.R.C.C. REPORT, *supra* note 8, at 33 (removes the requirement of a nonhuman source in the definition of the defense of necessity, but the commentary indicates that it is for natural sources or other situations not covered by specific defenses); L.R.C.C., CRIMINAL LAW, *supra* note 8, at 85, 90.

the trier of fact.

D. Justification or Excuse

Other arguments for distinguishing duress from necessity are based upon differences between justification and excuse.[55] Generally, justifications admit that conduct satisfies the definition of an offense but the conduct is not wrongful since such conduct is justifiable in the totality of circumstances. Justifications focus on acts. Thus, if an act is justifiable for one person, it is justifiable for anyone else in the same circumstances. For example, the justification of self-defense is available to all actors in the same circumstances.

Excuses, on the other hand, admit that an actor's conduct is wrongful but we can not properly hold the actor responsible for his behavior. Excuses focus on the actor. If conduct is excusable, only the particular person is excused. For example, an insanity defense is not available to all actors in similar circumstances.

The absence of a reasonable alternative implies that conduct is at least permissive because it produces greater net value than any alternative. Prohibiting the conduct would not prevent net harm. The argument addresses the rightness and wrongness of the act, not the responsibility of the individual. Thus, absence of a reasonable alternative should be treated as a justification.

Fletcher contends that while necessity is a justification, duress must be an excuse.[56] His reasoning hinges on the several undesirable consequences that would result if duress was a justification. First, one would never be justified in resisting a person coerced into action. Justified conduct is lawful and, therefore, resistance is inappropriate.[57] For example, if Collins is coerced into robbing a bank, the bank teller and guard would not be justified in resisting Collins. Second, others would be justified in assisting Collins. And third, those coercing Collins might not be guilty as accessories because one cannot be guilty as an accessory to justifiable conduct.

However these arguments are not persuasive. First, justification does not necessarily establish the inappropriateness of resistance or interference. Justification shows only that conduct is not wrongful and that one has no duty to refrain from engaging in such conduct. The sole

---

[55] *See* G. FLETCHER, *supra* note 23, at 759; 1 P. ROBINSON, *supra* note 8, §21.

[56] G. FLETCHER, *supra* note 23, at 830.

[57] *See* 2 P. ROBINSON, *supra* note 8, §121(d).

conclusion is that the conduct is permissible.[58] For resistance to be wrong, the conduct must be more than permissible; others must also have a correlative duty not to interfere.

Two arguments might be raised for the wrongness of interference with justifiable conduct. First, if justification is based on the absence of reasonable alternatives, then a justified actor is producing more net value in his activity than in any alternative act. Consequently, resistance would produce less net value and be wrong. However, this argument assumes that it is always wrong to reduce net value. Such a proposal is disputed in ethics and not supported in law. Second, people have a general duty not to interfere forcibly with persons engaged in permissible conduct. Although some interference might be justifiable, forcible interference is not.

Even conceding this second argument, the consequences Fletcher predicts are not disastrous. Indeed, they appear appropriate. For example, Collins may be saving lives by robbing the bank and thus producing the greatest net value. It would therefore be appropriate to assist him and wrong to interfere unless one could prevent the harm Collins is try to avoid.[59] Police do not usually intervene in such situations unless they anticipate a reasonable chance of saving lives. However, the bank employees have no way of knowing that Collins is being coerced; they reasonably believe that he is engaged in an ordinary robbery. Thus, they have reasonable grounds for resistance. Finally, as Fletcher partially admits,[60] the argument fails because we can hold the coercers guilty as principals operating through wholly innocent parties. The *Model Penal Code* provides that one is criminally liable for causing "an innocent or irresponsible person" to engage in unlawful conduct.[61] Consequently, it is not necessary to treat the absence of a reasonable alternative due to human threats as an excuse rather than a justification.

E. Homicide

Another issue is whether the absence of a reasonable alternative, or lesser evils, will not justify certain harms or evils, such as killing a human being. The absence of a reasonable alternative justifies killing one person to save two or more persons. It does not normally justify killing one person to save another, even oneself. Except for the uncertainty of the threat being fulfilled, the values are balanced and one alternative is no more reasonable

---

[58] *See* Bickenbach, *The Defence of Necessity*, 13 CAN. J. PHIL. 88, 92, 94 (1983).
[59] 3 J. FEINBERG, *supra* note 11, at 154-55.
[60] G. FLETCHER, *supra* note 23, at 830 n.63.
[61] MODEL PENAL CODE §2.06(2)(a); *see* W. LAFAVE & A. SCOTT, *supra* note 49, at 380.

than the other. Morally, however, either alternative is permissible. In light of the ineffectiveness of deterrence in such a situation, the defense should arguably include this situation.[62] However, since the inability to choose rationally defense would also cover many such cases, it is preferable to maintain the narrow scope of the lesser evils defense.

The law is ambiguous about a necessity defense for killing. Necessity should, of course, be a defense when the alternative is between one death and many deaths. For example, diverting a runaway train from a track where it will kill many to a track where it will kill only one person is justifiable. However, other cases are less clear.

Two classic necessity cases involved killing. In *The Queen v. Dudley*,[63] three sailors and a cabin boy had been in a lifeboat for twenty days without food and water following a shipwreck. Two of the sailors killed the weakened cabin boy and ate his body to stay alive. They were rescued four days later. The court rejected the defense of necessity.

In the *United States V. Holmes*,[64] another shipwreck case, several crew members and a number of passengers were in one lifeboat. Because the overcrowded boat was unlikely to survive an oncoming storm, the crew threw several male passengers overboard. While the court did not directly reject the defense of necessity, the judge instructed the jury that the crew had a duty to the passengers to sacrifice themselves first, except for those crew members necessary to operate the boat, and then lots should have been drawn among the passengers. The lack of a reasonable alternative warranted some method of selecting who would be sacrificed. The judge noted it would have been unreasonable to sacrifice all the crew members.[65]

Traditionally, duress has not been recognized as a defense to murder and other serious crimes.[66] However, in an extensive review of American cases, Hall did not find a single case involving a clear choice between self-sacrifice and the death of an innocent person in which the court rejected duress as a defense.[67] Two recent British cases indicate that duress may be a defense to murder. In *Director of Public Prosecutions v.*

---

[62]One might still object that taking an innocent life is morally worse than permitting oneself to be killed, because one is the causal agent of harm. I have considered this objection in another context. *See* Bayles, *A Problem of Clean Hands; Refusal to Provide Professional Services*, 5 SOC. THEORY & PRAC. 165 (1979).

[63]14 Q.B.D. 273 (1884).

[64]26 F. Cas. 360 (E.D. Pa. 1842) (No. 15,383).

[65]*Cf.* 2 P. ROBINSON, *supra* note 8, §124(g)(5)(E).

[66]J. HALL, *supra* note 2, at 439; W. LAFAVE & A. SCOTT, *supra* note 49, at 376.

[67]J. HALL, *supra* note 2, at 440.

Lynch,[68] Irish Republican Army members threatened to kill Lynch, a fellow member, if he did not drive a getaway car for a murder. Lynch was tried as an accessory, a principal in the second degree. The court permitted a defense of duress. In *Abbott v. The Queen*,[69] Abbott held the victim's arms while others stabbed the victim. Abbott was tried as a principal in the first degree in the homicide. He contended he had been threatened by a notorious killer, but the court rejected the duress defense. Thus, with regard to homicide, British law permits a duress defense for accessories, principals in the second degree, but not for principals in the first degree.

The *Lynch* and *Abbott* decisions have provoked criticism. Lord Kilbrandon, who was in the minority in Lynch and the majority in Abbott, contends that the distinction between principal in the first degree and principal in the second degree, or accessory, is too fine a distinction on which to base the availability of the duress defense.[70] He would prefer to permit the duress defense for both charges, but only as a mitigating factor rather than as a complete defense.[71] Anthony Kenny agrees that the current law is unsatisfactory, but rejects duress, and perhaps necessity as well, as a defense for either a principal or an accessory to murder.[72]

As an objection to full exculpation, both Kilbrandon and Kenny raise the issue of how many persons one can kill to save one's life.[73] However, the absence of a reasonable alternative defense solves this problem. Killing many to save one would not be the alternative producing the greatest value. However, the objection could be modified to a series of killings. For example, Davis may be threatened by terrorists and therefore kill one person. If he uses the threat as a successful defense, then the terrorists, knowing that he is susceptible to duress, might again threaten him to kill another person. By this process, several lives may be lost to save one.

The absence of a reasonable alternative does not necessarily justify killing to save a single life, even one's own. The evils are balanced, so one alternative is a reasonable as the other. Indeed, given a chance that the threat to take one's life might not be carried out, it might even be more reasonable to refuse to kill another. This would not be true if the threat was

---

[68]1975 A.C. 653 (H.L.).

[69]1977 A.C. 755 (P.C.).

[70]Kilbrandon, *Duress per* Minas *as a Defence to Crime*: I, 1 LAW & PHIL. 185, 191-92 (1982).

[71]*Id.*

[72]Kenny, *Duress per* Minas *as a Defence to Crime*: *I*, 1 LAW & PHIL. 197, 200, 202-203 (1982).

[73]Kenny, *supra* note 72, at 200 (approving an argument by Lord Salmon); Kilbrandon, *supra* note 70, at 191.

that unless one killed the other person, both would be killed. In any case, after two such murders coerced through duress, the police should increase its protection to the coerced killer to avoid the recurrence of the situation.

Kenny presents another argument against permitting necessity or duress as a defense to murder. He contends that although resisting duress by refraining from homicide might call for heroism in some circumstances, it does not follow that it is morally permissible not to resist. The only available action might require heroism in sacrificing one's life since the absence of a reasonable alternative does not justify taking one life to save another, even one's own.[74] Kenny concludes that taking an innocent life is wicked. This is not a necessary conclusion because the fact that resisting duress might require heroism does not imply anything about the permissibility of alternatives. It does not follow that killing an innocent person is morally wrong if the evils are balanced. Indeed, any reasonable alternative seems morally permissible. Finally, Kenny carefully restricts his objections to the duress defense to the taking of one life for another. Consequently, none of these arguments against a defense of duress for homicide applies to the absence of a reasonable alternative defense.[75]

F. Lesser Offenses

One commentator also urges that duress should not even be a defense against lesser crimes.[76] He argues that the duress defense encourages criminals to sue coercion, especially to get witnesses to commit perjury. Perjury strikes at the root of the administration of justice, and witnesses who are caught in their own lies may easily manufacture evidence of coercion.

---

[74]Kenny, *supra* note 72, at 203.

[75]Kenny also argues against the claim that punishment in such cases will not deter. The logic, he suggests, is to increase the punishment, although he does not support this solution for humanitarian reasons. *Id.* at 204. Nevertheless, he thinks humanity towards victims supports not mitigating the punishment. The defense of no reasonable alternative does not rest on the inability to deter; therefore, this argument is irrelevant to that defense. Moreover, Kenny's argument assumes the conclusion of his previous argument, namely, that it is wicked or morally wrong to kill another to save one's life. Otherwise, there would be no point in deterring the conduct. But the previous argument is not valid. Furthermore, if imminent death is the ultimate evil for a person, the only way to obtain a legal threat to overcome it would be to punish the person's loved ones also, but that would clearly be wrong. *Id.* at 205. Finally, the argument basically supports punishing victims of coercion to deter coercers, which can hardly be a recommendation of justice. Baker, *Duress, Responsibility, and Deterrence*, 24 DIALOGUE 605, 611 (1985).

[76]Anton, *Duress per* Minas *as a Defence to Crime: III*, 1 LAW & PHIL. 207, 210 (1982).

This argument is unconvincing. Although perjury can cause significant harm, such as the conviction of an innocent person, this does not always occur. Moreover, to determine whether perjury was a reasonable alternative, the harm caused by perjury in a particular case must be balanced against the harm threatened. The courts may apply the same standard of availability of a reasonable alternative to evaluate duress whether the defendant is accused of homicide or perjury.

One further consideration is relevant to allowing the absence of a reasonable alternative defense to both homicide and other offenses. The defense always requires that the available alternatives involve less net value so as not to be reasonable alternatives. However, the more serious the harm caused, the greater the difference there must be between such harm and the harm avoided to render the latter an unreasonable alternative.[77] Thus, the difference between the threat and harm caused must be greater for perjury leading to the conviction of an innocent person than for perjury exculpating a guilty person.

G. Responsibility for Situation

The last issue to be considered is whether the absence of a reasonable alternative defense should be available when the actor was responsible for getting into the situation. Some statutory formulations bar the defenses of necessity and duress if the defendant was at fault in getting into the situation.[78] Gross supports restricting the defense in such cases, arguing that if an actor was reckless or careless in getting into the situation, then the actor should not be able to violate the interests of others to protect his interests.[79] Although, it need not always be the actor's interests that are in jeopardy, such interests should be weighed as the actor weighs them in determining the reasonableness of alternatives. That is, the actor's interests can be discounted if the actor gave them little weight or was reckless or careless about them.

Robinson argues that it is sufficient to hold the actor liable for any offense committed while getting into the situation.[80] If the actor ignores risks to others, he could be held liable for reckless endangerment. For

---

[77]*See* 3 J. FEINBERG, *supra* note 510, at 158, 209.

[78]*See* W. LAFAVE & A. SCOTT, *supra* note 49, at 376; *cf.* MODEL PENAL CODE §§2.09(2), 3.02(2) (reckless or negligent behavior no defense to offenses requiring only those degrees of culpability).

[79]H. GROSS, *supra* note 20, at 171, 285.

[80]2 P. ROBINSON, *supra* note 8, §123 (c); *see also Perka,* 13 D.L.R.4th at 19; W. LAFAVE & A. SCOTT, *supra* note 49, at 388.

example, such liability would cover a "grand schemer" who sets a fire so that he may set a backfire on his enemy's property to save a town. While setting the backfire is justified, the actor is liable for setting the original fire with the intent of burning his enemy's property. Not to allow the defense when the actor is careless or reckless in getting into the situation discourages him from taking appropriate action to minimize harm.[81]

IV. The Inability to Choose Rationally Defense

This section considers a defense based on the inability to choose rationally due to fear of lack of time. Formulations of the duress defense may contain elements based on the inability to choose rationally, but none rests exclusively on the ground. Robinson comes closest in proposing that persons be excused if, faced with a coercive threat that a person of reasonable firmness would not have resisted, they lacked sufficient control of their conduct to be held accountable.[82] Robinson's proposal differs, however, in several respects from a defense based exclusively on the inability to choose rationally. It focuses on the inability to control one's conduct rather than the inability to choose rationally. Although the inability to choose rationally deprives one of control, not all loss of control involves the loss of ability to choose. For example, loss of control might merely involve the inability to make the choice effective. Robinson's proposal also does not fully consider the inability to choose due to lack of time. A person who reacts quickly to an immediate threat still has control of his physical movements.

A defense should be recognized when, due to lack of time or overwhelming fear, a person is unable to choose rationally, regardless of whether a person of reasonable firmness would have been able to do so. Common limitations of the defense of duress deny the defense to persons who are unable to choose rationally. Since the inability to choose renders a person not responsible for conduct, this violates the fundamental principle that one should not be criminally liable for conduct for which one is not responsible. Most of the usual limitations involve situations for the trier of fact to consider in deciding whether a person was actually unable to choose rationally.

The difficulty of distinguishing between a person unable to choose rationally and a person who must make a greater effort to do so creates a practical problem. Traditional limitations on duress attempt to avoid the difficulty by providing objective criteria. The proposed solution is to treat a

---

[81] G. Fletcher, *supra* note 23, at 797.

[82] 2 P. Robinson, *supra* note 8, §177a.

defense based on inability to choose rationally as mitigating rather than excusing. This solution reduces the problem of distinguishing between those unable to choose rationally and those whom it is simply difficult. This proposal reaches beyond the strict logic of the inability to choose rationally ground, but leaves the question of responsibility in the hands of the trier of fact to reflect community views.

A. Reasonable Firmness

A central issue involving the inability to choose rationally is whether the defense should be available only if a person of reasonable firmness would not be able to resist the threat. The logic of the defense does not support this condition, for whatever others might have been able to do, the individual in question was not able to choose rationally and thus was not responsible. Such a limitation imports an objective standard not usually present in criminal liability.[83]

An argument is that the limitation is required to ensure that the defendant was unable to choose rationally. Whether a person was able to choose rationally is largely determined by the imminence and severity of the threat. It is difficult for a defendant to convince the trier of fact that he was unable to choose rationally in the face of a minimal threat. We need not make it impossible, in principle, for such proof to be offered by imposing an objective standard.

A similar but distinct approach is discussed by Fletcher. Fletcher proposes that the test should be whether an actor can fairly be expected to take the risk.[84] The merit of this approach is that it sets a higher standard for individuals in roles such as police officers or soldiers. For example, if both an ordinary citizen and a police officer were held hostage by terrorists, the defense might be available to the citizen but not the officer. On policy grounds this might seem desirable, however, it does not fit the inability to choose rationale. The rationale is that the actor is not responsible because he is unable to choose. That a police officer should have been able to choose rationally, rather than be overcome by fear, does

---

[83]Frequently, a person of reasonable or ordinary firmness would not have resisted because it would have been unreasonable to do so, that is, no reasonable alternative existed. A justification based on the absence of a reasonable alternative should be available. However, a reasonable alternative might exist but the ordinary person is too terrified to attempt it. Therefore, even limited to what ordinary persons could resist, an inability to choose rationally defense differs from the absence of a reasonable alternative defense.

[84]G. FLETCHER, *supra* note 23, at 833 (German code); *see also Perka*, 13 D.L.R. 4th at 22 ("society's expectation of *appropriate* and normal resistance to pressure") (emphasis added).

not make the officer a responsible actor.[85]

B. Limitations Rejected

1. Interests Threatened

The inability to choose rationally defense might also be limited by the type of interests that are threatened. There is no reason for such a limitation. It does not matter what the fear is if it negates the ability to choose rationally. The defense of duress is often limited to oneself or those under one's protection.[86] Gross suggests that this limitation should be supported because harm to oneself or those under one's protection is "more serious than harm to...a stranger."[87] Gross' claim confuses the strength of a person's interest in avoiding a harm with the seriousness of the harm. One child dying is no more serious than another child dying, but people are more concerned when the child is their own. Alternatively, the claim imports the notion of a greater duty or responsibility to protect oneself and those under one's protection than others. However, the inability to choose defense does not involve weighing relative harms or duties. Such a weighing pertains to the absence of a reasonable alternative. Limiting the defense to threats to oneself or others confuses the grounds of inability to choose and no reasonable alternative. Moreover, it is counterproductive to deny the defense to individuals who care enough for strangers that they lose the ability to choose rationally out of fear for the strangers' welfare. Surely the law should promote, not punish, concern for others.

The duress defense is also commonly limited to threats of death or

---

[85]One might also claim that placing either version of the limitation of the defense would be to require heroism. Some commentators argue that the law should not require heroism. Bickenbach, *supra* note 58, at 86, 92; *see also* H. GROSS, *supra* note 20, at 291-92. However, a defense based on the absence of a reasonable alternative might require a significant sacrifice, perhaps a form of heroism. In any case, the moral heroism argument does not apply to the limitations. Requiring reasonable firmness or what can reasonably be expected is not to require heroism. It is not heroism to act as an ordinary person would or as can reasonably be expected of persons in a role. Ordinary fire fighting by fire officers is not heroism, although some acts go beyond what can reasonably be expected of them and thus are heroic.

[86]W. LAFAVE & A. SCOTT, *supra* note 49, at 376; L.R.C.C., CRIMINAL LAW, *supra* note 8, at 87. *But see* L.R.C.C., REPORT, *supra* note 8, at 32 (eliminates limitation to those under one's protection).

[87]H. GROSS, *supra* note 20, at 284.

bodily harm.[88] This limitation is also unnecessary and contrary to the rationale of the inability to choose rationally ground.[89] For example, Erlanger owns a new Porsche in which she has invested all her savings for a number of years. She values the car highly and takes care to protect it. Two thugs meet her in a deserted parking garage and threaten to smash the Porsche with a sledgehammer unless she reveals the names of two companies for which her law firm is arranging a merger. After one blow to the car, she is overcome with fear and gives them the information. The circumstances seem to be a plausible defense to complicity in securities fraud. The less significant the threat, the more difficult it will be to convince the court of the inability to choose. Consequently, it is unnecessary to restrict the threatened interests that will support the defense.

2. Offenses

An inability to choose rationally defense should be available for any charge, including homicide. If one is lacking the ability to choose rationally, then one is not responsible for one's conduct. The fact that great harm will result will not make the persons more responsible and capable of choosing. The harm caused by perjury will have no effect on a witness overcome by fear. Normally, the defense will only be offered when significant harm occurred. If the defendant's act produced the greatest net value of all the available alternatives, then an absence of a reasonable alternative defense could be offered. Thus, an inability to choose defense to homicide would be raised primarily in cases other than self-defense. Of course, given time to choose, the claim must be that one was overcome by fear. If the particular individual was not so overcome, even this defense will not apply.

3. Source of Threat

Nor does the inability to choose ground require that the defense be restricted to human threats. Thus, it is best not to formulate the defense as involving coercion, as Robinson does,[90] because "coercion" implies a

---

[88]W. LAFAVE & A. SCOTT, *supra* note 49, at 374, 376; L.R.C.C., REPORT, *supra* note 8, at 32 ("serious harm")' L.R.C.C., CRIMINAL LAW, *supra* note 8, at 87 ("serious and immediate bodily harm").

[89]*See* Anton, *supra* note 76, at 211.

[90]2 P. ROBINSON, *supra* note 8, §177(a), (e)(1).

human agent.[91] One might argue that threats from humans are more frightening because they usually are more difficult to avoid.[92] For example, a coercer will make adjustments to carry out a threat when one attempts to escape; whereas, an avalanche can not change directions to stop one's escape. This consideration goes to the probability of danger and is more appropriate for a defense based on the absence of a reasonable alternative. It might be relevant to whether a persons was actually overcome by fear, but it is irrelevant when the inability to choose is due to lack of time.

4. Imminence of Harm

Similar considerations apply to a limitation of imminent harm. Obviously, imminence is relevant to an inability to choose rationally due to lack of time. In addition, the more imminent the danger, the more likely a person is to be overcome by fear. Nevertheless, fear of a nonimminent disaster can overcome a person's capacity to choose rationally. An example is an individual verging on irrationality from fear of nuclear war or nuclear power plants, although the danger is not imminent. [93]

5. Responsibility for Situation

Similarly, the defense should not necessarily be limited to cases in which the actor was not at fault for getting into the situation.[94] As with the absence of reasonable alternative justification, one may be liable for any crime one commits in getting into the situation. One factor, however, differs. For example, suppose Faherty knows that he has a great fear of snakes. If he goes camping in the woods, sees a poisonous snake, and sets the woods on fire to kill it, then a defense of inability to choose due to fear of snakes seems unacceptable. This example is similar to the violent drunk who should know better than to drink too much. The best approach to intoxication as a defense is debatable, but most scholars agree that a persons prone to violence when drunk should be liable for getting drunk and being violent. The same rationale should apply to Faherty.

C. Excuse or Mitigation

---

[91]M. BAYLES, PRINCIPLES OF LEGISLATION 19 (1978); Bayles, *A Concept of Coercion*, in COERCION: NOMOS XIV 19-20 (J. Pennock & J. Chapman eds. 1972).

[92]H. GROSS, *supra* note 20, at 290.

[93]*See* State v. Warshow, 138 Vt. 22, 410 A.2d 1000 (1979).

[94]*See* Anton, *supra* note 76, at 211-12.

The inability to choose rationally exculpates a person from responsibility. A fundamental principle of criminal law is not to hold liable or punish a person who is not responsible for his conduct. Consequently, the inability to choose rationally should logically provide an excuse. However, it is difficult to determine when someone is overcome by fear. The difficulty is analogous to determining whether, under an insanity defense control tests, people could not control either conduct or simply did not do so. However, most successful insanity defense claims require a showing of a continuing disease or defect. No continuing mental disability is likely with an inability to choose due to danger defense.[95]

The question then becomes how one can avoid allowing a defense based on spurious claims of inability to choose. Most of the suggested limitations on duress function to prevent duress claims. Restricting a defense to threats that a person of reasonable firmness would not have resisted, threats to oneself or those under one's protection, threats of death or serious bodily injury, human threats, and imminent threats, each make it more likely that a person was in fact overcome by fear. Although actual inability to choose should be left to the trier of fact, this provides less protection against spurious claims.

Instead of limiting the defense, one may view claims of duress as mitigating rather than completely exculpating the offense or punishment.[96] In this respect, the inability to choose rationally due to fear is analogous to provocation that reduces a charge of murder to manslaughter. With provocation, the powerful emotion is anger; with duress or inability to choose rationally, the powerful emotion is fear. A defense of provocation requires four elements: first, a reasonable provocation must have existed; second, the defendant must have actually been provoked; third, insufficient time must have elapsed between the provocation and offense so that a reasonable person would not have cooled off; and fourth, the defendant must not have cooled off in fact.[97] The usual duress defense parallels these features. There must be a threat that a person of reasonable firmness would not have resisted, one must have had fear and not controlled it, and the danger must have been imminent.

---

[95]*See* 2 P. ROBINSON, *supra* note 8, §177(c)(1). Robinson incorrectly suggests a state or coercion as a disability that vanishes. A state of coercion, even coercion to which people of reasonable firmness would succumb, need not be a disability. As Robinson recognizes, not everyone will be disabled by such coercive threats; rather, uncontrollable fear is the disability. *Id.* §177(d).

[96]*See* BAKER, *supra* note 75, at 609-10.

[97]W. LAFAVE & A. SCOTT, *supra* note 49, at 573.

Lord Kilbrandon has analyzed the effect of duress as "weakening the resolution" to refrain from an act one would not otherwise have performed.[98] This analysis is applicable in most cases. Some will be completely unable to choose rationally, and others only less able to choose rationally. The strict logic behind both the inability to choose rationale completely excuses the former, and not the latter. Treating the inability to choose as mitigation gives weight to the latter and avoids the nearly impossible task of determining whether the actor in fact could have chosen rationally. Moreover, as a mitigating factor only, the defense will not significantly weaken the general deterrence effect of the law.[99] Given that the conduct was wrong, condemnation of the conduct is appropriate.

One could implement an inability to choose defense as mitigating several ways. For example, provocation reduces a charge. Frequently there is a lesser offense to which a charge can be reduced. However, reducing the charge might change the requisite elements of an offense and make conviction easier. Alternatively, one might simply reduce the penalty. For example, assuming attempts are punished less than completed offenses, the penalty could be limited to that for an attempt of the offense. The court can vary the amount of punishment in accordance with the likelihood that a persons could not choose rationally or the difficulty of doing so. If the court is convinced that a defendant could not have chosen rationally, it may merely impose a minimal probation or no punishment.

V. Utilitarianism and mistakes

A utilitarian concern with the deterrence effect of criminal law requires modifications of the strict logic behind both the inability to choose rationally and absence of reasonable alternative defenses. One modification is to treat a defense of inability to choose rationally as mitigating rather than excusing. Another is to restrict mistakes about the absence of reasonable alternatives to objectively reasonable mistakes. Finally, even if no reasonable alternative in fact existed, the defense should not be available unless the defendant reasonably believed that no alternative existed.

A. Utilitarian Concerns

The traditional utilitarian argument for excuses is the pointlessness of

[98]Kilbrandon, *supra* note 70, at 193.

[99]*See* Anton, *supra* note 76, at 211; Baker, *supra* note 75, at 610.

punishing particular offenders.[100] For example, some scholars argue that punishment will not deter people who act from necessity to save their own lives. However, as several commentators have pointed out,[101] while punishment might not deter the individual or individuals in similar situations, it might increase general deterrence. The ground of involuntary behavior, no reasonable alternative, and inability to choose rationally focus on individual behavior. From a more general perspective, the admission of broad defenses on these grounds might weaken the general deterrence of the criminal law. Perhaps due to such utilitarian concerns, courts have usually restrictively interpreted and applied the defense of necessity and duress.[102]

The argument that an inability to choose rationally defense should be treated as mitigating rather than excusing appeals to utilitarian concerns. The argument does not depend strictly on the implications of the inability to choose rationally ground, but includes concerns about the utility of a rule recognizing an excuse. These concerns include the questionable accuracy of judgments regarding the inability to choose and the effect on the denunciatory force of law and general deterrence.

Utilitarian concerns differ for the absence of a reasonable alternative defense. The availability of reasonable alternatives focuses on the circumstances of the crime rather than the defendant's mental condition.[103] Moreover, as this defense is a justification, utility would be promoted if people acted on the defense, because in each case the greater value would be chosen. Acts with no reasonable alternative are always rational and utility-maximizing. On the other hand, acts for which a defense of inability to choose rationally is available do not necessarily produce the greater value or promote utility. In short, if everyone acted to choose the greater value, or lesser evil, utility would be increased. One cannot make this claim about conduct resulting from an inability to choose rationally.

However, if the actor mistakenly believes that no reasonable alternative exists, the conduct does not produce the greater value or lesser evil. Hence, if the defense is permitted even when people are mistaken about the absence of a reasonable alternative, utility will be decreased. The treatment of mistakes regarding the existence of the justifying

[100] J. BENTHAM, *supra* note 16, at 171.

[101] G. FLETCHER, *supra* note 23, at 914-17; H.L.A. HART, *supra* note 21, at 43.

[102] Bickenbach, *supra* note 58, at 89.

[103] Absence of a reasonable alternative due to threats by others requires consideration of the likelihood of the coercer fulfilling the threats, and this requires consideration of the coercer's mental state.

circumstances thus becomes important. The issue is whether mistakes must be reasonable or merely sincere.

Whereas commentators recommend that mistakes must be reasonable,[104] penal codes often permit a necessity defense involving only a sincere mistake.[105] Requiring mistakes about the absence of a reasonable alternative to be reasonable stems directly from the underlying ground. The objective is to maximize value, or at least minimize losses. Permitting unreasonable conduct does not promote this objective. Consequently, the absence of a reasonable alternative ground supports a requirement that mistakes be reasonable.

Another argument for requiring reasonable mistakes about the absence of a reasonable alternative is suggested by Fletcher. He states that furthering a greater interest over a lesser interest is too broad a formulation for a defense, because it would leave to individual citizens the legislature's task of balancing competing interests.[106] One might thus view the absence of a reasonable alternative defense as permitting citizens to substitute their judgments for those of the legislature.[107] To allow citizens to substitute their judgments, no matter how unreasonable, for those of the legislature is incompatible with the function of law and the democratic process.

In addition, permitting unreasonable mistakes to exculpate might result in confusing grounds for defenses. Under the inability to choose or involuntary behavior ground, reasonableness is not at issue. If behavior is involuntary, the actor is not responsible--he could not have done otherwise even if he had so chosen--and thus mistake is irrelevant. An actor unable to choose rationally is also not responsible for his act. The unreasonableness of fear does not make an actor more capable of choosing. Similarly, requiring a reasonable response to duress that destroys the ability to

---

[104]Gross and Robinson make reasonableness a requirement for all mistakes about justifications. H. GROSS, *supra* note 20, at 281-82; 2 P. ROBINSON, *supra* note 8, §184(a)(1).

[105]The *Model Penal Code* defense of necessity requires only that the actor believed his conduct was necessary to avoid a lesser evil. MODEL PENAL CODE §3.02(1). The Law Reform Commission of Canada's proposed defense of necessity is silent regarding the actor's belief, and thus apparently applies only when the justifying circumstances actually exist. L.R.C.C., REPORT, *supra* note 9, at 33; L.R.C.C., CRIMINAL LAW, *supra* note 8, at 96. However, if one applies the Commission's mistake of fact defense to an actor's judgment that an act is necessary, then a sincere belief, absent wilful blindness, should suffice. L.R.C.C., REPORT, *supra* note 8, at 39; L.R.C.C., CRIMINAL LAW, *supra* note 8, at 74-75.

[106]G. FLETCHER, *supra* note 23, at 793.

[107]*See Perka*, 13 D.L.R.4th at 14 (disallowing defense because permitting defenses beyond specific code defenses would invite courts to second guess the legislature).

choose also confuses the grounds.[108]

More likely, unreasonable mistakes are permitted due to confusion with a mistake of fact defense. A mistake of fact defense concerns a circumstance or consequence that is part of the definition of an offense.[109] Consequently, the mistake negates the mens rea necessary for the offense. However, a mistake about a justification does not negate mens rea for an offense and thus does not automatically exculpate the defendant. One can logically treat the two defenses differently, and good policy reasons exist for so doing.

B. Objective and Subjective Interpretations

Suppose, however, the actor mistakenly believed there were reasonable alternatives but did not choose one of them. The question arises whether the actor should be entitled to a defense based on the absence of a reasonable alternative. Robinson defends an objective theory of justifications. His theory is objective in that it ignores the "knowledge, purpose, disregard, or ignorance" of the actor.[110] The actual circumstances are decisive rather than the actor's belief regarding the circumstances. Consequently, even if the actor believes justifying circumstances do not exist, the act is justified if such circumstances do in fact exist.

Robinson's theory parallels an interpretation of the ethical principle of utility. The objective interpretation of the principles that an actor's duty is to perform the act that will in fact maximize utility. If the actor reasonably believes his act will maximize utility, but it does not, then the act was wrong. However, the actor might be absolved of blame by an excuse of reasonable mistake. Contrarily, if an actor did not believe his act would maximize utility, but in fact it did, then the act was right. However, the actor might still be blameworthy.

The contrasting subjective interpretation of the principle of utility is that an actor's duty is to act in a manner that he reasonably expects to maximize utility. If the actor does so, the act is correct and the actor blameless even if the act does not in fact maximize utility. Contrarily, if the actor does not choose the act that he reasonably expects to maximize

---

[108]*See, e.g.*, L.R.C.C., REPORT, *supra* note 8, at 32 (requiring a "reasonable response"); L.R.C.C., CRIMINAL LAW, *supra* note 8, at 86. However, the Law Reform Commission of Canada's proposed duress defense apparently rests primarily on the absence of a reasonable alternative ground.

[109]G. FLETCHER, *supra* note 23, at 696-97; H. GROSS, *supra* note 20, at 259-62.

[110]2 P. ROBINSON, *supra* note 8, §122(f).

utility, the actor has violated his duty and deserves blame even if the chosen act does in fact maximize utility.

The issue then it to determine which interpretation is most appropriate for the criminal law. In practice, people can only act on the basis of what they reasonably believe to be the likely consequences. Thus, even if one adopts Robinson's objective view, people can, at best, act on the basis of reasonable beliefs about whether justifying circumstances exists. As the purpose of law is to guide people's conduct,[111] it is best to state the law in terms they must apply, namely, subjective terms. Under an objective interpretation, people must still consider whether they have a reasonable basis for believing that justifying circumstances exist.

Two replies can be made on behalf of Robinson's view.[112] First, if a reasonable belief is included in the definition of a justification, then one would not be justified in resisting persons who reasonably, but mistakenly, believe they have a defense. However, a justification does not necessarily show that interference is wrong. Moreover, if the actor is mistaken, his act does not produce the greatest value. Therefore, reasonable resistance to prevent the act would increase value. Even if interference is an offense, it will be justified if no reasonable alternative exists.

Second, a plausible requirement for criminal liability is the commission of a wrongful act. Thus, an actor who in fact is justified but does but not believe himself justified, does not commit a wrongful act. However, this argument begs the question, as the act is wrong under a subjective interpretation. Even if one uses an objective interpretation, one may question whether criminal liability attaches to wrongful acts or blameworthy actors. The law of impossible attempt illustrates these tensions. Robinson concedes that if one is willing to punish impossible attempts, then an actor with evil intent who is in fact justified might be convicted of an attempt.[113] With that concession, the practical differences between the objective and subjective analyses diminishes.

However, the utilitarian concern with general deterrence remains. General deterrence is weakened if persons who set out to commit crimes but are in fact justified in the circumstances are not held liable or only held liable for a lesser offense. Some people might engage in conduct they believe to be criminal in the hope that they might in fact have a justification. This claim might sound implausible--who would act on the

---

[111]RAZ, *On the Functions of Law*, in OXFORD ESSAYS IN JURISPRUDENCE 281 (A. Simpson ed., 2d series 1973).

[112]*See* 2 P. ROBINSON, *supra* note 8, §184(c).

[113]*Id.* at §§85(c), 122(d).

basis of such hope? Many people purchase lottery tickets in the hope that they will win, when the expectable utility of the ticket is well below its costs. There is not reason to expect criminals will be more rational. Thus, general deterrence requires that the mistake be reasonable, which will also deter criminal acts based on the chance of justification.

VI. CONCLUSION

Three possible grounds exist for the defenses of necessity and duress. The formulations of the defenses in traditional law, most proposed codes, and commentators are based on mixed rationales. The involuntary behavior ground requires that the actor's movements be involuntary in the minimal sense of not being able to do otherwise if he so chose. Consequently, this ground supports only a limited defense of lack of voluntary act or actus reus, which is usually treated as the absence of a necessary element of the crime.

The absence of a reasonable alternative justifies an act fulfilling the definition of an offense if it has more value, or less evil, than any act that complies with the law, thus making compliance unreasonable. This rationale has predominated in the traditional defense of necessity, but various unjustifiable limitations have been added. In particular, unjustifiable requirements include the requirement that the danger be imminent, that it be from a nonhuman or natural source, and that the actor not be at fault in getting into the situation. The first two considerations can be left to the trier of fact in determining whether a reasonable alternative existed. The third is best left to liability for separate offenses committed by the actor in getting into the situation. The logic of no reasonable alternative justifies killing another person when doing so will save more lives. However, it does not generally justify taking one life to save another.

The inability to choose rationally supports an excuse when, due to lack of time or being overcome by fear, an actor cannot choose rationally. This rationale underlies some recent definitions of duress. However, the rationale does not support such limitations as those requiring that a person of reasonable firmness would have resisted, that the threat must be to interests of the actor or those under his protection, that the threat must be of death or serious bodily injury, of human source, or imminent, or that the actor must be innocent in getting involved in the situation.

Epistemological and utilitarian considerations support two general limitations on the defenses. In view of the difficulty of distinguishing between inability to choose rationally and mere difficulty in doing so, a defense based on the inability to choose should mitigate, not excuse. To avoid weakening general deterrence, a defense based on the absence of a reasonable alternative should permit only reasonable mistakes about the nonexistence of alternatives. The pure logic of the grounds must yield to general utilitarian aims of criminal law.

MARRIAGE AS A BAD BUSINESS DEAL: DISTRIBUTION OF PROPERTY ON DIVORCE

> While reasonableness is rarely the main ingredient in the decision to marry, the law should not make the choice to marry unreasonable *per se*.[1]

Although many factors can be involved in the reasonableness of marriage, this essay focuses on only one--the financial settlement in the event of divorce. Recent changes in divorce law and in demographic patterns of marriage and divorce are making marriage an unreasonable decision for an increasingly large segment of the population. If marriage is to become an economically reasonable decision for persons affected by these changes, divorce laws pertaining to financial settlements need to be revised.

Ironically, the recent changes in divorce law were intended to correct inequities in the law. While the changes may produce more equity in divorces that conform to past patterns of marriage and divorce, they unfortunately tend to produce inequity in those that conform to more modern patterns.

Recent changes in laws concerning financial settlements upon divorce concern what property is to be divided, how that property is to be divided, and if and how much alimony or maintenance is to be awarded. A pervasive trend has been to increase the property to be divided. One aspect of this trend has been the classification of more property as marital or community and, therefore, less as nonmarital or separate.[2] Another aspect has been the expansion of the category of property to include, for example, unvested pensions.[3] Additionally, there has been a decrease in the

---

[1]H.D. KRAUSE, FAMILY LAW IN A NUTSHELL 365 (2d ed. 1986).

[2]Some states permit courts to distribute both marital or community property and separate property. *See* Freed & Walker, *Family Law in the Fifty States: An Overview*, 21 FAM. L. Q. 417, 453-54, Table IV (1988); *see also* J.J. GOLDEN, EQUITABLE DISTRIBUTION OF PROPERTY §2.02 (1983).

[3]*See, e.g., In re* Marriage of Campa, 89 Cal. App. 3d 113, 152 Cal. Rptr. 362 (cal. Ct. App. 1979), *appeal dismissed for want of a substantial federal question*, 444 U.S. 1028 (1980) (pension); Evans v. Evans, 96 Mich. App. 328, 296 N.W.2d 248 (Mich. Ct. App. 1980) (social security); Elliott v. Elliott, 274 N.W. 2d 75 (Minn. 1978) (social security); *see also* M.A. GLENDON, THE NEW FAMILY AND THE NEW PROPERTY 67 (1981).

W. L. Robison (ed.), The Legal Essays of Michael Bayles, 243–254.
© 2002 *Kluwer Law International. Printed in the Netherlands.*

importance of marital fault to the division of property upon divorce.[4] Finally, alimony as a life-long award to a dependent spouse has generally been replaced with short-term "rehabilitative" alimony to enable a dependent spouse to acquire job training and become economically independent.[5]

During the 1970's, partly in response to the drive for equality of the sexes, equal division of property and diminution of alimony were emphasized. An equal division of property supposedly reflects the equality of the sexes, while alimony if often considered demeaning and is, in practice, usually not fully collected. Recently, however, equal division of property has been viewed less favorably.[6] To provide an equal division of property, the family home may have to be sold, sometimes leaving a spouse having custody of children with inadequate housing. Moreover, one spouse, usually the husband, may have a higher earning capacity. Consequently, postdivorce economic equality and, thus, sexual equality, does not necessarily result.[7]

Recent divorce law changes, as well as some suggestions for further changes, have been based on the most prevalent past pattern of marriage and divorce. This traditional pattern was of couples marrying at a young age, the wife staying home to raise a family, and the couple divorcing after a substantial number of years. However, two other patterns of marriage are becoming increasingly significant. One prominent pattern involves the rise in the number of second and subsequent marriages.[8] These marriages naturally occur at a later age than first marriages.[9] Moreover, one or both of the participants in these marriages may have been through a financially difficult divorce and, therefore, may be more apt

---

[4]Freed & Walker, *supra* note 2, at 462-63, Table V, 467.

[5]L.J. WEITZMAN, THE DIVORCE REVOLUTION 163-64 (1985); *see also* H.H. CLARK, THE LAW OF DOMESTIC RELATIONS IN THE UNITED STATES 175 (2d ed. 1987).

[6]*See, e.g.*, L.J. WEITZMAN, *supra* note 5, at 105-09.

[7]*See id.* at 378 ("For without equality in economic resources, all other 'equality' is illusory.").

[8]In 1970, 31.4% of marriages taking place in the United States involved at least one previously married partner. By 1975, this percentage had risen to 39.9%, and by 1980, to 43.8%. By 1985, this percentage had risen to 45.7%. BUREAU OF STATISTICS, U.S. DEP'T OF COMMERCE, STATISTICAL ABSTRACT OF THE UNITED STATES 85, Table 129 (109th ed. 1989) [hereinafter STATISTICAL ABSTRACT].

[9]In 1985 the median age at first marriage was 23.0 years for women and 24.8 years for men. The median age for divorced people remarrying was 32.7 years for women and 36.0 years for men. *Id.* at 86, Table 130.

to consider the financial aspects of marriage than people entering their first marriage. The other growing pattern is simply marriage at an older age.[10] Because marriages that fit into both of these patterns involve older people, it is more likely that both partners will enter the marriage with established jobs or careers in which they expect to continue. In both of these newer patterns, spouses are more likely to bring significant property into the marriage than in the traditional pattern.

This essay focuses on the law governing the division of financial assets and concludes that the law, as it now exists, can make marriages that fit into the newer patterns unwise and unfair. Because both partners in such marriages are more likely to have established employment or careers, the decrease in alimony awards is less significant. Additionally, the classification of property as marital and nonmarital, together with the current method of distribution, is unreasonable and unfair when applied to marriages that fit into these new patterns and that end in divorce.

A significant minority of states classify all property as marital. Even in the majority of states which distinguish between marital and nonmarital property, the classification is likely to be unfair in marriages conforming to these newer patterns. New ways of treating pensions on divorce also contribute to making such marriages financially unwise. The principles of distribution do not correct and may exacerbate the problems that arise from the classification of property.

---

[10]In 1975, 65.3% of people who got married in the United States were 24 years old or younger. By 1980, this percentage had dropped to 58.2%. By 1985, people 24 or younger accounted for only 48.3% of people married in the United States. While these percentages were dropping, the percentage of people who got married between the ages of 25 and 34 role from 21.1% in 1975, to 28% in 1980, and to 34.1% in 1985. Likewise, the percentage of people who got married between the ages of 35 and 44 rose from 6.7% in 1975, to 7.8% in 1980, and to 11.1% in 1985. *Id.* at 85, Table 128.

If, as argued, the divorce law discourages marriage, one might wonder why marriage rates continue to be so high. Four possibilities suggest themselves. First, the rates would be even higher were it not for the divorce laws. Second, the effect is not so much discouragement of marriage but discouragement of marriage outside of one's economic class. Thus, divorce law affects who people marry but not whether they marry. Third, economic considerations are not the only factor involved in determining the overall reasonableness of marriage, so when other factors are considered, marriage might still be reasonable. Fourth, perhaps some decisions to marry are simply not rational or reasonable; whom one loves does not seem to be rationally based. Whatever the case may be, the law need not and should not contribute to marriage being economically unreasonable.

I. Marriage As An Economic Partnership

Divorce law's purposes can significantly affect its contours. Divorce law, especially as it relates to property distribution, can be assumed to have at least three purposes. First, the law should provide a sharp and clean break so that the ex-spouses can get on with their lives with minimal personal and financial contact. Of course, where there are children, continued contact regarding them should occur. Second, the law should have predictable results so that spouses can plan for the consequences of divorce. Third, the law should be fair,[11] since fair laws tend to diminish disputes.[12] Basic to these purposes is the concept that marriage should not be discouraged by society.

The traditional concept of marriage underlying the law has both moral and economic aspects. The moral aspect involves public recognition and protection of an intimate sharing and loving relationship that provides a setting deemed desirable for child rearing.[13] Historically, this moral aspect was reflected in the law by the prohibition of adultery, by fault-based divorce, and by the distinction between legitimate and illegitimate children. With the trend against legal enforcement or morality and the demise of fault-based divorce, the moral aspect has become less significant, especially for divorce.

The historical economic aspect of marriage was an identity in the husband. That concept has been replaced by one of an (equal?) economic partnership.[14] Three principles underlie the economic partnership concept of marriage.[15] First, the principle of "all efforts" is that each spouse will contribute all time and effort to thc marital unit. Second, the "enablement" principle is that homemaking enables the income producer's activities. Third, the "sharing" principle is that spouses expect to share in the financial fortunes of the marital unit. The reasonableness and fairness of current laws for second[16] and late marriages that result in divorce depend largely on the appropriateness of these principles.

---

[11]Whatever "fair" is.

[12]Of course, the public interest in fairness transcends dispute minimization.

[13]*See* Bayles, *Marriage, Love and Procreation*, in PHILOSOPHY AND SEX 130, 138-42 (R. Baker & F. Elliston 2d ed. 1984).

[14]*See* H.H. CLARK, *supra* note 5, at 194.

[15]Krauskopf, *Classifying Marital and Separate Property--Combinations and Increase in Value of Separate Property*, 89 W. VA. L REV. 997, 1019 (1987).

[16]The expression "second marriage" is used throughout to describe any marriage after the first.

The partnership conception of marriage omits some considerations relevant to the total well-being of the marital unit and its partners. For example, in the partnership model there is no consideration of psychological well-being or of love and commitment. Although the principles of "all efforts" and "enablement" are meant to include intangible as well as tangible aspects, the concept is of a semi-arm's-length relationship and does not represent a full conception of marriage, especially as viewed by participants. Nonetheless, the law probably cannot adequately handle a full concept of marriage. The following criticisms reveal that the partnership model is inadequate even as a concept of the economic aspects of marriage.

The "all efforts" principle is both psychologically and economically inappropriate. The once popular notion that couples should share everything no longer seems realistic. To maintain their separate identities and independence, people now expect to have some separate and individual activities. This is especially true of persons marrying for a second time or at a late age. They have significant past lives as separate individuals. Psychological identity and independence often depend on financial independence. Financial independence can rest on individual income or separate property brought to the marriage that one may expect to manage and retain. If both spouses are working, they often think of at least some of their income as separate; not all efforts are devoted to the marital unit.[17]

The "enablement" principle seems more plausible. Surely, one spouse managing all homemaking chores enables the other spouse to devote more time to producing income.[18] However, this principle assumes that the income producing spouse can devote more time to producing income and that the time spent performing homemaking chores comes from time spent producing income. Neither of these assumptions is necessarily true. People in hourly paid jobs cannot unilaterally increase their hours of work, and salaried workers are not directly paid for overtime. Moreover, homemaking activities usually decrease recreational time rather than work time. The "enablement" principle becomes even less plausible if it is interpreted to mean that the enablement function's value

---

[17]In roughly one-third of marriages where both spouses work, they view their earnings as individual, not family, income. M.A. GLENDON, *supra* note 3, at 65 n.55.

[18]I have found that I have more time for professional activities when single, even performing household chores myself, than when married. The loss of time when married stems from activities that might be considered their own reward--for both partners. These self-rewarding aspects are not considered in the partnership model, but as each partner benefits, they do not affect the economic aspects.

increases in proportion to the income produced.[19] If one simply values homemaking time as the cost of hiring someone to do the work, then of course it does not increase proportional to the income produced. If one thinks of it as saving the income producer time, then it would be proportional. However, this view is based on the mistaken assumption that homemaking time is taken from time that would be used to produce income rather than from time that would be used for recreation.

Although this proportionality interpretation of the "enablement" principle is incorrect, a concept of the "sharing" principle abased on proportionality is possible. A general formula for each spouse's share of marital assets is $S=Sf x T$, where T is the total of marital assets and Sf is one spouse's fractional share. Thus, even if a spouse's activity is homemaking, assuming Sf remains constant, the value of that spouse's share increases in proportion to the total. However, the general formula does not indicate what fraction of the total marital assets belongs to a spouse. That is, the division need not be in proportion to the amount each contributed or produced. Spouses probably have different conceptions about appropriate shares, and the expectations of a particular couple might change over time. These expectations cannot be the sole basis for determining what the law should be, for they are shaped partially by what the law is. Consequently, while a minority of states divide marital property equally, a large majority distribute it equitably, which allows for unequal shares.[20]

II. MARITAL AND NONMARITAL PROPERTY

Partners' expectations of the share of assets they will receive on divorce can reasonably be understood to depend in part on the amount of property they bring to the marriage. In first marriages at a young age, neither partner usually has much property. However, that is often not the case in second and late marriages. For people contemplating such marriages, marriage can be viewed as economically unreasonable. Consider an example of each of these trends. Person *A*, who is considering a second marriage, owns a car, furniture, and a house valued at $85,000 with a remaining mortgage of $50,000. Person *B*, who is contemplating a first marriage, is thirty years old, has a full-time job that pays $28,000 a year, owns a car and 135 shares in the employer's company bought under an employees' stock purchase program, and has $5600 in a mutual fund. Suppose that each is contemplating marriage to a person who, though

---

[19]*See, e.g.*, Krauskopf, *supra* note 15, at 998.

[20]*See* Freed & Walker, *supra* note 2, at 453-54, Table IV.

employed, has an income some $5000 to $10,000 less per year and no significant property other than an automobile.

A and *B* can both lose a significant amount of their property should their marriages end in divorce in, say, five years. Crucial to this potential loss is the classification of property as marital or nonmarital. In a significant minority of states, no distinction is made between marital and nonmarital property.[21] In these "hotchpot" states, the judge dividing the assets presumably considers how much property each person brought to the marriage.[22] However, that is only a presumption, and the judge need not do so. Consequently, both *A* and *B* risk losing a portion of the property they bring to their marriages if the marriages end in divorce. In this respect, marriage is economically unreasonable and unfair for *A* and *B*.[23]

Community property and common law states that distinguish between marital and nonmarital property face similar problems.[24] In the majority of states which make such a distinction, property possessed prior to marriage and property acquired by gift of inheritance during marriage are normally classified as nonmarital. Moreover, except in one state,[25] the classification of property as marital or nonmarital largely depends on the source of funds expended to buy the property. In these states, *A*'s and *B*'s separate property seem secure. Not so!

The doctrine of transmutation provides several ways by which the actions of one or both spouses can cause separate property to become marital property.[26] First, property can be transmuted by gift or by placing it in joint title.[27] For example, suppose *B* sells a few shares of the mutual fund to purchase a stereo television as a christmas gift for *B*'s spouse. In some states, the gift becomes the recipient spouse's separate property. However, other states explicitly except interspousal gifts from being separate property, in which case the gift becomes marital property.[28]

---

[21]*See id.*; L.J. GOLDEN, *supra* note 2, at §2.02.

[22]*See* C. FOOTE, R.J. LEVY & F.E.A. SANDER, CASES AND MATERIALS IN FAMILY LAW 658 (3d ed. 1985).

[23]*See* M.A. GLENDON, *supra* note 3, at 63.

[24]H.H. CLARK, *supra* note 5, at 177-78. Actually, the common law states have often incorporated community property doctrines. *See id.*

[25]*See* Freed & Walker, *supra* note 2, at 453-54, Table IV, 455 (In Mississippi the classification of property depends solely upon the state of title to that property.)

[26]*See generally* Krauskopf, *supra* note 15, at 1002-09.

[27]*See, e.g.*, Carter v. Carter, 419 A.2d 1018, 1022 (Me. 1980).

[28]*See, e.g.*, FLA. STAT. §61.075 (3)(a)(3) (Supp. 1988).

Similarly, suppose that after a few years *A* and *A*'s spouse decide to sell their house and purchase a larger one. In many states, mortgage lenders require that the new house be taken in joint title. In this case, the house becomes marital property, and *A*'s previously separate equity is converted to marital property.

Second, suppose *A* avoids placing the house in joint title. It still could be readily transmuted to marital property through the doctrine of commingling. *A*'s income is marital property. If this income is used to make mortgage payments, marital and nonmarital property has been commingled and the nonmarital property is therefore possibly subject to division upon divorce.[29] The same occurs if *B* purchases more shares of stock under the employee plan or buys more shares of the mutual fund. When marital property is combined with nonmarital property, the resulting whole will usually be classified as part marital and part separate property, the percentages depending upon the source of the funds.[30] Thus, if *A* had $35,000 worth of equity in the house at the time of marriage, at least that much will remain *A*'s separate property.

A has not, however, avoided the possibility of having the equity at marriage transmuted to marital property. A third form of transmutation occurs when property is used by the marital unit. Thus, if *A* and *A*'s spouse live in the house and use the furniture, this property can become marital.[31] With this version of transmutation, *A*'s only method of retaining the house as separate property is to refrain from using it as the marital home. *B*, however, will avoid this form of transmutation, because the stock and mutual fund are not "used" by the marital unit.

There is another way *A* and *B* can find marriage financially disadvantageous. Suppose *B*'s mutual fund is a high income bond fund with the income re-invested. In some states, the income received from separate property during marriage is marital property,[32] so the shares bought by re-investing are also marital. Similarly, if *A* rents the house, the rental income is often marital property. Accordingly, if this rental income is used to pay off the mortgage, that part of the equity in the house becomes marital property. In short, if income from separate property is

---

[29]*In re* Marriage of Marsden, 130 Cal. App. 3d 426, 181 Cal. Rptr. 910 (Cal. Ct. App. 1982); Sturgis v. Sturgis, 663 S.W.2d 375 (Mo. Ct. App. 1983).

[30]*See* Krauskopf, *supra* note 15, at 1000.

[31]*See, e.g.*, FLA. STAT. §61.075(3)(b)(3) (Supp. 1988) (Income from separate property ceases to be separate if "treated, used or relied upon....as marital asset.").

[32]*See, e.g.*, H.H. CLARK, *supra* note 5, at 189; Krauskopf, *supra* note 15, at 1000; IDAHO CODE §32-906 (1983).

marital property, separate property brought to a marriage cannot increase due to re-investment of income.

A and *B* might still be able to increase the value of their separate property; they might have capital gains. Whether this is so depends on the principles used for dividing the appreciation in value between commingled marital and nonmarital property. In some cases, appreciation other than that caused by inflation is simply classified as marital property.[33] If this principle is employed, *A* and *B* will not retain as separate any growth in the real value of their separate property.

Two other principles are often used, especially for private businesses, depending on whether the major source of funds invested in the business is marital or nonmarital.[34] If the primary source of increase to separate property is the skill and activity of one spouse, such increase will likely be categorized as marital property.[35] If the primary source of increase to separate property is independent of the marital unit, then such increase will likely be categorized as separate property. Thus, if *A* rents the house, the marital unit is entitled to reasonable compensation for *A*'s managerial effort. If *B* does nothing with the shares of stock and does not re-invest dividends, then *B* might be able to retain their full value as separate property, even if the shares appreciate in value.[36]

The point is that *A* and *B* have little chance to do better than retain as separate property the value they bring to marriage adjusted by inflation. At best, they can retain full appreciation of unmanaged assets. At worst, the whole could become converted to marital property. If their intended spouses have little property, no property, or property of significantly less value, they are not entering the economic partnership on equal terms. Without assurance that the division of marital assets upon divorce will reflect their greater contributions, *A* and *B* are faced with a bad business deal.

III. Pensions

Pension rights brought to marriage are separate property, but those acquired during marriage are now generally considered marital property.

---

[33] *See, e.g.*, Sousley v. Sousley, 614 S.W. 2d 942 (Ky. 1981) (appreciation in value treated as income and divided).

[34] *See generally* Krauskopf, *supra* note 15, at 1024-33.

[35] Remember that any effort put into managing a business is, by the principle of all efforts, a marital contribution.

[36] *See, e.g., In re* Estate of Ney, 212 Cal. App. 2d 891, 28 Cal. Rptr. 442 (Cal. Ct. App. 1963); Cord V. Cord, 98 Nev. 210, 644 P.2d 1026 (1982).

The distribution of marital pension rights upon divorce is complex. Only a few points regarding possible unfavorable distributions are mentioned here. Suppose *CH* and *CW* have approximately equal incomes, but *CW* has a better pension plan because her employer contributes more. Upon divorce, pensions acquired by both during their marriage are treated as marital property. Suppose they are divided equally. In this case, *CW* receives a smaller pension for the years of marriage than she would receive if she had been single during those years. But, one might say, this is appropriate if one assumes that marriage is an equal partnership. Nonetheless, it is an unwise economic decision to put more into a partnership than the other partner if assets are to be divided equally. Moreover,the variety of pension plans and methods of valuing them render it difficult to be sure that one will not lose simply by miscalculation of benefits.

IV. Other Considerations

Persons entering a second or late marriage with significantly more property than their intended spouses are making a bad business deal. All of the property they possessed before the marriage might be considered in the distribution of assets upon divorce. Some of their formerly separate property may become marital property, the income from property retained as separate may be considered marital property, and the appreciation in value of property retained as separate may be considered marital property.

However, mere classification of property as marital does not necessarily imply that one will lose it upon divorce. One might lose some of such property in equal division states, but, even there, judges often consider the source of the funds with which the property was purchased. In states in which property is divided equitably, if one has an equitable claim to a larger share of marital assets, that claim may be recognized. The classification of assets as marital or separate, though, is not the dispositive issue. Regardless of what property will be considered available for distribution, whether marriage is economically unwise depends crucially on how property is to be divided.

The problem with the current laws is the uncertainty of what will be considered an equitable distribution. In effect, equitable distribution is discretionary distribution.[37] In some states, statutes provide courts only general guidance with regard to the distribution of assets.[38] In other states,

---

[37] *See* M.A. GLENDON, *supra* note 3, at 63-64.

[38] *See, e.g.*, ALASKA STAT. §25.24.160 (Supp. 1988); MICH. COMP. LAWS ANN. §25.99 (West 1984).

statutes require that certain factors be considered.[39] These factors include the length of the marriage, the age and health of the parties, the occupations of the parties, the amounts and sources of each party's income, the vocational skills and employability of each party, and each party's contributions to, or dissipations of, the marital assets.[40] No reasonably precise formula exists to determine what distribution will result from the application of these factors. Some of these factors pull in opposite directions. For example, contribution supports a larger share for the person who brought greater assets into the marriage or who has a higher income. Vocational skills and employability, on the other hand, can support a greater share for the person who has fewer vocational skills and is less employable, even though that person probably contributed less to the marriage than did the more highly skilled and employable spouse. In the final analysis, one must marshal a large amount of data to support one's claim, and then trust in judicial discretion.

If the preservation of formerly separate property upon divorce is uncertain, then one can make an antenuptial agreement to provide specific guidelines for the division of property upon divorce.[41] However, the validity of an antenuptial agreement is uncertain.[42] Indeed, the uniform marriage and divorce act merely cites an antenuptial agreement as another factor for a judge to consider in the division of the property.[43] Thus, the remedy for uncertainty is itself uncertain.[44]

V. CONCLUSION

Second and late marriages are two growing patterns of marriage and divorce. Persons entering such marriages are more likely to have substantial financial assets than those marrying earlier in life. Divorce law primarily regards marriage as an economic partnership. The underlying principles of "all efforts," "enablement," and "sharing" are questionable.

A party entering a marriage with substantially more assets than the other party faces significant risks of losing those assets in the event of divorce. In some states, no distinction is made between marital and

---

[39] *See, e.g.*, FLA. STAT. §61.075(1) (Supp. 1988).

[40] For a more complete list, see Freed & Walker, *supra* note 2, at 465-66.

[41] *See* Krauskopf, *supra* note 15, at 1034.

[42] *See, e.g.*, Posner v. Posner, 233 So. 2d 381 (Fla. 1970); Mulford v. Mulford, 211 Neb. 747, 320 N.W.2d 470 (1982); Duncan v. Duncan, 652 S.W.2d 913 (Tenn. Ct. App. 1983).

[43] UNIF. MARRIAGE AND DIVORCE ACT §307(A), 9A U.L.A. 238 (1973).

[44] Moreover, antenuptial agreements can involve significant legal expense.

nonmarital property for purposes of distribution on divorce. Even if a distinction is drawn, separate property can be transmuted into marital property by joint title, use by the marital unit, and perhaps mere commingling with marital property. Income from separate property is often marital, and the property's appreciation in value can become mostly marital. In addition, one might lose some of the value of a pension accrued during marriage. Consequently, marriage can be an economically unreasonable decision for people with significant property.

In the majority of states, equitable distribution upon divorce can provide such a person a greater portion of the assets. However, various principles compete, and several support giving a larger share to the person who probably contributed less. The results depend on judicial discretion and are uncertain. Antenuptial agreements might provide protection for assets brought to a marriage, but their validity is sometimes risky, and even if valid they are not always decisive.

Consequently, many second and late marriages are bad business deals. Considerable uncertainty exists about how marital property will be distributed should divorce occur. The economic reasonableness of marrying decreases, and marriage is thus discouraged. The uncertainty undermines predictability of results, thus fostering disputes. The law's fairness is also doubtful, at best depending on the discretion of judges. As one scholar put it, "what persons will enter a business or professional partnership or joint venture if the only liquidation rule is that a court will have discretion to make any order it thinks fit in regard to all the money and property?"[45] Finally, the economic partnership concept of marriage is misleading.

Financial assets possessed prior to marriage should not so readily be considered a contribution to the marriage. Those assets, and their income and increase in value, should normally remain nonmarital property. They should become marital only if the owner makes an affirmative act to contribute them to the marriage. Mere use of tangible assets such as a house or automobile should not count as such an act. Use of income to purchase assets for joint use would be such an act. If such assets are the primary source of income, such as a business, then at least all income should be deemed marital. Unless stronger protection is given to assets brought to a marriage as separate property, many potential second and late marriages will be economically unwise and could be discouraged. The laws governing the division of property upon divorce must be revised if the law is to encourage, or at least not discourage, marriage.

---

[45]Baxter, *Family Law Reform in Ontario*, 25 U. TORONTO L.J. 237, 261 (1975).

Publications

Books

Editor, *Contemporary Utilitarianism*. Garden City, NY: Doubleday and Company, Anchor Books, 1968. Reprint edition: Gloucester, MA: Peter Smith, 1978

Editor, *Ethics and Populations*. Cambridge, MA: Schenkman Publishing Co., 1976

Co-editor with Dallas M. High. *Medical Treatment of the Dying: Moral Issues*. Cambridge, MA: G. K. Hall & Company and Schenkman Publishing Co., 1978

Principles of Legislation: The Uses of Political Authority. Detroit: Wayne State University Press, 1978

Morality and Population Policy. University, AL: University of Alabama Press, 1980

Professional Ethics. Belmont, CA: Wadsworth Publishing Co., 1981. Excerpt from Ch. 4 reprinted in N. Abrams & M. D. Buckner, eds., *Medical Ethics* (Cambridge: The MIT Press, 1983) and Albert Flores, ed., *Professional Ideals* (Belmont, CA: Wadsworth Publishing Co., 1987)

Co-editor with Kenneth Henley. *Right Conduct: Theories and Applications*. New York: Random House, 1983

Co-editor with Bruce Chapman. *Justice, Rights, and Tort Law*. Dordrecht: L D. Reidel Publishing Co., 1983

Co-editor with Douglas Ray and Ann Harley. *Values, Life-Long Education and an Aging Canadian Population*. London, Canada: Third Eye, 1983

Reproductive Ethics. Englewood Cliffs, N.J.: Prentice-Hall, 1984. Ch. 2 reprinted in Rem B. Edwards & Glenn Graber, eds., *An Introduction to Bioethics* (New York: Harcourt, Brace Jovanovich, 1987)

Principles of Law. Dordrecht: L D. Reidel Publishing Co., 1987

Co-editor with Robert C.L. Moffat and Joseph Grcic, *Perspectives on the Family*, Studies in Social and Political Theory, Vol. 8 (Edwin Mellen Press, 1990)

Procedural Justice: Allocating to Individuals, Law and Philosophy Library, Vol 10 (Kluwer Academic Publishers, 1990)

Hart's Legal Philosophy: An Examination, Law and Philosophy Library, Vol 17 (Kluwer Academic Publishers, 1992)

PAPERS PUBLISHED

'Singer's Moral Principles and Rules.' *Philosophical Studies* 16 (1965): 61-64
'Utilitarian Justice.' *Rendevous: Idaho State University Journal of Arts and Letters* 2 (Winter 1967): 23-32
'A Rule-Utilitarian Moral Code.' *Journal of Value Inquiry* 3 (1969): 258-69
'The Justification of Civil Disobedience.' *Review of Metaphysics* 24 (1970): 3-20
'Hart on Problems in Legal Philosophy.' *Metaphilosophy* 2 (1971): 50-57
'Legal Principles, Rules and Standards.' *Logique et Analyse* 14. Nos. 53-54 (1971): 223-28
'The Human Right to Population Control' & 'Axinn, Kant and Rights of Collective Persons.' In *Human Rights: Amintaphil 1*, ed. by Ervin H. Pollack, pp. 396-409, and 411-15
'In Defense of Authority.' *Personalist* 52 (1971): 755-58
'A Concept of Coercion.' In *Coercion: Nomos XIV*, edited by J. Roland Pennock and John W. Chapman, pp. 16-29. New York: Aldine-Atherton, 1972
'Comments: Offensive Conduct and the Law.' In *Issues in Law and Morality*, edited by Norman S. Care and Thomas K. Trelogan, pp. 111-26. Cleveland: Press of Case Western Reserve University, 1973
'Reparations to Wronged Groups.' *Analysis* (1973): 182-84. Reprinted in *Reverse Discrimination*, edited by Barry R. Gross, Buffalo, NY: Prometheus Books, 1977.
'Compensatory Reverse Discrimination in Hiring.' *Social Theory and Practice* 2 (1973): 301-12
'Dismantling the Criminal Law System.' Co-editor of special symposium issue of that title. *Wayne Law Review* 19, No. 3 (1973): 824-1007, article on pp. 827-46
'The Complexity of "Why Be Moral?"' *Personalist* 54 (1973): 309-17
'Criminal Paternalism.' In *Limits of Law: Nomos XV*, edited by J. Roland Pennock and John W. Chapman, pp. 174-88. New York: Lieber-Atherton, 1974
'Mill's *Utilitarianism* and Aristotle's *Rhetoric*.' *Modern Schoolman* 51 (1974): 159-170
'Coercive Offers and Public Benefits.' *Personalist* 55 (1974): 139-44
'Mental Abnormality and the Criminal Process.' In *Punishment and*

Human Rights, edited by Milton Goldinger, pp. 57-71. Cambridge, MA: Schenkman Publishing Co., 1974

'Marriage, Love and Procreation.' In *Philosophy and Sex*, edited by Robert Baker and Frederick Elliston, pp. 190-206. Buffalo: Prometheus Books, 1975, 2d edn. 1984. Reprinted in *Occasions for Philosophy*, edited by James Edwards and Douglas MacDonald, Englewood Cliffs, NJ: Prentice-Hall, 1979; *Philosophy for Adults*, edited by Thomas O. Buford, Washington, D.C.: University Press of America, 1980; *Contemporary Readings in Social and Political Ethics*, edited by G. Brodsky, J. Troyer, and D. Vance, Buffalo: Promethesus Books, 1984

'Ideals and the Concept of Morality: A Fanatic's Reply to Granrose.' *Idealistic Studies* 6 (1976): 62-68

'The Function and Limits of Political Authority.' In *Authority: A Philosophical Analysis*, edited by Ransom Baine Harris, pp. 101-11. University, AL: University of Alabama Press, 1976

'Legislating Morality.' *Wayne Law Review* 22 (1976): 759-80

'Harm to the Unconceived.' *Philosophy and Public Affairs* 5 (1976): 292-304

'Hume on Blame and Excuse.' *Hume Studies* 2 (April 1976): 17-35

'Limits to a Right to Procreate.' In *Ethics and Population*, pp. 41-58. Reprinted in *Having Children*, edited by Onora O'Neill and William Ruddick, New York: Oxford University Press, 1979; and *Human Values and the Law*, edited by James H. Wilbur, Geneseo, NY: State University College of Arts & Science at Geneseo, 1979

'Selective and Conditional Population Aid: Some Moral Issues.' Occasional Paper, Project on Cultural Values and Population Policy. Hastings-on-Hudson, NY: Institute of Society, Ethics and the Life Sciences, 1977. Pp. 22. In *Ethical Issues in Population Aid*, edited by Daniel Callahan and Phillip Clark. New York: Irvington Publishers, 1981

'Genetic Equality and Freedom of Reproduction: A Philosophical Survey.' *Journal of Value Inquiry* 11 (1977):L 186-207

'Participation: An Overvalued, Impractical Ideal.' In *Equality and Freedom: International and Comparative Jurisprudence*, edited by Gray Dorsey, pp. 351-57. Dobbs Ferry, NY: Oceana Publications: The Netherlands: A. W. Sijthoff, 1977

'On Legal Reform: Legal Stability and Legislative Questions.' *Kentucky Law Journal* 65 (1977): 631-55

'National Health Insurance and Noncovered Services.' *Journal of Health Politics, Policy and Law* 2 (1977): 335-48

'Sterilization of the Retarded: The Legal Precedents.' *Hastings Center*

Report 8 (June 1978): 37-41. Reprinted in *Mental Retardation and Sterilization*, edited by Ruth Macklin and Willard Gaylin, New York: Plenum Press, 1981

'Obedience to Lawful Authority.' *San Diego Law Review* 15 (1978): 669-75

'Famine or Food: Sacrificing for Future or Present Generations.' In *Ethics, Free Enterprise, and Public Policy*, edited by Richard T. DeGeorge and Joseph A. Pichler, pp. 291-307. New York: Oxford University Press, 1978. Partially reprinted in *What Do We Owe Posterity?* edited by Ernest Partridge, Buffalo, NY: Prometheus Books, 1981

'Population Policy Proposals: Population Distribution.' With Martin P. Golding. *Encyclopedia of Bioethics*. Edited by Warren T. Reich et al. New York: Free Press, 1978

'Against Professional Autonomy.' *National Forum: The Phi Kappa Phi Journal* 68 (Summer 1978): 23-26. Reprinted in *Engineering Professionalism and Ethics*, edited by James H. Schaub and Karl Pavlovic, New York: John Wiley & Sons, 1983

'Medical Fallibility and Malpractice' and 'Response to Gorovitz.' With Arthur Caplan. *Journal of Medicine and Philosophy* 3 (1978):L 169-86 and 192-95

'Euthanasia and the Quality of Life.' In *Medical Treatment of the Dying*, pp. 128-52

'Physicians as Body Mechanics,' 'Internal or External Physician-Patient Relationships, Response to Clements,' and 'Comments on "Protecting the Unconceived".' In *Contemporary Issues in Biomedical Ethics*. Edited by J. W. Davis, C. B. Hoffmaster, and S. J. Shorten, pp. 167-77, 187-89, and 101-08 respectively. Clifton, NJ: Humana Press, 1978. Revised version of 'Physicians as Body Mechanics' reprinted in *Concepts of Health and Disease*, edited by T. Tristram Engelhardt, Jr., Arthur Caplan, and James T. McCartney, New York: Addison-Wesley, 1981

'Rationales for Environmental Legislation' and 'Reply.' In *Law and the Ecological Challenge: Amintaphil II*, edited by Eugene E. Dias, pp. 122-36 and 150-53, respectively. Buffalo, NY: Wm. S. Hein, 1978

'The Price of Life.' *Ethics* 89 (1978): 20-34. Reprinted in *Death and Dying: An interdisciplinary Approach*, edited by Sandra Wilcox and Marilyn Sutton, 2d edn., Sherman Oaks, CA: Alfred Publishing Co., 1982

'Morality and the Constitution.' *Arizona State University Law Journal*, 1978, pp. 561-71

'Catch-22 Paternalism and Mandatory Genetic Screening.' In *Philosophical Issues in Medical Ethics*, edited by Michael S. Pritchard and Wade L. Robison, pp. 29-42. Clifton, NJ: Humana Press, 1979
'The Capacity and Power to Consent.' In *Consent: Concept, Capacity, Conditions, and Constraint*, edited by Lyman Tower Sargent, pp. 159-65. *Archiv für Rechts-und*
'A Problem of Clean Hands: Refusal to Provide Professional Services.' *Social Theory and Practice* 5 (1979): 165-81. Reprinted in *Moral Responsibility and the Professions*, edited by Benjamin Freedman and Bernard Baumrin, New York: Haven Publishing, 1983; and *Ethics and the Legal Profession*, edited by Michael Davis and Frederick Elliston, Buffalo, N.Y.: Prometheus Books, 1986
'Political Process and Constitutional Amendments.' *Southern Journal of Philosophy* 18 (1980): 1-8
'Hercules or Proteus? The Many Theses of Ronald Dworkin.' With Lawrence Alexander. *Social Theory and Practice* 5 (1980): 267-303
'The Value of Life: By What Standard?' *American Journal of Nursing* 80 (1980): 2226-30. Reprinted in *Death and Dying: An Interdisciplinary Approach*. edited by Sandra Wilcox and Marilyn Sutton, 3rd edn., Palo Alto, Calif.: Mayfield Publishing Co., 1985
'Justice and the Dying.' In *Justice and Health Care*, edited by Earl E. Shelp, pp. 109-17. Dordrecht: D. Reidel Publishing Co., 1981
'Character, Purpose, and Criminal Responsibility.' *Law and Philosophy* 1 (1982): 5-20
'Punishment for Attempts.' *Social Theory and Practice* 9 (1982): 19-29
'Law and Politics.' In *Memoria del X Congreso Mundial Ordinario de Filosofia del Derecho y Filosofia Social*. Vol. VII, pp. 137-44. Mexico: Universidad Nacional Autonoma de Mexico, 1982
'Betwixt and Between: Juggling Ethical Responsibilities on Today's Nursing Scene.' *Canadian Nurse* 78 (June 1982): 36-38, 40. 'The Author Replies.' *Canadian Nurse* 78 (Oct. 1982): 6
'Acceptable Risk and the Public: Nonprofessional Involvement in Safety Design.' In *Designing for Safety: Engineering Ethics in Organizational Contexts*, edited by Albert Flores, pp. 127-38. Troy, NY: Center for the Study of Human Dimensions of Science and Technology, Rensselaer Polytechnic Institute, 1982
'Professionals, Clients and Others.' In *Profits and Professions: Business and Professional Ethics*, edited by Joseph Ellin, Michael S. Pritchard, and Wade L. Robison, pp. 65-73. Clifton, NJ: Humana Press, 1983

'When the Baby Won't Be Perfect.' *Westminster Institute Review* 2 (Fall 1982):: 11-13

'Introduction: The Purposes of Contract Law.' Co-editor of Symposium 'Jurisprudential Perspectives on Contract.' *Valparaiso University Law Review* 17 (1983): 613-752, Introduction on pp. 613-26

'Ethical Issues of Purchasing Management.' *Business Quarterly* 48 (Spring 1983): 42-47

'Value Issues of Lifelong Education in an Aging Society.' In Values, *Life-Long Education and an Aging Canadian Population*, pp. 177-93

'Moral Theory and Application.' *Social Theory and Practice* 10 (1984): 97-120. Reprinted in *Ethical Principles and Practice*, edited by John Howie, Carbondale, IL: Southern Illinois University Press, 1987

'Intuitions in Ethics.' *Dialogue* 23 (1984): 439-55

'Ethical Theory in the Twenty-First Century.' *Southern Journal of Philosophy* 22 (1984): 439-51. Reprinted in *New Directions in Ethics*, edited by Richard M. Fox and Joseph P. DeMarco, Boston: Routledge & Kegan Paul, 198

'Brand Name Extortionists, Intellectual Prostitutes, and Generic Free Riders.' *International Journal of Philosophy* 2, 2 (1984): 13-25

'Introduction: Labour, Law, and Society.' Editor of Symposium 'Rights, Work, and Collective Bargaining,' *Valparaiso University Law Review* 19 (1984): 1-152, introduction on pp. 1-13

'Equal Human Rights and Employment for Mentally Retarded Persons.' In *Moral Issues in Mental Retardation*, edited by R. S. Laura and A. F. Ashman, pp. 11-27. London: Croom Helm, 1985

'Courts vs. Legislatures as Protectors of Human Rights.' In *Juristic Logic, Rationality and Irrationality of Law: Proceedings of the XI World Congress*, Vol. I, edited by Andre-Jean Arnaud, Risto Hilpinen, and Jerzy Wroblewski, pp. 291-304. *Rechtstheorie, beiheft* Nr. 8, 1985

'Legally Enforceable Commitments.' *Law and Philosophy* 4 (1985): 311-42

'Mid-Level Principles and Justification.' In *Justification: Nomos XXVIII*, edited by J. Roland Pennock and John W. Chapman, pp. 49-67. New York: New York University Press, 1986

'Principles for Legal Procedure.' *Law and Philosophy* 5 (1986): 33-57

'The Value of Life.' In *Health-Care Ethics: An Introduction*, edited by Donald VanDeVeer and Tom Regan, pp. 265-89. Philadelphia: Temple University Press, 1987

'The Justification of Administrative Authority.' In *Authority Revisited: Nomos XXIX*, edited by J. Roland Pennock and John W.

Chapman. New York: New York University Press, 1987, pp. 287-301.
'Reconceptualizing Necessity and Duress.' *Wayne Law Review* 33 (1987): 1191-1220
'Interprofessional Ethics in Health Care.' *International Journal of Applied Philosophy* 3, 3 (Spring 1987): 21-28
'Professional Power and Self-Regulation.' *Business and Professional Ethics Journal* 5, 2 (1987): 25-43
'Ethical Case Studies in Teaching Philosophy: Comment.' *Teaching Philosophy* 8 (198)
'Procedural Due Process.' In *Philosophical Dimensions of the Constitution*, edited by Diana T. Meyers and Kenneth Kipnis Boulder, Colorado: Westview Press, 1988, pp. 206-221
'Marriage As A Bad Business Deal: Distribution of Property in Divorce.' *Florida State University Law Review*, Winter 1989, Vol. 17, No. 1, pp.95-106

Book Reviews and Minor Publications

'Stop Light for Government.' *Balanced Living* 17 (1961): 311-313
'The Two Worlds of Graduate Assistants.' *Wayne State University Graduate Comment* 6 (1963): 23-25
Reason in Society, by Paul Diesing. *The Humanist* 23 (1963): 71
'Narveson's Private Language.' *Graduate Review of Philosophy* 5 (1963): 25-29
'A Note on Nagel's Requirements for Explanations.' *Graduate Review of Philosophy* 6 (1964): 8-10
Prisoners in America, edited by Lloyd E. Ohlin. *Wayne Law Review* 20 (1974): 191-209
'Comments.' *In Vitro* 13 (1977): 55, 56, 85, 95, 96, 97, 108, 140
'Case Study: Eavesdropping on Medical Assault.' *Hastings Center Report* 7 (1977): 24. Reprinted in *Cases in Bioethics*, edited by Carol Levine and Robert M. Veatch. Hastings-on-Hudson, NY: The Hastings Center, 1982
Taking Rights Seriously, by Ronald Dworkin. *Villanova Law Review* 22 (1977): 1266-72
World Hunger and Moral Obligation, edited by William Aiken and Hugh LaFollette; *Obligations to Future Generations*, edited by R. I. Sikora and Brian Barry; and *Food Policy: The Responsibility of the United States in the Life and Death Choices*, edited by Peter G. Brown and Henry Shue. *National Forum* 69 (Spring 1979): 40-42

'Confusion Over Values.' *Westminster Institute Review* 1 (1981): 3-4
'Moral Law.' In *Guide to American Law*. St. Paul, Minn.: West Publishing Co., 1984
Basic Rights, by Henry Shue. Review of Metaphysics 36 (1983): 947-48
The Reverse Discrimination Controversy, by Robert K. Fullinwider, and *Justice and Reverse Discrimination*, by Alan H. Goldman. *Journal of Philosophy* 79 (1982): 455-64
The Surrogate Mother, by Noel P. Deane with Dennis L. Breo. *Westminster Institute Review* 1 (April 1982): 14
'The Westminster Institute for Ethics and Human Values.' *Eidos* 2 (1981): 177-81
'No Easy Answers on Question of Surrogate Mothers.' *Toronto Star*, 10 July 1982, pp. B1, B7
'The Notwithstanding Clause: A Defense.' *Westminster Institute Review* 2 (Winter 1983): 16-18
'To Treat or Not to Treat.' *Essex County Medical Society Bulletin*, September 1983, pp. 2-4
Criminal Law, The General Part: Liability and Defences, Law Reform Commission of Canada. Dialogue 22 (1983): 553-55
'Ethics, Public Policy, & Society.' *Access* 2, 2 (May-June 1984): 19
The Good Lawyer: Lawyer's Roles and Lawyers' Ethics, edited by David Luban, *Law and Philosophy* 3 (1984): 431-36
'Canada: The Mandarin Bureaucracy.' With Benjamin Freedman. *Hastings Center Report* 14 (Dec. 1984): 17-18
'Introduction.' In *Man, Law and Modern Forms of Life*, edited by Eugenio Bulygin, Jean-Louis Gardies, and Ilkka Niiniluoto, pp. xi-xvi. Dordrecht: D. Reidel Publishing Co., 1985
'Commentary: Trust, Risk, and Possible Benefits.' In *Nuclear War: Philosophical Perspectives*, edited by Michael Allen Fox and Leo Groarke, pp. 241-4. New York: Peter Lang Publishers, 1985
Harm to Others, by Joel Feinberg. *Law and Philosophy* 4 (1985): 423-32
'Reply to Davis.' In *Ethics and the Legal Profession,* ed. Michael Davis and Frederick Elliston, pp. 458-60. Buffalo, NY: Prometheus Books, 1986
Offense to Others, by Joel Feinberg. *Law and Philosophy* 5 (1986): 268-69
Madness and the Criminal Law, by Norval Morris. *Nous* 20, 2 (1986): 268-69
'Population Control.' *Encyclopedia Americana*. Danbury, CT: Grolier, 1987, pp. 410-412
The Nature and Limits of Authority, by Richard T. DeGeorge. *American Political Science Review* (1987): 260

'Commentary on Nagan.' *University of Florida Law Review* 39 (1987): 491-96
Harm to Self, by Joel Feinberg. *Law and Philosophy* (1988): 260
'Life, Death, and Health Care.' *Westminster Affairs* 4 (1990): 4-5

INDEX

Law and Philosophy Library

1. E. Bulygin, J.-L. Gardies and I. Niiniluoto (eds.): *Man, Law and Modern Forms of Life*. With an Introduction by M.D. Bayles. 1985 ISBN 90-277-1869-5
2. W. Sadurski: *Giving Desert Its Due*. Social Justice and Legal Theory. 1985 ISBN 90-277-1941-1
3. N. MacCormick and O. Weinberger: *An Institutional Theory of Law*. New Approaches to Legal Positivism. 1986 ISBN 90-277-2079-7
4. A. Aarnio: *The Rational as Reasonable*. A Treatise on Legal Justification. 1987 ISBN 90-277-2276-5
5. M.D. Bayles: *Principles of Law*. A Normative Analysis. 1987 ISBN 90-277-2412-1; Pb: 90-277-2413-X
6. A. Soeteman: *Logic in Law*. Remarks on Logic and Rationality in Normative Reasoning, Especially in Law. 1989 ISBN 0-7923-0042-4
7. C.T. Sistare: *Responsibility and Criminal Liability*. 1989 ISBN 0-7923-0396-2
8. A. Peczenik: *On Law and Reason*. 1989 ISBN 0-7923-0444-6
9. W. Sadurski: *Moral Pluralism and Legal Neutrality*. 1990 ISBN 0-7923-0565-5
10. M.D. Bayles: *Procedural Justice*. Allocating to Individuals. 1990 ISBN 0-7923-0567-1
11. P. Nerhot (ed.): *Law, Interpretation and Reality*. Essays in Epistemology, Hermeneutics and Jurisprudence. 1990 ISBN 0-7923-0593-0
12. A.W. Norrie: *Law, Ideology and Punishment*. Retrieval and Critique of the Liberal Ideal of Criminal Justice. 1991 ISBN 0-7923-1013-6
13. P. Nerhot (ed.): *Legal Knowledge and Analogy*. Fragments of Legal Epistemology, Hermeneutics and Linguistics. 1991 ISBN 0-7923-1065-9
14. O. Weinberger: *Law, Institution and Legal Politics*. Fundamental Problems of Legal Theory and Social Philosophy. 1991 ISBN 0-7923-1143-4
15. J. Wróblewski: *The Judicial Application of Law*. Edited by Z. Bańkowski and N. MacCormick. 1992 ISBN 0-7923-1569-3
16. T. Wilhelmsson: *Critical Studies in Private Law*. A Treatise on Need-Rational Principles in Modern Law. 1992 ISBN 0-7923-1659-2
17. M.D. Bayles: *Hart's Legal Philosophy*. An Examination. 1992 ISBN 0-7923-1981-8
18. D.W.P. Ruiter: *Institutional Legal Facts*. Legal Powers and their Effects. 1993 ISBN 0-7923-2441-2
19. J. Schonsheck: *On Criminalization*. An Essay in the Philosophy of the Criminal Law. 1994 ISBN 0-7923-2663-6
20. R.P. Malloy and J. Evensky (eds.): *Adam Smith and the Philosophy of Law and Economics*. 1994 ISBN 0-7923-2796-9
21. Z. Bańkowski, I. White and U. Hahn (eds.): *Informatics and the Foundations of Legal Reasoning*. 1995 ISBN 0-7923-3455-8

Law and Philosophy Library

22. E. Lagerspetz: *The Opposite Mirrors*. An Essay on the Conventionalist Theory of Institutions. 1995 ISBN 0-7923-3325-X
23. M. van Hees: *Rights and Decisions*. Formal Models of Law and Liberalism. 1995 ISBN 0-7923-3754-9
24. B. Anderson: *"Discovery" in Legal Decision-Making*. 1996 ISBN 0-7923-3981-9
25. S. Urbina: *Reason, Democracy, Society*. A Study on the Basis of Legal Thinking. 1996 ISBN 0-7923-4262-3
26. E. Attwooll: *The Tapestry of the Law*. Scotland, Legal Culture and Legal Theory. 1997 ISBN 0-7923-4310-7
27. J.C. Hage: *Reasoning with Rules*. An Essay on Legal Reasoning and Its Underlying Logic. 1997 ISBN 0-7923-4325-5
28. R.A. Hillman: *The Richness of Contract Law*. An Analysis and Critique of Contemporary Theories of Contract Law. 1997 ISBN 0-7923-4336-0; 0-7923-5063-4 (Pb)
29. C. Wellman: *An Approach to Rights*. Studies in the Philosophy of Law and Morals. 1997 ISBN 0-7923-4467-7
30. B. van Roermund: *Law, Narrative and Reality*. An Essay in Intercepting Politics. 1997 ISBN 0-7923-4621-1
31. I. Ward: *Kantianism, Postmodernism and Critical Legal Thought*. 1997 ISBN 0-7923-4745-5
32. H. Prakken: *Logical Tools for Modelling Legal Argument*. A Study of Defeasible Reasoning in Law. 1997 ISBN 0-7923-4776-5
33. T. May: *Autonomy, Authority and Moral Responsibility*. 1998 ISBN 0-7923-4851-6
34. M. Atienza and J.R. Manero: *A Theory of Legal Sentences*. 1998 ISBN 0-7923-4856-7
35. E.A. Christodoulidis: *Law and Reflexive Politics*. 1998 ISBN 0-7923-4954-7
36. L.M.M. Royakkers: *Extending Deontic Logic for the Formalisation of Legal Rules*. 1998 ISBN 0-7923-4982-2
37. J.J. Moreso: *Legal Indeterminacy and Constitutional Interpretation*. 1998 ISBN 0-7923-5156-8
38. W. Sadurski: *Freedom of Speech and Its Limits*. 1999 ISBN 0-7923-5523-7
39. J. Wolenski (ed.): *Kazimierz Opalek Selected Papers in Legal Philosophy*. 1999 ISBN 0-7923-5732-9
40. H.P. Visser 't Hooft: *Justice to Future Generations and the Environment*. 1999 ISBN 0-7923-5756-6
41. L.J. Wintgens (ed.): *The Law in Philosophical Perspectives*. My Philosophy of Law. 1999 ISBN 0-7923-5796-5
42. A.R. Lodder: *DiaLaw*. On Legal Justification and Dialogical Models of Argumentation. 1999 ISBN 0-7923-5830-9
43. C. Redondo: *Reasons for Action and the Law*. 1999 ISBN 0-7923-5912-7

Law and Philosophy Library

44. M. Friedman, L. May, K. Parsons and J. Stiff (eds.): *Rights and Reason*. Essays in Honor of Carl Wellman. 2000 ISBN 0-7923-6198-9
45. G.C. Christie: *The Notion of an Ideal Audience in Legal Argument*. 2000 ISBN 0-7923-6283-7
46. R.S. Summers: *Essays in Legal Theory*. 2000 ISBN 0-7923-6367-1
47. M. van Hees: *Legal Reductionism and Freedom*. 2000 ISBN 0-7923-6491-0
48. R. Gargarella: *The Scepter of Reason*. Public Discussion and Political Radicalism in the Origins of Constitutionalism. 2000 ISBN 0-7923-6508-9
49. M. Iglesias Vila: *Facing Judicial Discretion*. Legal Knowledge and Right Answers Revisited. 2001 ISBN 0-7923-6778-2
50. M. Kiikeri: *Comparative Legal Reasoning and European Law*. 2001 ISBN 0-7923-6884-3
51. A.J. Menéndez: *Justifying Taxes*. Some Elements for a General Theory of Democratic Tax Law. 2001 ISBN 0-7923-7052-X
52. W.E. Conklin: *The Invisible Origins of Legal Positivism*. A Re-Reading of a Tradition. 2001 ISBN 0-7923-7101-1
53. Z. Bańkowski: *Living Lawfully*. Love in Law and Law in Love. 2001 ISBN 0-7923-7180-1
54. A.N. Shytov: *Conscience and Love in Making Judicial Decisions*. 2001 ISBN 1-4020-0168-1
55. D.W.P. Ruiter: *Legal Institutions*. 2001 ISBN 1-4020-0186-X

Volumes 1–55 were published by Kluwer Academic Publishers.

56. G. den Hartogh: *Mutual Expectations*. A Conventionalist Theory of Law. 2002 ISBN 90-411-1796-2
57. W.L. Robison (ed.): *The Legal Essays of Michael Bayles*. 2002 ISBN 90-411-1835-7

KLUWER LAW INTERNATIONAL – THE HAGUE / LONDON / NEW YORK